The Goal Gourmet

The Peter Kitchen Story

Second Edition

Neilson N Kaufman

Peter Kitchen
Sevenoaks, Kent
United Kingdom

THE GOAL GOURMET

The Peter Kitchen Story
Second Edition

By
Neilson N Kaufman

This first edition of this book was published by the Derwent Press in 2006.

Second Edition
Paperback: ISBN: 978-0-9934042-0-7
Ebook (.mobi) ISBN: 978-0-9934042-1-4

Photographs:

Photographs supplied by the Author, Peter Kitchen and his family, Leyton Orient FC, David Dodd, Stephen Jenkins, Mike Childs, Doncaster Rovers FC, Steve Uttley, John Coyle, Rod Stewart Vagabonds, Las Vegas FC, Fulham FC, Cardiff City FC, Happy Valley Club, Chester City FC, and Corinthian Casuals Vets, Lene Ahlmann - PhotoGraphIT, Steve Nichol - Official Leyton Orient FC Photographer, Peter Thurlow, Steve Uttley

Cover art and book design by:
Pam Marin-Kingsley, www.pammarin-kingsley.com

Published by:

Peter Kitchen
Sevenoaks, Kent
United Kingdom

For more information, contact:
email: thegoalgourmet@gmail.com
Facebook: @GoalGourmet

DEDICATION

From Peter Kitchen

This book is dedicated to my son Michael, his wife Yoko, , my grandsons Alfie and Tommy and my granddaughter Atalie in Japan.. A lovely family who has proved that different cultures are not a barrier to love and happiness.

Also, to the memory of my mother Dorothy and father Harry.

To my son Darren, who tragically died at twenty-eight during 2003, and who never fulfilled his potential.

Darren Kitchen

CONTENTS

ACKNOWLEDGEMENTS

First and foremost as the Author, I would like to thank All Mighty God for allowing me good health and for the opportunity to work on this book with Peter Kitchen and to make new friendships with many people connected with all the clubs Peter played for during his long career.

I would also like to thank my wife Debbie and twin daughters Amy and Samantha for their patience, love, prayers and support whilst working on this and a number of other projects.

Thank you to Kitch for allowing me this time in sharing his life and experiences with me and the readers and for all the time and effort he spent in the many emails between Kent and Johannesburg and for the posting of all the photographs and press reports over the past year, without which this book would not have been possible. Also, for checking of all the various drafts sent to him to ensure accuracy and for the opportunity of becoming a good friend with him, one of the greatest all-time Doncaster Rovers and Leyton Orient players.

To the others who have been a wonderful help in the compilation of this book, a very special thank you. I would especially like to first list the following, who have given their time and effort very generously and for the new friendships I have made with each one. Finally to Neil Cross, Pam Marin-Kingsley and all the staff at Derwent Press for their expert time and effort in the production of this book. The wonders of technology aided in producing this book since the Author lives in South Africa, the publisher in the UK and the designer in the States.

A very warm and special thanks to the following people

Gudrun Osborne, a long-standing O's supporter, she has spent many months at various Libraries in London and in particular at the British Library in Colindale researching and locating newspaper articles on Kitch and on the O's for use in this and other books I am busy with.

Shirley E. Kelly, an O's fan of fifty years, whose mother worked at the club for many years in the 1950s, she has spent many hours doing research and sending information and photographs for use in this and other books on a daily basis

Steve Uttley, a member of the Doncaster Rovers Football Club's media team, who has given much valuable assistance in supplying information on past players and taking of photographs in and around Mexborough for use in this book.

The Goal Gourmet

John Coyle and Tony Bluff, both authorities on the history of Doncaster Rovers FC, a big thank you to you both for supplying details on the club and its former managers and players.

I would also like to thank the following football clubs and people who have been a tremendous help in the compilation of this book.

The Football Clubs:

Cardiff City, Chester City, Corinthian Casuals Vets, Dagenham & Redbridge, Doncaster Rovers, Fulham, Happy Valley, Leyton Orient and Margate.

The People:

Peter Allen, Miljia Aleksic, Anthony Ambrosen, Stan Anderson, Brian Attmore, David Ballheimer, Dennis Barefield, Bob Bennett, Annamaria Bischoff, Ted Blair, Jim Brown, Neil Brown, Stephen Byrne, Peter Catt, Tim Carder, CJ Carenza, Alan Chandler, John Collings, Katherine Corbett, Tom Davies, Gary Dixon, David Dodd, Bob Dunning, Rita Ellis (née Kitchen), Bobby Fisher, Liz Forrest, Stella L. Fox, Bob Gilbert, David Godfrey, Michael Harker, Julie Haynes, Peter Holme, Steve Hossack, Matt Hudson, Barry Hugman, Stephen Jenkins, Paul Ann Holman, Joannou, Trefor Jones, Colin Jose, Michael Joyce, Jonathan Kaye, Michael Lamb, Andrew Lock, Joe Mayo, Ian Miller, Bob Mills, John Motson, Brendan O'Callaghan, Alan Parry, Christine Pandole, Ian Perkins, Andy Porter, Matthew Porter, Lois Pugh, Wilfred Pugh, Alan Ravenhill, Chrissy Rosenthal, Jim Rosenthal, Jim Ryan, Lloyd Scott, Michael Shea, Richard Shepherd, Adrian Sill, David W. Simpson, Roger Smith, Martin Strong, Chas Sumner, Brian Tabner, Geoff Thompson, John Treleven, Jeff Trice, Martin Tyler, Brian Wakefield, Edward Walton, Mark S. Waters, Alex White, Mark Whyman, Bill Yates, Tim Reder, Steve Jenkins, and David Dodd.

Thank you, one and all.

Neilson N Kaufman
Johannesburg, South Africa
Revised July 2015

FOREWORD

Geoff Thompson

Chairman of the Football Association and Executive Committee Member of UEFA

**Mr Geoff Thompson,
Chairman of the FA**

Geoff Thompson was at Doncaster Rovers replacing Tony Garnett as General Manager and Company Secretary, he stayed for one season before taking up a post with the Sheffield and Hallamshire FA. In 1979, he was elected to the FA Council and today he holds the powerful position of Chairman at the Football Association having been elected in 1999 and he was also elected to UEFA's Executive Committee in July 2000.

Peter Kitchen was already a promising young player at Doncaster Rovers in the 1970s when I was General Manager and Company Secretary at the club. Peter suited Rovers – a small club with a big heart, just as Peter's prolific goal scoring impressed all the more in light of his diminutive appearance. I remember his great sense of personal commitment to the club and the natural rapport he built with ease with the fans.

Peter's excellent record at the club formed the foundation for him for further his career, which he did in style with Orient, then two divisions higher. His passion and enthusiasm for his football and his prowess in front of goal made him quite literally a legend at both Belle Vue and with the East End Club.

It was Peter's brilliant goals, which paved the way for the Orient to reach the FA Cup Semi Finals, in 1978, for the first and only time in their history.

Peter's contribution to football in this country cannot be undervalued. With 210 career goals in 519(26) appearances in England, the statistics speak for themselves and I extend my congratulations to him for his excellent contribution to English club football.

A Message from John Ryan, Chairman of Doncaster Rovers FC

Peter Kitchen was one of the most skilful and gifted players to ever grace Belle Vue, Doncaster, and his partnership with Brendan O'Callaghan provided us with one of the most prolific goalscoring duos we have ever had.

Peter unfortunately was sold to Leyton Orient for the paltry sum of £30,000, something that wouldn't happen today in my chairmanship.

I reckon Rovers were short changed even in those days by some £300,000!

He had special skills when receiving balls from throw-ins and tricked the defenders each time. I have never seen anybody else do this in all the time I have been watching football.

He was a deadly finisher and in fact he scored in the first few minutes on his debut for Rovers.

**Peter with John Ryan,
Chairman of Doncaster Rovers**

His dribbling skills were amazing at times and he was compared to Jimmy Greaves, and without doubt he was one the best footballers Doncaster Rovers ever had, plus he was also a gentleman.

Peter is held in high regard by all Doncaster Rovers' supporters.

I met up with him in the year we returned to the Football League with our first game against Leyton Orient at Brisbane Road and both clubs presented him with a gift to mark the occasion as he gave both of us valuable service. He did a lap of honour, cheered by both Orient and Rovers fans alike.

Last season I also invited him to the Aston Villa Carling Cup tie, had a keepsake shirt made for him and he brought us a bit of luck as we beat them 3-0.

He also did a lap of honour and cheekily took a ball off an Aston Villa player in the warm up and showed he had lost none of his silky skills on the ball and quick feet of Peter Kitchen were still evident.

Peter will always be a hero of mine and many others and a footballer to be revered, plus, as I say, a true gentleman.

John Ryan

SPECIAL TRIBUTES -
Fans, Former Players,
Journalists, and Friends

Bob Bennett, the Sports teacher at Mexborough Grammar School informed the Author in April 2005 about his memories of a young Peter Kitchen.

At school, Peter studied very hard and he progressed impressively on both academic and footballing fronts, and gained three GCE 'A' level passes in English, Economics and Social History and in British and European Political History.

I followed Peter's career with great interest and I was very surprised that one of the bigger local teams didn't go for him before he went to London to join Orient. I know he would have liked to continue living in the area, he would have been a great buy for a big club. I know Peter supported Sheffield United as a boy and so their and other big teams' loss was Orient's gain.

At the time of the FA Cup semi finals between Orient and Arsenal, the local papers were full of the Kitchen and Alan Sunderland connection, unfortunately Alan had to pull out of the match with an injury, but he did score in the Wembley final against Manchester United. And so I was rooting for Orient, but in the end it was too big a mountain to climb for Peter and the O's.

Peter Scores 14 goals

Yes I remember the silky skills of a young lad named Peter Kitchen. I remember when the school team thumped local rivals Hinde House by 16-1 and Peter weighed in with fourteen goals, it was a fantastic performance and I noticed in that match that Peter wasn't a greedy player, he also made and liked to see other boys score some goals.

When Peter joined the lower sixth form from secondary school, we had at the school another big star in the making in Alan Sunderland who was in the first XI, but Peter didn't show his true capabilities until towards the end of the football season, when we began to realize just how good he was.

Peter and Alan played together in a few matches and were a great combination and for two years running the team got into the Yorkshire school final.

We saw Alan's potential, he was quick off the mark, strong in the air and had great ball control and he agreed to join Wolverhampton Wanderers after leaving school and was signed by Bill McGarry. On the over hand Peter was more of late developer and just about finishing his A-levels when Lawrie McMenemy began to take notice of him.

He played for Yorkshire Schools and got into the last twenty-two for the England youth squad. His great value was his sharpness inside the penalty area, half a chance and he was there. He could turn most defenders and score, he used to leave all the boys standing with his great turn of speed. He would get his head and shoulders down and he would be off and when he had the ball in the penalty area, believe me, he was just deadly.

In my opinion and to conclude, Peter Kitchen was a very good pupil and I would rate him as being in the same mould as the great footballer Jimmy Greaves, exceptional close ball control, the ability to turn on a sixpence, a predator's instinct who could score goals from either close-in, a long shot and the wonderful ability of being able to dribble past players and score.

Stan Anderson wrote:

When I became manager of Doncaster Rovers in February 1975, the club was in the relegation zone of the 'old' Fourth Division, so obviously I thought the team wouldn't have many decent players and I'd have my work cut out to avoid relegation.

After my first week at the club, I soon changed my mind and the main reason was that I had a forward line that could score goals. The main striker at the club was Peter Kitchen, who had he been given the opportunity at the time, could have played in a much higher division.

He had very good control of the ball and two good feet, Peter scored some wonderful goals for Doncaster and his partnership with Brendan O'Callaghan was the best in the Fourth Division.

We missed out on promotion for two seasons and eventually Peter was transferred to Orient, where he performed with his usual skill. A very popular player at Doncaster and well liked by the supporters.

I am delighted to have been asked to say these few words for a player who always worked hard for me and who was such a gentleman both on and off the field.

Peter, it was so nice to hear from you after such a long time, I wish you well for the future. *(Refer to Stan Anderson in Manager's section in Chapter 19.)*

Brendan O'Callaghan wrote:

I played at Doncaster Rovers for almost six years between 1972-78 with Peter

Kitchen mainly as my striking partner. Kitch, like me, was a former Grammar School student and I felt that some of the players and staff at Rovers resented that to some extent.

Peter and I certainly did not adhere to Manager Maurice Setters' vision of professional football. Setters wanted everyone to be a clone of himself, and we felt that too much time was wasted on trying to make some young players into something they were not.

When Stan Anderson took over, he gave everyone more scope to play and to be inventive and to concentrate on their strengths, rather than trying to expose their weaknesses.

Within this framework Kitch and myself struck up an immediate partnership, rather like Keegan and Toshack at Liverpool and Worboys and Bannister with Bristol Rovers.

Kitch was the best receiver of a ball on the ground that I played with in my career. His first touch, swerve and ability to avoid tackles were first class and his finishing was as good as anyone in the division. I mainly dealt with 'out' balls from defence and knew without looking or thinking where Kitch was. I also knew that if I won my fair share of headers from the excellent crosses from Ian Miller or Terry Curran, then Kitch would be on the end of them finishing with either left or right foot, it did not matter to him.

It seemed a little bit strange in hindsight, that in the four years that we had a partnership producing some 160 goals, I thought, we were never regarded as crowd favourites. I remember one game when we have scored five goals between us, Kitch was criticized by the crowd when he missed what would have been his fourth goal!

I suppose the best year we had together was in 1975-76 when Rovers scored 90 goals but incredibly conceded more! That season we also reached the League Cup Quarter Final but were well beaten at Spurs after twice being in the lead.

I think the highlight of that period was the wonderful draw we got against Liverpool at Anfield in 1974 when Kitch any myself both scored against the eventual Cup winners and Kitch hit the bar in the final minute! Another highlight when we were selected for the PFA divisional team, despite finishing in midtable.

It seems strange that although we had a telepathic relationship while playing, we were never the closest of friends off the pitch. Footballers rarely keep in touch with former players and I have not seen Peter since the early 80's, but I wish him all the best and I hope that the book receives the adulation that this terrific player deserves.

John Coyle, a writer on the history and players of Doncaster Rovers emailed:

Whenever Rovers supporters discuss the greatest players the club have had over the many years of its existence, one name always come up – Peter Kitchen. They think back to the golden era of attacking football and think of whenever Terry Curran or Ian Miller racing to the by-line, a panting full back in their wake Brendan O'Callaghan would meet the cross with a towering header and on hand was Kitchen to coolly slot the ball into a gaping net.

Just recently when I mentioned your biography on the mystical Kitchen, a Rovers supporter commented to the effect that: "They don't come like him anymore." His Rovers and also Orient goal tallies has not been surpassed since he left both clubs. Thanks for the wonderful memories Peter Kitchen.

Wilfred Pugh, a good friend of Peter's in Mexborough, wrote:

Peter and myself became good friends some thirty years ago when we met in the town where we were born in Mexborough, South Yorkshire. We spent many hours together in our local pub The Ferryboat Inn.

Peter was playing for Doncaster Rovers at that time and I fondly remember attending many games, both home and away and taking Peter's father Harry with me to the games.

It became obvious Peter had a knack of scoring goals and he scored within the first few minutes of his Rovers debut. As his game developed his great ability to be able to twist and turn and go by defenders was just wonderful to watch.

With scouts and managers from clubs such as Sheffield United and West Bromwich Albion and Orient present at home matches and it was only a matter of time before Peter moved on to bigger and better things.

At one point it seemed that he would go to Ipswich Town and I know he was bitterly disappointed when they could not agree a fee with Doncaster Rovers and so he returned home. The Ipswich manager at the time was (Sir) Bobby Robson, who later told Peter that it had been a big mistake not to sign him. Peter didn't stay long in Town and soon moved to London with Orient.

Peter was my best man when I married my wife Susan in Scunthorpe, the Vicar was a big West Brom fan and he recognised Peter the minute he saw him, he got so absorbed in talking football to Peter and I had to remind him that there was a wedding about to take place.

One other funny moment I recall attending a dinner in Doncaster where the late George Best was guest of honour. I approached him for his autograph after the dinner and while he was signing I said to him "Has anyone ever told you that you look like Peter Kitchen?" (they both had beards and long locks at the time). He looked startled at first and then said "Yes actually!! But usually it's the other way round – Peter Kitchen looks like me!" (See Page 146 for a photo of George Best).

(Peter Kitchen confirms the George Best look-a-like story, he remembers: "throughout my career a lot of people said that when I grew a beard, I looked like George Best (the eyebrows and shape of face, I recall one charity match, in 2004, I played at Ardingly School and we in a pub owned by the former Republic of Ireland and Brighton player Gerry Armstrong, a bloke wearing a Man City shirt at the bar came up to me with a book and a pen and asked for my autograph. I asked him if he was joking and no he said he genuinely thought I was George Best, now that George has died, I don't think this would happen again!!!").

I also remember the last time Peter played at Doncaster when he was in his second spell with Leyton Orient. Peter scored 2 goals when Orient won 3-1. The Doncaster crowd cheered every time Peter got the ball and the home fans gave him a standing ovation at the end of the game, even though we had lost.

Well, what can be said of Peter, an amazingly talented footballer and a natural-born goal scorer.

Best wishes to Peter from your friend,
Wilf Pugh and family

Bob Gilbert, a long time Doncaster Rovers Fan wrote:

I watched Peter grow from a young lad in Rovers youth and reserve sides and over seven years, into a brilliant lethal striker, forming one of the great striking partnerships in our club's history with big centre forward Brendan O'Callaghan. I know you and many of the older O's fans enthuse over Peter's goals in the League and FA Cup during the 1977–1978 season, I also saw his two FA Cup goals at Chelsea, I had a few too many that night to celebrate my hero's goals down in Chelsea and I re-enacted his dribble and his goal whilst walking from White City Tube, only to miss my footing and ending up in Hammersmith Hospital with a totally knackered ankle. Yes, he scored two brilliant goals.

However, the best goal I had ever witnessed of Peter's was for Rovers. It was on a very cold night in Wales, at Newport County on 21 February 1976, after I drove from Warwick University to watch the match. *(Refer to page 89.)*

Peter Catt, a sports journalist in Doncaster, who saw most of Peter Kitchen's games for Rovers, wrote:

I worked at the Doncaster Evening Post as a freelancer covering Doncaster Rovers matches for local, regional and national newspapers for over thirty years with another of the great local sports journalists Joe Slater, now, Joe, like me, was a great admirer of Peter Kitchen, he had fond memories of Peter, whom he talked about often and whom he rated very highly both as a player and a person, sadly, Joe died a few years ago after his retirement.

Today I'm the sports editor of the Doncaster Free Press.

It was a George Raynor who first mentioned Peter Kitchen's name to me, having spotted him playing for Yorkshire Grammar Schools team in a competition, George was a Rovers Scout for many years and spotted a number of good players for the club.

I remember him talking enthusiastically about this young striker with the unusual name of Kitchen and what is beyond doubt Kitch, as he was fondly known was one of the finest strikers to play for Doncaster Rovers.

I would say he would rank as second only to the incomparable Alick Jeffrey in my time watching and reporting on the club.

Peter was a natural goalscorer with head – although he was not that tall – or with either boot. He was a Denis Law type of player – difficult to mark, with a quick change of pace, skilful and tricky in the box and always had an eye for goal.

Kitch developed into an outstanding finisher during his time at Belle Vue, particularly when he scored over 20 League goals in three consecutive seasons – a feat only achieved by only one other legendary Doncaster player Tom Keetley in the 1920s.

The biggest surprise to me and many other fans at the time was that a bigger club did not come into sign him because he looked the type of player who could score goals at any level and he proved in that in Cup matches against the likes of Tottenham Hotspur and Liverpool.

He played in a forward line of Miller, O'Callaghan and Kitchen which at the time tripped off the tongues of all Rovers' fans – and was certainly as famous in their minds – as the Charlton, Law and Best trio at Manchester United.

Peter played his best football at Belle Vue under manager Stan Anderson, who brought the trio together, and was a manager fond of attacking football. In fact it is fair to say that if the Rovers had defended as well as they attacked around that time they would have most certainly won promotion more than once and Peter would not have had to leave the club to join Orient in the summer of 1977 to achieve his ambition of playing at a higher level.

It was Anderson who taught Peter to stick a hand out behind him when he was being closely marked with his back to a defender so he could judge whether he had enough room to swivel and turn. That became a Kitch trademark trick of his that he would turn and shoot and more often than not, score – just when his marker thought he had everything covered.

After leaving Belle Vue, Peter almost returned to the club twice. It was Billy Bremner who tried to sign Kitch when he became manager at Belle Vue in the 1980s and he also applied to become manager during the notorious reign of Ken Richardson in 1994, Ian Atkins got the job instead and, in a way, I'm glad it wasn't Peter who got the job because his name may have become tarnished by becoming associated with Richardson who became a hate figure for Rovers' fans. He was in good company when being rejected by the club as manager, applicants also included George Burley and Sam Allardyce. Atkins didn't last very long either once he realised Richardson wanted to sign his own players and pick the team!

Peter Kitchen was and still is to this day a massive hero among the Belle Vue fans, as can be seen by the reception he received at the match in the Carling League Cup against Aston Villa in November 2005.

Ted Blair, a Darlington fan wrote:

I remember Peter Kitchen and Brendan O'Callaghan, quite a formidable duo in Division Four, we lost a match at Belle Vue in October 1976 by 4-0 and Kitchen scored a couple of grand goals and they also had a young Tony Woodcock on loan from Forest.

Peter came out of their supporters club after the game with all his pockets filled with bottles of beer, I remember his long black hair and the Mexican styled moustache, the true spirit of the 1970s.

The man who signed Peter Kitchen for Orient, George Petchey, stated:

I had been watching Kitchen for three years, in the early days at Doncaster I watched him score twice for the reserves and thought: "Bloody hell, he's going to be some player."

I suppose I watched him four or five times after that – often he was not the main reason for being at the game – and each time he looked brave and sharp in the box. His finishing was brilliant and the way he struck the ball, it excited me."

Then followed a long dialogue with Doncaster manager Stan Anderson, after he had priced Kitchen at £70,000, I kept phoning to ask Stan: "How much is Kitchen today Stan?" The reply: "Still seventy grand, George."

Weeks passed, then I noticed a small paragraph in a daily newspaper, stating that Ipswich Town had released Kitchen back to Doncaster Rovers after a trial period.

I rang Stan again and asked: "How much is Kitchen today?" He told me to make an offer. I said "£15,000." Pause... When he came back and said, "How about £30,000?" I just replied: "It's a deal..." and that's exactly how Peter Kitchen came to Orient.

The well-known cellist and Orient supporter, Julian Lloyd Webber stated:

I admired the goal scoring ability of Peter Kitchen: One of my greatest O's moments ever was watching us knock out Chelsea in the FA Cup at Stamford Bridge back in 1978. Those two Kitchen goals were absolutely brilliant and his goal in the sixth round against Middlesbrough was just as good.

**At the Leyton Orient Supporters Club October 2005:
Neilson N. Kaufman, Author; Stephen Jenkins, Deputy Chairman
Leyton Orient Supporters Club, and Peter Kitchen.**

Stephen Jenkins, Deputy Chairman of the Leyton Orient Supporters Club, wrote:

I can still remember nearly thirty years ago reading in the local Waltham Forest Guardian about the great striker we had just signed from Doncaster Rovers in July 1977, alongside the article was a picture of Kitch wearing the new white braces kit. It seemed liked a new era was just beginning at the club and what an impression our new addition made to the squad in his first season.

I was at Craven Cottage to see Peter make his first full appearance in O's colours of red shirts and white braces when he scored in a 2-0 win over Fulham on 13 August 1977 in the League Cup. The match was played over two legs and the O's played both legs at the Cottage because the O's pitch was recovering from major repair work during the close season.

The highlight of the 1977-78 season was O's great FA Cup run when we reached the semi final of the competition, going out to Arsenal 3-0. I spent days prior to the big game making two huge banners, one of the O's crest and the second, which spelt out 'Kitchen Fries Rice' referring to the Gunners full-back Pat Rice. And I was proud to hear the great football commentator Brian Moore mention my banner in ITV's 'The Big Match'.

In the 5th Round of the competition they had held Chelsea at home to a 0-0 draw, thousands of O's fans, including myself made the trip to Stamford Bridge only to get held up in the awful traffic along the Embankment beside the Thames. There were four of us in a car and having just parked the car, we knew we had missed the start of the match. We made our way to the Stadium and just as we arrived we heard a loud roar of the Chelsea fans celebrating Bill Roffey's own goal that put the home side 1-0 up. Worse was to follow when we saw the turnstiles had been closed for safety reasons.

Despondently we made our way around the perimeter of the ground and headed towards the local pub to listen to the match on the radio, however, in the shadows a lone voice called to us "Are you lads Orient fans?" To which we answered "Yes!". "Give me a fiver and you can come in here" he said. It wasn't until we got close up that we realised that it was a policeman who was looking to get us into the game!

We did not ask any questions, we gave him our money and made our way into the stand only to realise that we were now in the infamous 'Shed' end of the ground!

We made sure our Orient scarves were well and truly hidden and whilst we were losing 1-0 things seemed pretty calm, typical of Orient, two goals from

Kitch (one of which was as good, if not better than the Ricky Villa goal for Spurs in the FA Cup Final), soon put us on red alert!

How we all winced and struggled to control our emotions, fearful of a 'good kicking' as all the drama of that great day in Orient's history unfolded in front of our very ours. We couldn't cheer and in fact did not celebrate until we got to a pub in Kings Cross where we met a group of Middlesbrough fans, whose club would become the next Peter Kitchen victim, with another 'wonder' FA Cup goal to take the O's to the Semi-Finals.

Alan Ravenhill, an O's supporter for around 50-years, who has seen all the notable O's players since 1946, wrote:

When in the summer of 1977 Orient signed Peter Kitchen from Doncaster Rovers, little did the club's supporters, myself included, think that O's had obtained a striker who would perform in such a way that he would quickly go on to join post-war forwards Tommy Johnston and Dave Dunmore as an Orient legend.

During his time with Fourth Division Doncaster Rovers, Kitchen had aroused the interest of several clubs including Ipswich Town, Liverpool and Sheffield United, but it was O's manager George Petchey who splashed out around £30,000 to bring him to Brisbane Road, who were two divisions higher than Rovers. And from hereon in we all know how this highly talented Yorkshire man fared.

Peter Kitchen was an excellent and prolific goalscorer, he was a splendid goal poacher, sniffing out the chances in the penalty boxes and cottoning onto big Joe Mayo's knockdowns, as he often did at Doncaster with Brendan O'Callaghan, but my abiding memory of Kitch, as he was affectionately known, was when he would receive the ball outside the penalty area then leaving a trail of opposing defenders left on the turf after a mazy dribble and often before slipping the ball into an empty net. Some of his great goals that come to mind were against teams like Chelsea, Stoke City, Hull City, Oldham Athletic, Sunderland and Millwall, but there quite a few others greatly admired.

Of all the great goals Kitch scored for the O's, there is one in my view, that could hardly be bettered and it was one of the most important goals of all, that being the one he netted in the FA Cup 6th round replay against Middlesbrough at Brisbane Road. Receiving an awkward bouncing ball from Phil Hoadley with his back to goal and being closely man-marked, but controlled the ball with a superb first touch, he hooked the ball over his shoulder from over 20 yards, turning to see the ball bounce into the net off the top of the post. A truly incredible goal.

I could add so much more regarding Kitch's ability and qualities but would just like to say finish by saying this:

Thank you Peter Kitchen for some tremendous memories and I feel with the wonderful talent you had I feel you should had been given the opportunity in the top division and I honestly believe you would have achieved much in the higher grade.

Alan Chandler, a long-standing O's fan, wrote:

The first time I ever saw Peter Kitchen, it was on his League debut at Luton Town in August 1977, having played and scoring in the League Cup at Fulham a few days earlier.

I can still to this day, remember him twisting and turning his opponent and I thought to myself, Hmm, this bloke is not a bad player, his close control was just brilliant and this – and his many wonderful goals - will remain with me forever.

Although he didn't look like a footballer, he certainly seemed to know where the goal was and, in the most honoured phrase, was a wonderful 'goal poacher'.

I couldn't make the FA Cup replay at Stamford Bridge against Chelsea but listened to the game on the car radio and the commentator was going bananas when he described PK's goals.

I suspect Mickey Droy, Chelsea's Gargantuan centre half, still to this day has a twisted gut from the pasting he got from PK that night.

O's fan of many years, Mark Waters wrote:

I saw Peter Kitchen play many times, while he was in the side you always felt that he would get a goal, and the team a result. His partnership with Joe Mayo was the best front pairing we've had since I've supported the club. What can one say about Kitch, a truly great striker.

Martin Strong, another faithful O's fan, wrote:

Orient had not been blessed with many decent strikers and when I first saw this bloke who had come down from Doncaster named Peter Kitchen, he looked a bit silly with a Mexican moustache, he was short, lazy, couldn't defend, liked his pint, yet one thing was for sure, he knew where the goal was. At long last we had a hero down at Brisbane Road. As the 1977-78 season progressed I was unable to believe when looking at the Sunday papers for hours to see our Peter Kitchen on the leading goal scorers lists with the likes of the Latchfords and Dalglishs of this world. Many years have since passed since the days of Peter Kitchen, yet I still miss that dreadful moustache and him in the supporters club after every match, for me he will never be replaced, a true Brisbane Road superstar.

Another O's fan, Michael Shea, wrote:

I witnessed every home game Peter Kitchen played for O's. I distinctly remember his comeback goal with us.

It was on 17 December1982, a match against Preston North End, watched by a meagre crowd of 1,668 – not unusually O's were struggling in the League, and Peter wearing his number 10 shirt, looking a little overweight at just over eleven stone, he scored near the end of the game with a superb, characteristically cool low drive to earn us a 2-1 win.

O's boss Ken Knighton acknowledged that no one else at the club could have taken the chance, and he was just so right, yes, it was the Kitchen of old.

Shea ended by saying: I got the impression that Frank Clark didn't hit it off with Kitchen, which appears to me ultimately brought his O's League career to an end as he was still scoring goals at the end of the 1983-84 season when he was released.

Jimmy Bloomfield, the Orient manager, summed up Kitchen back in 1978, when he said:

Goalscorers are born. Kitch has the happy knack of being in the right place at the right time. But his greatest asset is that he believes he will score goals. I stressed to him that so long as he is in the right place he will go on scoring.

Joe Mayo, Kitchen's great striking partner at Orient, wrote:

The first time I really knew about Peter Kitchen was what I read about him in the first away programme at Fulham. Peter and myself were signed by O's manager George Petchey to bring some Northern steel to a team of Southern softies and when I first saw the size and shape of Kitch, I thought to myself, he's a little guy, and I'm on my own upfront, but Peter and myself hit it off straight away both on and off the pitch, so much so that he almost single handily took Orient though to the semi final of the FA Cup, one of the most successful stages of the club's history.

I know that playing in that team was one of the highlights of my career and even though we lost in the Semi Final of the FA Cup, it is a time I will always remember and I think how close we came to achieving the impossible.

I enjoyed playing alongside Kitch straight away, and one of our first home matches together was home to Cardiff City, from our very first corner kick I managed to get a flick on the ball and there was Kitch to finish it off, the first of three goals that day for him.

This formed a pattern that we managed to build on over the season that culminated in our successful Cup run in 1978. That year the thrill of he FA Cup for both the players and fans, especially for Kitch and he scored some fantastic goals to keep our dream alive.

Even though you need a bit of lady luck to go that far in any competition, I think we beat our more illustrious opponents on merit until our lady luck ran out at Stamford Bridge against Arsenal.

During that Cup run I'll always remember the two goals Kitch scored against Chelsea, both fantastic pieces of individual skill against top class opposition. I don't think old Micky Droy ever recovered from that night and Peter Bonetti retired shortly afterwards.

There was also the goal he scored against Middlesbrough in the quarter final - absolutely brilliant, but just as important was the amount of effort we had to put in as a team at Ayresome Park to earn a reply to get Boro back to Brisbane Road and after our great victory, I don't think the O's fans have seen any better celebrations that night.

It was sad that we never made it to Wembley, we would have loved to be there in the FA Cup final.

I loved my time at Orient and especially the games I played with Kitch, his awareness and confidence in front of goal was a real eye-opener to me, not only that, he was never afraid to roll up his sleeves for the good of the team.

Being a Northerner he was obviously very easy to get on with, even though like most of these guys, he didn't have a tattoo.

Kitch was one of the best goalscorers I've ever played alongside and he was right up there with the like of the great Jeff Astle and Tony Brown, both fantastic players.

The only regret I had was that Kitch left the Orient too soon, I knew he was ambitious, but I knew he never really settled at any other club after he left the O's, with people like Harry Zussman and Brian Winston, who made it a family club
and made all the players feel at home.

We also had some fantastic young players like John Chiedozie, Glenn Roeder, Bobby Fisher, Paddy Grealish, we also had the youngest of them all our keeper Jacko, who must have been close to his pension?

Good luck Pete, I wish you every success in the future and thanks for the many wonderful memories,

Almost thirty years on, seems like yesterday, I wish it was?

Peter Allen, one of O's few true greats (He still holds the record of total games made for the club with 473(8) senior appearances, and a former colleague of Kitch in the 1977-78 season) writes:

What can I say about Peter Kitchen, well over 13-years with the club, I can truly say that Peter was bye far the best finisher I had the privilege to play with.

I battled with a spate of injuries in 1978, yet was re-called for the famous FA Cup tie at Stamford Bridge against Chelsea, the goals Peter scored that evening were stunning and a prime example of his art as a top class striker.

In ending, I think the strike partnership of Peter and Joe Mayo was ideal and 'if only' they were in our squad when we were pushing for promotion to the First Division back in 1974, I'm sure we would have been promoted.

As a member of the new Orient Ex-Players Association, I hope to see Peter again soon at one of their evenings, to rekindle some wonderful O's memories.

Bobby Fisher, a former O's team-mate, who was also in the side that defeated Chelsea 2-1 at Stamford Bridge, wrote in 1995:

Kitch was never a player who liked to run himself in the ground. Rumours had it that he once came back into his own half to collect a pass – and needed a compass to find his way back into the opposing team's area.

He was always a goal-hanger and most of his goals were tap-ins. But some of his more spectacular efforts are forever etched in my mind.

The classic goals against Chelsea in our great FA Cup run of 1978 were just superb and the strike against Middlesbrough that took us into the semi-finals still brings me out in goose pimples every time I remember it.

The tactics of that side revolved around getting the ball to Kitch inside the box as quickly and as often as possible and he did the rest.

Even when he was getting some mega media attention, it never went to his head and he remained one of the boys.

Whenever we see each other at a game, he still has me running around for him, fetching his tea and a hot pie at half time.

But after all those goals he scored for us, I still don't mind running around for the lazy old so and so.

Comedian and O's fan Bob Mills

Born in London during 1957, he began his career as a valet in King's Cross and in fact he was booed off stage in his first concert, but today Bob Mills is a great live stand-up comedian and TV host, notable for his appearances in cult TV series such as 'In bed with Medinner', 'The Show', also the daytime quiz 'Win, lose or draw' on ITV1, also 'Dial Midnight', Goals on Sunday and the acclaimed 'There's only one Brian Moore' and today he is also a great scriptwriter and also hosts from time-to-time a radio show on BBC London.
Bob recalls:

Yes, I remember Peter Kitchen our great striker. I told the following story on the ITV' football programme 'There's only one Brian Moore'

I started by talking about how great and terrific the O's striker Kitch was, and recalled the first time I actually met him back in 1978 in a pub in Chingford, after the O's were knocked out by 'lucky Arsenal' which I attended due to obtaining a ticket from an 'Gunners' friend of mine.

I was a rather young and intense person at the time and saw Peter sitting with a few friends and I rushed up to them and launched into a long-winded tribute to the great man and then went on about how fortuitous MacDonald's two 'own goals' were and the pride we O's fans feel of his great performance and goals and of the whole team's efforts.

I even included a 'leftist' rant about the O's morale victory in O's playing a few local lads of African decent against Arsenal's all British squad of mercenaries!! Trust me, I was young and loved the sound of my own voice.

I remembered PK just stared at me for a while, politely listening to my diatribe, before interrupting me in his broad Yorkshire accent. 'Are you an O's fan, then?

I answered, honestly. That I hadn't been, but I was now (Let be known, and I have remained a loyal fan ever since).

He replied: "You'll be wanting to buy me a drink then," so I did. I then sat down and shut up. Bless Him. That in truth was the one and only time I have met the great Peter Kitchen.

Hope the book is a great success and I look forward to reading about a great O's player, one who I have greatly admired.

(Peter Kitchen also remembered the above incident, and recalls 'I didn't know of Bob at the time or whether he was famous or not. I have since admired his great talent and for the fact that he continues to support the O's after all these years').

Jeff Trice, the Historian of Margate Football Club wrote:

Yes, Peter Kitchen did play for us in 1991, at the age of thirty-nine he was brought in by the manager Tommy Taylor to give some experience to a young and not very good side at the time and even though he was getting on a bit, he looked a class above the rest. (*His comments appears in Chapter 13*)

Roger Smith worked with Kitch at Wimbledon, they are still great friends to this day.

Roger Smith was a trainee and then a professional with Tottenham Hotspur in the early sixties, never quite making the grade, he then moved to Exeter City and played a couple of seasons before moving into Southern League football. In 1980 he was a part-time youth coach with Arsenal and scouting at the same time. In 1990 he was offered the job of Head of Youth development at Wimbledon and over the twelve years with them he had a good degree of success. Sadly, after the move to Milton Keynes many of the staff, including Smith were made redundant in September 2002. Nowadays, he works part-time for Arsenal in a scouting capacity, both home and abroad.

Roger Smith wrote:

I must say from the outset that it is a pleasure to contribute to this biography, despite the much good-natured banter from myself towards Kitch. I am never ceased to be amazed at the esteem he is held in by Orient supporters in particular on occasions especially since I have been scouting again for Arsenal, he has accompanied me to a match at the Orient where I have lost count of the times a 'punter' has suggested, that Kitch could still do a job up-front for the club. I'm less than amused when Kitch actually discusses the merits of these suggestions!

As previously mentioned, we first met when he was encouraged to play for 'The Commentators' team who were originally formed by guys who obviously worked in the industry and wanted to primarily enjoy a 'relaxing' friendly game of football on a Sunday afternoon. Not that many of the games were always that friendly as several of the guys were very competitive.

I'm not sure myself and Kitch would have made a great partnership if we had played together professionally, as I was a wide left player who liked scoring goals and as everyone knows Kitch was used to being the main goalscorer for every team he played for!

I remember on one occasion when I deemed to have a shot from rather a narrow angle and Kitch complained to me at the lack of a cross, I allegedly questioned whether I had used my quota of shots up for the game. His favourite participation at half time was to remind all who would listen to 'get the ball forward, quicker' whilst I would tell them I wanted it played wider.

In all fairness, even at the age of over forty at the time, he was still an excellent finisher, and was very composed in front of goal (Something he never tired of reminding us of over our weekly drink at his local on a Friday night in Epping).

When I became head of Youth development at Wimbledon FC in the nineties, he was one of the first people I encouraged on to our coaching staff with schoolboys. Apart from obvious footballing pedigree, his manner with youngsters was first-class, and I knew for sure they were in good hands. It was only the pressure of work that eventually meant he could not regularly meet the demands of the new Academy programme that was installed at the club in the late nineties.

Since Wimbledon we have remained firm friends and meet on regular occasions for a meal on our annual trip to the O's.

I'm sure this biography on Peter Kitchen will meet with great approval from all the fans who ever watched him play.

HASTA LUEGO AMIGO

A great friend of Peter's, Bill Yates, contributed the following:

I have not, unlike most of the other people who will contribute to Peter's biography, been involved in the world of professional football, except as a spectator. I have for most of my working life been involved in international banking and financial futures markets.

My first experience of professional football was on the terraces of Boundary Park watching Oldham Athletic in the days of the old Third Division North. My heroes at that time were Bobby Johnson (Ex Manchester City and Scotland) and Jimmy Frizzell, who later became manager).

In the mid 1960's, I also started to go to watch Manchester United, watching the greats like Bobby Charlton, George Best, Dennis Law and Nobby Stiles. I also watched Manchester City.

I first met Peter in 1994, though business when he was manager of the White Oak Leisure Centre in Swanley, Kent. Having grown up as an Oldham fan on the other side of the Pennines from Peter, I knew nothing about his football career with Doncaster Rovers and later with Orient. However, having moved to London in the 1970's, I can remember reading an article in the paper on the eve of the 1978 FA Cup semi-final about the Arsenal striker Malcolm MacDonald and the Orient striker Peter Kitchen.

Peter was in the process of separating from his partner Sharon at the time that we met and, having gone through the same experience myself, we became ageing playboys on the loose.

Things have calmed down now, but I remember the first of our many trips away, when we went to the coastal resort of Cocoa Beach in Florida. Peter had been there many times before but it was my first visit.

Another friend Roger Smith (he has also made a contribution to this book) joined us two days later. On our first day, Peter and I were lazing in the sun, having a quiet drink in the beach bar of a local hotel, when an extremely beautiful young lady, who, having heard our English accents, asked if we would like to judge the Florida heat of a national beauty competition. She offered us free drinks all afternoon, which we thought was manna from heaven, so we willingly accepted.

After Roger had arrived we found the local pole-dancing club – the least said the better. Certainly being with Peter was most interesting. I have also been with him on a trip to Japan to visit his son and spent a most enjoyable and interesting trip to various destinations in Europe.

Although I never went to watch Peter play football professionally, I have seen a number of his matches on video and can see he was a most skilful striker with the ability to read the game. I have seen him play for Corinthian Casual's Vets team many times and although he was not as quick as in the past, his skills were still there to be seen and I have seen him score many great goals for the Vets.

I am proud to have Peter as a friend, not because he is Peter Kitchen, the Doncaster Rovers and Orient cult hero, but because he is a nice, genuine loyal guy and a real good friend.

Katherine Corbett, who is Peter's current partner and close friend, wrote:

I first met Peter (or PK as he is affectionately known at work) in 1993 when I was trying to start a business venture as a beauty therapist by renting a room at the White Oak leisure centre where he was the Centre manager. In work he was perceived by the staff as a very professional manager, who had a very 'cool' personality and he was always very smartly dressed and renowned for his flamboyant taste in Ties. He was a manager who had a

Peter and partner Katherine Corbett, 2004

caring approach to his staff and he enjoyed socializing with them and at staff parties he was always first (and last) in the bar. At this stage, I knew nothing of his previous career as a professional footballer, and when we talked it was not something that he ever spoke about.

Changes in both our personal lives, Peter separating from his long term partner in 1996 and me divorcing my husband in 2000 led to us developing a relationship in 2001. It was at this time that I learned about his career as a footballer which I didn't know very much about like a lot of women except what I read in the paper or heard on the news.

It was only when I went to a few matches with him that I realized how passionate people are about the game. I went with Peter to a Leyton Orient 'Star man' dinner at which Peter presented an award and I then realized just how popular and highly regarded he is by the Orient fans.

He was inundated with requests for autographs and everyone was always ready with a tale or memory of his skill and goal scoring feats for the club.

In 2003, I went with Peter to the Orient v Doncaster Rovers game where he was presented with two crystal decanters by both clubs and considering that he hasn't played for these clubs for over twenty years, it was incredible to see the ovation he got from both sets of supporters when he did a lap of honour around the pitch at half time. As usual Peter treated the whole day with his usual coolness although I could see he was visibly moved and emotional by the reception he received.

I have also been with Peter when he has met up with some of the well-known TV Commentators and it is clear that he is well respected by all of them also.

In the cellar at his home he has an amazing collection of football memorabilia which chronicles some of the events in his football career, which includes programmes, posters, football shirts, press cuttings, books and videos which I know have been invaluable in producing this biography.

Peter and I both share a passion for travelling and foreign climes. We try and squeeze as many trips as possible around our work commitments and have had some very memorable holidays together. Christmas and New Year 2004 was celebrated on South Beach, Miami, Florida and for my birthday in July 2005 we had a great trip to the Loire Valley in France, sampling the local wines and delicious food.

In September 2005 we visited Peter's son Michael and his family in Japan, which was a very different sort of holiday where technology and tradition merge very effectively together. The friendliness and hospitality of the people we met was absolutely wonderful. We also try to fit in as many visits as we can each year to my property in Andalusia in Spain.

I feel very lucky to have met Peter and for us to be so close as he is the most level headed, open minded and intelligent and fair person I have ever met.

Peter Kitchen is quite a unique man.

Mark Whyman

Mark is the Managing Director of the Sencio Community Leisure Group and is Peter's boss.

He wrote:

I first met Peter Kitchen when we both had full heads of hair and moustaches that would have done justice to a scene from the good, the bad and the ugly. Peter was then manager of the Edenbridge Leisure Centre and I was the Supervising Officer for Leisure in the crazy days of the Thatcher administration, when compulsory competitive tendering split councils into two distinct companies, the provider and the supplier camp.

Although Peter and I were in opposite camps, we found an ability to be able to work across the divide, this was an early indication of Peter's pragmatic approach to life, and an insight to how he can adapt in differing environments.

Moving on some fifteen years later, we now both have less hair, its more grey that anything else and the moustaches have all but gone. The working relationship has change to one where Peter is my Operating Director in a company which we formed as a management team nearly two years ago called Sencio Community Leisure, which is responsible for the operation of Leisure centres throughout West Kent.

During these past 15 years I have come to value Peter's loyalty, support and common sense approach. Peter is still an out and out sportsman and a great believer in giving young people opportunities and assistance, be it on the playing field or in their careers with us. Which I am pretty sure goes back to Peter's appreciating those that saw him as a younger player struggling to get a foothold in the professional football world.

If there are good influences in our lives there is also the more darker and destructive influences and I know from some of Peter's stories where screaming coaches and managers did not always seem to be to Peter, the best way of motivating players.

Again, from these experiences Peter not only had a strong motivational impact on the organisation but can always be relied on to be the balance and a calming influence to ensure that all points of view are explored and to sometimes temper my impetuous and impatient MD desires.

The way in which Peter dealt with the death of his son Darren is an insight into the resourcefulness and inner strength that Peter can demonstrate and this I'm sure will help others to deal with similar problems.

To close I would like to say that as you pass through life you meet a handful of people that truly enhance and add value to life. Peter Kitchen is one of those and I am proud and honoured to be able to call him a colleague and friend.

Special Tributes
From the Great TV Commentators

John Motson

Motty, as he is known, is considered an icon and the voice of football and commentating on over 1000 matches in over 25 years. It all started for the son of a Methodist minister, as an 18-year old working at a Barnet newspaper before going to work in Sheffield for the Morning Telegraph where he first covered league football and then for BBC Radio Sheffield. Three years later he joined the BBC's Match of the Day team and when Kenneth Wolstenholme departed, he became the lead commentator. Since he has covered well over 1500 matches for the BBC, when football highlights returned to ITV, he joined the Radio 5 Live team. He resumed his place on Match of the Day when the rights retuned to the BBC in 2004. He has narrated over thirty football videos and has also written four books.

John Motson was awarded the OBE in June 2001.

**Peter with John Motson at
"Motty's" 60th birthday bash July 2005**

He wrote:

Peter Kitchen was already an Orient legend before I met him in the 1980s. His contribution to their FA Cup run in 1978 has been well documented in this biography, although it was really at Doncaster Rovers where Mexborough-born Michael Peter Kitchen first made his name, scoring 89 league goals in 221 appearances. John Motson (His full name is Michael Peter Kitchen, but uses 'Peter' as his first name)

I mention the name 'Michael' because Peter named one of his sons after himself, and it was Michael Kitchen who looked after my BBC team so well when we visited Osaka for the Japan World Cup of 2002.

By then I had the privilege of knowing Peter as a footballer and a friend. His professional career had also embraced spells at Doncaster, Fulham, Cardiff City and Chester City before his retirement from the professional game in 1985.

Anxious to keep his scoring record, Kitch came down in the world, to lend a hand to his great friend Roger Smith, who was running the commentators Sunday team in which I attempted to play alongside Jim Rosenthal, Alan Parry and Martin Tyler.

But it was not the goals he scored and there were two or three in nearly every game, for which I remember Kitch most fondly.

One day in the mid-nineties Peter and I went to watch a league match at Orient on one of my off days. I can't remember whom the O's were playing, the day was just unforgettable for me because of the reception we got even before we reached the main entrance. I lost count of the number of supporters who wanted to shake Peter's hand as we walked down Brisbane Road. They literally forced him into the social club with me in his wake, where we got free drinks for the rest of the afternoon simply because they were pleased to be in his company.

The other memory I have is not to be taken too seriously, but one foggy Sunday morning at Aylesbury I scored my only headed goal for the commentators. Since the mist obscured the view of most of the other players, there weren't many spectators, I can tell you without fear of contradiction that Kitch actually crossed the ball from the left and I did a belly flop as I nodded in a perfect delivery past a despairing goalkeeper. Anyone else would have called it a diving header.

Since Kitch was known as more of a finisher that a provider, maybe he will add this to his list of few assists. He certainly assisted the Commentators team in a lot of other ways, not least arranging a fantastic occasion when we played against Rod Stewart and his team on his private pitch at Epping.

Finally, I had the pleasure of entertaining Peter at my 60th birthday bash in the Cotswolds in July 2005. Most people were kind enough to bring me a present. Typically, Kitch arrived with three gifts, which I shall always treasure.

This man Peter Kitchen has got a lot about him. I have personally opened two of his sports centres, have shared a glass or two with him on many occasions, and always enjoyed his sense of humour.

I am privileged to be associated with this well deserved biography tribute to a great goalscorer of the modern game and a terrific bloke.

Jim Rosenthal

One of the most famous faces on ITV Television Sport, having first presented football, and he has since presented every motor racing Grand Prix since 1997 and has been voted the sports presenter of the Year in both 1997 and 1990. He also has a strong portfolio of corporate work hosting conference and award ceremonies. Jim Rosenthal returned to covering football in 2006 as host of ITV's coverage of the Champions League.

He wrote:

Playing alongside the Kitch was a footballing education, a close-up example of the chasm that exists between those of us who talk a good game and the select band of professionals who have the equipment to perform at the highest level.

Kitch had the touch – close control and speed of thought that is worth millions in the modern game. I use the present tense because even deep down into his fifties those skills are still there. I vividly remember a Christmas Charity match at Cookham Dean in 2003, the village where I live in Berkshire. Conditions underfoot were awful – the pitch a mixture of ice and mud – sleet and snow were in the air.

The Kitch produced a master-class: he looked like a thoroughbred among carthorses. An immaculate hat trick had the villagers open-mouthed. It was vintage Kitch at an age when most of the spectators would settle for taking the dog for a walk to the local.

If truth be known, we commentators and presenters had no right to be playing in the same team as someone with Kitch's talent - but, despite our shortcomings – he was always patient and encouraging. Perhaps we gave him in return in that we furthered his love affair with the game he so graced.

I'm delighted that this book will be a permanent reminder of the Michael Peter Kitchen footballing legend and for many years a good Samaritan to the Commentators XI.

Alan Parry

One of the best-known voices in football having been a commentator for more than thirty years with BBC, ITV and Sky. After a normal education in his native Liverpool he left school at the age of sixteen to become a trainee on a local newspaper.

He is the only commentator to play a more active role in the game being a Director of Wycombe Wanderers, helping them from non-league football to League status. His partner Gill is an avid West Ham United fan.

He wrote:

As one of the original members of the Commentators XI football team, I've been privileged to play with some great stars over the years and Peter Kitchen is right up there with the best of them. The walls of my office are lined with photographs of some memorable games and memorable players from the period when the Commentators would travel the country playing charity games almost every weekend.

I am just a Sunday morning pub player who never rose above the dizzy heights of the Liverpool Sunday League Division Eight so I was always thrilled to be playing in the same team as legends like Kitch. This is a guy that I've commentated on and admired from afar and here I was getting changed in the same dressing room.

Kitch was always so patient and understanding with myself, and the likes of John Motson, Jim Rosenthal and Martin Tyler. We could all talk about the game far better than we could play it, but Kitch never showed the frustration he must have felt when one of us screwed up a flowing move started by him or one of the other ex-pros who turned out for our team on a regular basis.

Kitch may have lost some of his fitness and sharpness in front of goal, but he never lost his skill. To see beefy young defenders turned inside out by that familiar drop of the shoulders and clever turn was always a delight. He scored some wonderful goals for our team despite a distinct lack of service from team-mates like me.

But the thing that I most liked about Kitch was his modesty and natural friendliness. Instead of being embarrassed to be playing in the same team as amateur cloggers like us, he gave the impression that he genuinely enjoyed the experience. He was always one of the last to leave the bar after games - and sometimes before kick-off as well!

I've lost count of the number of times when star-struck members of the opposition would be crowded around Kitch in some smoky clubhouse trying to persuade him to relive a few memories from the great days of his career. Normally, he would just shrug his shoulders in a matter-of-fact way and recall some goal that Orient fans are still raving about even now.

Now that our Commentators team no longer plays, I don't see Kitch as often as I would like, but I still regard him as a true pal. Kitch is a bloke that I know I could rely on in time of need and that is the hallmark of true friendship.

He's a great mate who was - and still is, in my eyes - a great player and I will always remember one particular game that we played in together for the Commentators. Somehow, I summoned up the energy to cross the half-way line from my position at full-back. Even more amazing, I managed to cross the ball for Kitch to score a trademark goal. As he trotted back for the re-start, Kitch turned to me and said: "Good ball, Al." Little old me - the Sunday league hacker from Merseyside - getting a compliment from a true football legend.

I treasure it to this day.

Martin Tyler

Last but not least, the great Martin Tyler.

After graduating from University, Tyler began his career on Marshall Cavendish's Book of Football. He then moved into television on London Weekend Television and later worked for Southern TV, Yorkshire TV, Granada and ITV. He joined BSB's Sports Channel in 1990 and onto Sky Sports for its launch in 1991. In

December 1999, he celebrated the 25th anniversary of his first television commentary and in April 2003, he won the commentator of the decade award from votes cast on the Premiership League website.

He wrote:

Here are some of my recollections of Kitch.

I joined Yorkshire Television as their football commentator in October 1976 and knew all about Peter's exploits at Doncaster Rovers particularly in partnership with Ian Miller on the wing and big Brendan O'Callaghan knocking the crosses down for Peter to score. Kitch left for London at the end of that campaign

At YTV we were always interested to highlight Yorkshire men in visiting teams so that when Orient played in Yorkshire in front of the cameras Peter would get a special mention. Of course, he was quickly in the limelight when he was the main man in the Orient run to the FA cup semi-final in 1978. I remember Peter going into the ITN studios in the West End so that we could do an interview with him from our Leeds studio. He was very helpful and gradually we got to know each other better.

I went to the O's win at Stamford Bridge and the replay against Middlesbrough in that Cup run, largely to see Kitch play, and of course it was time very well spent. In those days the BBC and ITV each had one semi-final for television highlights. Each ITV region would send their own commentator so I was dispatched to the Orient-Arsenal semi final to do the Yorkshire "version" of the match. How Malcolm Macdonald was credited with his two goals I'll never know because they were both own goals on a very unlucky day for Kitch and his O's team-mates.

Little did I realise then that I would be playing up front with the great man in many, many matches to come. Peter reminded me that we bumped into each other at a Footballer of the Year dinner when his full-time career was coming to an end and I actually suggested he might like to play in a few charity matches with the Commentators XI. Some of the games were glamorous affairs in front of big crowds at League grounds. We did play at Brisbane Road one day, when if I remember Peter lined up against us. But the majority were scruffier affairs in front of the proverbial man and his dog.

What Peter did appreciate was that we all took the matches very seriously and of course we were thrilled to have him and his wonderful eye for goal. He always encouraged the lesser lights as well.

I did play in the Isthmian League (making my League debut at centre forward For Corinthian Casuals away at Leytonstone) and incidentally had been much helped by the former Leyton Orient goalkeeper Pat Welton. But that was many years earlier. Alongside Peter, I became a poor man's Joe Mayo and loved every minute of it!

The team would still be going now but for the advent of Premiership games on Sundays, which meant that the actual Commentators in the side like Motty, Alan Parry, Jim Rosenthal and myself had to go to work rather than Indulge us on the pitch!!

Peter was a great team-mate to all of us and had a fund of stories from his time in the professional game. He was and still is terrific socially and I'm delighted to have this chance to say thanks publicly to him for giving us so much of his time.

Peter, thanks for the many great memories!

INTRODUCTION

The ball started rolling on this biography of Peter Kitchen on the 21st March 2005, after I first emailed Stephen Jenkins, the Deputy Chairman of the Leyton Orient Supporters Club to ask if he knew the whereabouts of the Orient's former Gourmet Striker of the seventies and eighties, Peter Kitchen.

After the successful Biographical publication on the life and times of O's greatest striker Tommy Johnston 'The Happy Wanderer' in November 2004, a number of O's fans had asked…'what about a biography on some of other great strikers, like Peter Kitchen and Phil Woosnam.' I knew that the Welsh Wizard Phil Woosnam, who wrote the foreword to the Tommy Johnston book and who now lives in the States, told me in 2004, that he hadn't the time to sit down and think about his memories and put pen to paper.

Having just finished the Complete Record book on the O's for their 100 years as members of the Football League with Breedon Book Publishing for publication during August 2006, and in celebration of the club's 125th anniversary and promotion to League One, and also before, and before I start on a very exciting project, a book on all the clubs and top players to have appeared in the Football League in celebration of the 120th anniversary of the Football League for November 2007, I thought, it might be interesting to see what Peter Kitchen himself has to say, once I get a reply from Stephen.

The following morning - 22 March - at 11.59am a reply came back from Stephen with Kitchen's work email address in Sevenoaks, Kent. I sent a long email to that address at 12.10pm and to my surprise a reply was received from Peter at 2.21pm saying: 'How great it was to hear from someone connected to the Orient' and he ended by saying the following: 'Yes, I would consider a biography on my life and playing career, it sounds quite an interesting and exciting project. I have lots of interesting stories to tell.'

So the project from my side had began with more emails bring sent to Peter and to my two publishers and emails to Doncaster Rovers Football Club, where Peter enjoyed much success during the early part of his career and to the websites of both Rovers, Orient, and also the other clubs with whom Peter played, Fulham, Cardiff City, The Happy Valley Club in Hong Kong, Dagenham, The Las Vegas Americans, the indoor soccer team Peter played for in the States, Chester City and Margate with whom Peter ended his professional playing career at the age of thirty-nine under their manager Tommy Taylor and playing in the same side with another former O's player Bill Roffey. Also emails were sent to Peter's old school Mexborough Grammar, also to his former sports teacher Bob Bennett and to Steve Uttley, the Media Manager at Doncaster Rovers and to that club's historian John Coyle and to the various friends and former playing colleagues.

To my surprise, the responses were just amazing with people offering to do research, find programmes, to take photos of Mexborough where Peter was born and to share their memories of Peter Kitchen. It showed me one thing, and that was, how much enjoyment Peter must have given all the fans around the country during his playing days since making his League debut on 27 November1970 at Shrewsbury Town aged just eighteen and scoring within ninety seconds of his debut.

In a Millennium poll released during December 1999, votes cast by both Doncaster Rovers and Orient fans, Peter Kitchen was voted by both sets of supporters as one of their top all-time first team players, this out of a total of 950 odd Orient players and 890 Rovers players to have played first team football for their clubs since their respective entries in to the Football League. In a poll carried out by the BBC Football Focus in 2004 to identify each Clubs 'Legend' Player, Peter Kitchen received almost 60% of the votes cast by the Orient supporters

In a poll during 2005 conducted by the *'Popular Stand Fanzine'*, to celebrate Doncaster Rovers' 125th anniversary, a poll was conducted and nominees included anyone connected with the club, including players, managers, fans and backroom staff.

Given the fact that such polls tend to be biased towards recent events and players, for Peter Kitchen to be included in the Top Ten of all votes cast by Rovers fans shows how much of a legend he still remains at Belle Vue and according to John Coyle, the doyen of the history of the club, all today's new strikers are still measured against Peter's remarkable goal scoring.

The Top Ten were:

1. Alick Jeffrey
2. Billy Bremner
3. Ian Snodin
4. Dave Penney
5. John Ryan
6. Glynn Snodin
7. Paul Barnes
8. Peter Doherty
9. Peter Kitchen
10. Syd Bycroft

In the April 2005 edition of *'FourFourTwo'* magazine, in a special supplement, readers were asked to vote for their best and worst players of the club that they supported, and the player voted as the overall greatest player for Leyton Orient Football Club was ***Peter Kitchen***.

In a BBC book of every English, Scottish and Welsh football club, compiled by Steve Boulton in 2006, Peter Kitchen was voted by Leyton Orient fans as their all time 'CULT HERO.'

Finally, in the FA Cup Semi Final programme Orient versus Arsenal, played at Stamford Bridge during May 1978 it stated: " Orient may not start today's race at the front of the grid, but as outsiders they have nothing to lose psychologically. Their secret weapons are *Peter Kitchen*, the Dead-Eyed Dick, the Fagin pickpocket of goals and the tall Joe Mayo up front."

Meeting with Peter in October 2005.

To end this introduction, due to the death of my Brother – Alan Kaufman – in October 2005, I had to be in London for the funeral, it was a chance to meet Peter at Orient's home match versus Lincoln City on 15 October and it was just amazing when we were in the Supporters Club rooms to see just how many young and old O's fans just wanted to shake Peter's hand and have him sign an autograph, almost thirty years since Peter first arrived at the club, something which had been noted by others in this book but quite remarkable to witness first hand.

It was also amazing just to sit next to Peter during the match, where he could pick up on O's strengths, playing it down the flanks, the touch and control of Gary Alexander and some of the team's weaknesses, like some of the players' lack of urgency at dead ball situations and the slackening off in the second half and not going for the 'kill', something he hoped would not be the cause of Martin Ling's boys losing out on promotion.

In December 2005, it appeared the publication of this book would have to be delayed until 2007, then a 'chance' email to Neil Cross, MD of Derwent Press, who was very keen in publishing the book, and so in February 2006 the ball starting rolling again.

Chapter 1
Mexborough and My Early Years

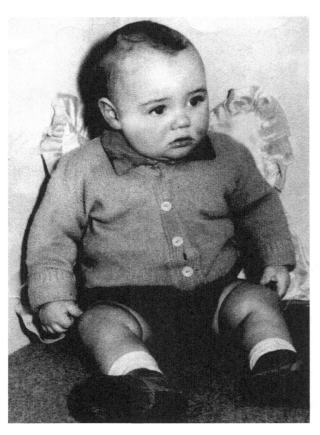

Peter aged 10 months.

I was born in Mexborough, South Yorkshire on 16 February 1952, ten days after the death of King George V1. I was christened Michael Peter Kitchen, my parents Harry and Dorothy chose my first names after the names of two of God's Angels. Although as I grew up, I was always referred to as Peter by all the family members and friends and so it was Peter that stuck over all the years, and therefore I was only ever associated with the name of Peter.

(In later years it became quite a pain, as I have to sign all official documents and cheques as Michael Peter and things like autographs and for non-official things, I signed only as Peter).

Mexborough was known in the 18th century as Mekesborough, located in the Borough of Doncaster, in South Yorkshire, in the triangle between Rotherham, Barnsley and Doncaster. It is located on the north bank of the River Don. Originally a market town, Mexborough grew around coal mining and steel, particularly after the construction of the Sheffield to Doncaster railway line, which ran through the town.

I affectionately always refer to Mexborough as 'The land that time forgot' because the entire major road system seem to bypass the town and unless you live there or have a reason for visiting then you would probably never know it ever existed.

It was and still is a tough area to grow up in and I jokingly say that 'We used to eat nails for breakfast'. There was a 'xenophobic' attitude to living in one of the surrounding towns, so as we grew up, we would rarely venture past the railway crossing into the next town, Denaby unless you were with a parent or a school teacher and at night it would definitely be a 'No-Go' area for a teenager outside of that town. It certainly made me grow up quickly and learn how to look after myself.

Today, Mexborough has a thriving shopping centre running from Bank Street through to Main Street and an excellent outdoor market, it is believed the town had had an outdoor market since the year 1177, known as the 'Mexborough Feast' and of course there is the River Don, which runs through most of the surrounding towns in South Yorkshire through the Don Valley for 70 miles (112 km).

Known Football League players born in Mexborough:

There have been a few famous sportsman and personalities, born in Mexborough over the years, there were forty-two men, other than Peter Kitchen, who played in the Football League, namely:

Percy Beaumont born 1897 and played with Sheffield United, Barnsley and Southend United between 1910-1926, *Charles Bembridge* (no DoB), Mexborough FC, Barnsley and Rotherham United between 1929-1933. *George Bennett* born 1882, Mexborough Thursday FC and Barnsley in 1901. *Harry 'Tip' Bennett* born 1873. Mexborough Town and Barnsley between 1899 and 1904. *Frederick William 'Billy' Biggar* born 1874, Birtley, Sheffield United (1899 to 1901), West Ham United, Fulham, Watford, Rochdale and Leyland Motors, he died in 1935. *Clarence Charles 'Charlie' Bisby*, born in 1904, between 1926 and 1936, he played for Notts. County, Coventry City, Mansfield Town, and Peterborough United. *Fred Bisby,* born in 1880 and was with Kinhurst Town and Grimsby Town between 1905-1907, he died in 1948. *Walter Brayshaw*, a forward with Mexborough Rovers, Sheffield United, Denaby United, Blackburn Rovers, onto Southend United and back with Denaby United, playing between 1919 and 1927. *Abraham 'Abe' Burkinshaw* born in 1886, played for Barnsley, Mexborough Town and Rotherham United between1908-1909. *William Cooper* (No DoB) with Denaby United and Barnsley in 1902. *John S. Cowley* born 1886 with Mexborough Town and Barnsley in 1907, *Samuel Cox* born in 1920 and between 1947 and 1952 played for Denaby United, West Bromwich Albion, Accrington Stanley and Scunthorpe United. *Pat Cullen* born in 1949, he was an England Amateur international, who between 1967 and 1973 was with Halifax Town. *Sidney Dawson* born in 1893 with Denaby United, Sheffield Wednesday, Kinhurst Town, Northampton Town and Grimsby Town between1910 and 1921. *Victor Edward Dodsworth* born in

1911 with Gainsborough Trinity, Manchester United (0 appearances) and Doncaster Rovers between 1930 and 1936, he died in 1986. *Jack Flaherty* (No DoB), with Wolverhampton Wanderers and Bournemouth & Boscombe Athletic between 1934 and 1935. *Herbert A. Garner* born in 1899 with Denaby United, Lincoln City, Wombwell, Rotherham Town, Mansfield Town, Leicester City and Stockport County between 1920 and 1930. *Steve Goulding born in 1954 who between 1971 and 1975 was with Sheffield United,* ***Charles Frederick (Fred) Gregory*** *born on 24 October 1911, the defender played for* Brodsworth Colliery, Doncaster Rovers, Manchester City, Reading, Crystal Palace, Hartlepool United and Rotherham United, between 1929 and 1947, making a total of 228 League appearances, scoring 20 goals. He also made nearly 100 appearances in WW2, Gregory died in 1985. *John Thomas 'Tommy' Hakin* born 1882 and played with *Grimsby Town, Plymouth Argyle, Portsmouth and Rotherham County between 1906 and 1910.* *Norman Hammond was in 1910 with Denaby United, Sunderland and Swindon Town in 1929 to 1931.* *Daniel 'Danny' Robert Hudson* born 25 June 1979, the midfielder started as a trainee with Rotherham United in 1996 and during his seven year stay made 31(20) League appearances with 6 goals, and also played for Doncaster Rovers, on loan in 2002-2003, he joined Halifax Town in 2003, more recently he was with Belper Town, *Joseph 'Joe' Langford* born 1911 and was with Torquay United in the 1933-34 season. *William Lawley* (No DoB) with Barnsley in 1902. *Harry Lee* born in 1933 was with Thames Hill YC, Derby County, Doncaster Rovers and Mansfield Town between 1949 and 1955. *Matthew 'Matt' Moralee,* (No DoB) with Mexborough Town, Sheffield Wednesday and Doncaster Rovers between 1900 and 1905.*Ray Mountford* born 28 April 1958, the goalkeeper was with Rotherham United and Bury (loan), he retired in 1984 to join the Mexborough Police force and rose to rank of Inspector. *Horace Nicholson* born 1895 with Mexborough Highthorne Mission, Sheffield Wednesday and Bradford Park Avenue between 1910 and 1922. *Robert Eric Thompson* born in1944, was with Leeds United as an apprentice and Doncaster Rovers between 1961 and 1963, making 9 League appearances, he later moved to Buxton. *Mike Walker* born in 1952, with Bradford Park Avenue in the 1968-69 season. *Albert Ward* (No DoB), with St. Albans City, Fulham and Rotherham between 1928 and 1930. *William Webb* born in 1932, with Rochdale, Leicester City and Stockport County between 1950 and 1957. *Richard Wright,* born in 1931 and was with Leeds United, Chester and Bradford City between 1949 and1955.

There were a further nine players who achieved great things during their careers in the Football League, they were:

Ian Banks was born on Monday 9 January 1961, as a youngster, he was nurtured by Peter Kitchen and who turned out to be a very talented midfield player who started with Barnsley as an apprentice and he went onto have a long and distinguished career for seventeen years with, Barnsley, Leicester City, Huddersfield Town, Bradford City, West Bromwich Albion, Barnsley, Rotherham United, before ending his Football League career with Darlington in 1995, making a career total of 580 League appearances, scoring 87 goals. He joined non-league Emley in 1995 and later became their manager. He retired from being involved in football during 1999 to take up a position as a financial advisor but returned to Emley as manager in July 2003, but resigned for personal reasons four months later after only seventeen games in charge.

Walter Bennett was born in 1874, an outside right who started his playing career with Mexborough Town after working down the Denaby Pit, he joined Sheffield United in 1891 and during his nine year stay, he won two England caps (1901) and a championship medal in 1898, he played 195 League games for the Blades, scoring 64 goals. He moved to Bristol City, 48 League appearances and 22 goals before moving out of the League with local side Denaby United in 1906. He also returned to the pit and was killed in a mining accident down the Denaby Pit in 1908, leaving a wife and four children. His England shirt and Championship medal are both displayed in the Sheffield United Hall of Fame Museum having been found with a member of his family, still living in Mexborough.

Eric Frederick Brook, was born on 27 November 1907, the 5ft 6ins outside left first attended Mexborough School and started his football career with Oxford Road YMCA, Swinton Prims, Mexborough FC, Dearne Valley Boys and Wath Athletic before signing for Barnsley in 1925, he joined Manchester City in a £6000 joint-signing with Fred Tilson. He became *a great goal scorer with 177 League and cup goals from 494 appearances* and he still jointly heads the list of top League goal scorers for City on 158 with Tommy Johnson. He also *won eighteen caps for England*, it should have been nineteen, he was travelling to Newcastle with another City player Sam Barkas, but were both injured in a car accident and could not play. Brook died in 1956.

George Hunt was born on 22 February 1910, the 5ft 8ins forward played for Regent Street Congregationals in Barnsley, but turned down an offer to play for the senior club in the town. After unsuccessful trials with Sheffield United and Port Vale, he secured a professional contact with Chesterfield in September 1929 and at the end of the season he netted nine goals from 14 appearances. In June 1930 he moved south to join Tottenham Hotspur and claimed 25 goals for their reserve side.

Once given his chance in the first team, he never looked back and was a real crowd pleaser with his fast solo runs, scoring 89 goals in three seasons, including promotion to the First Division in 1933.

He won three full England caps, all in the space of 49 days against Scotland, Italy and Switzerland in 1933. He moved to Arsenal in October 1937, for a reported £7000 fee and scored 3 goals from 18 League appearances winning a League Championship medal, he moved to Bolton Wanderers in March 1938 after another spell with Sheffield Wednesday, he retired in 1947, taking the job as coach at Bolton Wanderers, and was with that club until September 1968. He died on 19 September 1996.

He scored 124 League goals for Spurs from 185 matches, and he held their club League goal scoring record for more than twenty-years until Bobby Smith broke it in 1960. He made a total of 297 League appearances and scoring 169 goals.

Rowan 'Lee' Mills was born on 10 July 1970, a 6ft and one inch centre forward, whose game was simple of getting the ball into the box and have a shot at goal. He started off in 1991 with Stocksbridge Park Steels FC, and went onto to play more than fourteen years in the game and involved with transfers of more than £1.8m and played for Wolverhampton Wanderers, Derby County, Port Vale, Bradford City, Manchester City, Portsmouth, Coventry City, Stoke City. He left the Football League in July 2003, joining Telford United, the following year he was with Conference side Hereford United, but after their failure to gain promotion back in the Football League, the thirty-four year old was released in May 2005, and he retired the following July. Mills made a total of 276(73) Football League appearances, scoring 102 goals.

James Sayer, was born in 1892 and started off in amateur football with Mexborough, Heeley and Sheffield Wednesday. He joined Stoke City in 1888, making just 14 League appearances and scoring once. On 5 February 1887, *his one claim to fame was when he won his one and only cap for England,* in a 7-0 victory over Ireland, played at Sheffield before 6000 fans.

Lionel Smith was born on 23 August 1920, the 6ft and 14stone left back started playing for Mexborough Albion and then Yorkshire Tar Distillers FC. He joined Denaby United before going to Arsenal as an amateur in May 1939 and turning professional with the Gunners three months later. During the war years, he was a guest player with Notts. County. After the war he returned to Arsenal, making 162 League appearances, scoring 18 goals, during his seven seasons at Highbury, *also winning six England caps.* He later played for Watford (7 League appearances) and finishing his career as player-manager with Gravesend and Northfleet. Before resigning in April 1960. Smith died in Stoke Newington, London on 8 November 1980, aged sixty.

Geoff Salmons was born on Wednesday 14 January 1948, the midfielder started as a junior with Sheffield United in 1967 and his career spanned some fifteen years, also playing for Stoke City, Leicester City, Chesterfield, ending up with Gainsborough Trinity in 1982. He *made a total of 449 League appearances with 41 goals.* In recent years, he ran the Pasteurs Lodge in Mexborough.

Alan Sunderland who was born on Wednesday 1 July 1953 and famous for his bubble-permed hairstyle, a product of Wath Wanderers, who joined Wolverhampton Wanderers in 1971 and stayed six years at Molineux before joining Arsenal in November 1977 for £220,000 and continued his successful career at Highbury, he scored the late winner in the 1979 FA Cup to secure a famous 3-2 win over Manchester United. He had a loan spell with Cambridge United and ended his league career with Ipswich Town. He made a total of 394(28) League appearances with 96 goals. Sunderland made one appearance for England on 31 May 1980, in a 2-1 win over Australia.

After four years running a public house in Ipswich, he moved to Malta in 1995 to manage the local side Birkirkara FC, today is now retired and lives in a small village called Mellieha. The News of the World newspaper brought him back to England in May 2005, as a commentator for the Arsenal and Manchester United FA Cup Final in Cardiff. The only connection with football today, he will occasionally coach some Maltese children, watches TV when Arsenal are playing, and he has a cockatiel named Rooney.

There were of course many footballers born in Mexborough, who never made it into the Football League, one of note was a *Fred Kirkham*, who was born in Mexborough on 26 April 1921. He joined Blackpool from the Fylde club in March 1939, and was described as a player of 'great promise' and played for the Blackpool 'B' side in the Lancashire League. He was close to a first team call up when WW2 started and he joined the RAF in June 1941. He played a few games for Bath City and Blackpool during the war years but he sustained a severe knee injury, which ended his playing career. Sadly, he was taken ill during November 1947, and died of pneumonia on 30 March 1949, aged just twenty-eight, never to claim his fame in the Football League.

Other famous sporting, acting and broadcasting personalities who were born in Mexborough:

Dan Clarke born on 4 October 1983, during 2005, he was a top class British Formula 3 Championship racing driver with the Raikkonen Robertson racing team. Racing boss Kimi Raikkonen said of Clarke: 'He is fast, he is determined and has the mind of a champion'. Clarke started racing as a ten year old, when he won many karting championships and at the age of eighteen he was crowned BRDC Formula Ford Champion. In 2006, he joined the Champ World Car series in USA, racing for the CTE Racing –HVM team.

William Ian 'Iron' Hague a former British Heavyweight champion between 1908 to 1911, he was born on 6 November 1885, he had 30 fights with 22 wins (17 ko's), the story goes that he worked in a local iron factory where they cast anvils, he could carry 2 anvils, one under each arm and challenged anyone to beat him and he offered to pay them a Pound if they could so, he never ever paid out anything. Hague died on 18 August 1951, aged sixty-five.

John Michael Hawthorn was born 10 April 1929, Mike Hawthorn was a very famous racing driver. He started his Formula One campaign in 1952 and he was the winner of the 1955, 24 hours Le Mans race, despite being involved in a terrible accident during the race, which killed 80 spectators. In 1958 he was the Formula One Championship and came one point ahead of Stirling Moss, he retired soon after and devoted his time in writing motor racing stories and restoring a 1935 Riley Sprite car. On 22 January 1959, Hawthorn died in a car accident whilst driving his 3.4 Jaguar, he went into a tree whilst travelling on the A3 Guildford by-pass.

Dennis Priestley was born on 16 July 1950 and he became one of the great darts players of all-time, winning the Embassy World Champion in 1991, and also with many other titles to his name. 'The Menace', as he is known, is by his admission finding it harder to take on the competition the older he gets.

Malcolm Walker, born on 14 October 1933, who played first class cricket for Somerset between 1952 and 1958. He had 52 innings and scored 574 runs, with one century, and he took 28 wickets with his right-arm off-break's, with a best of 5/45. He died in September 1986 in Retford, Notts, and aged 52 years and 323 days.

There have been a few top actors born in Mexborough over the years including:

Keith Barron was born on 8 August 1934 (*some references show his birth as being in 1936*), a famous actor who started at the Sheffield Repertory and has starred in many TV series and films, the latest TV series being 'Brief Encounters' in 2005, as Ted Deary, he has also appeared on stage with Bristol Old Vic. He is currently cast in the role as the father of *DCI Banks* in the ITV series of that name

Brian Blessed was born 9 October 1937 (*some references show his birth a being in 1936*) the son of a coal miner, who came from a very poor background. An actor who became best known for his hearty, king-sized portrayals in many film and TV productions and he creates an impressive screen presence.

As well as his acting, he had been a great love of mountaineering and has been on three expeditions to Mount Everest, he has also completed a trek to the North Pole and was on an expedition to the Lost World in Venezuela.

I met Brian Blessed in Newfoundland Park,on the Somme battlefields in Northern France in 2007, when he was filming a TV documentary. He was actually standing in one of the trenches in the park and he laughed out loudly in his very distinctive voice when I told him I was also originally from Mexborough

Tony Capstick was born on 27 July 1944, he was a comedian, actor, folk singer and guitarist and was a broadcaster on BBC Radio Sheffield for more than 30-years until being dismissed in January 2003, he also wrote a regular column for the Rotherham Advertiser. The fifty-nine year old was found dead at his cottage in Hoober, near Wentworth, South Yorkshire on 24 October 2003.

Kenneth Haigh born 25 March 1930, an Actor who took part in Cleopatra and in the Beatles film 'A Hard Days Night', he also played in a number of British TV series during the seventies'.

And finally Politician, *Brian O'Malley* who was born on 22 January 1930, he became Labour MP for Rotherham in 1963 and he worked in the Whip's Office in the Ministry of State of Health and Social Security, he died on 6 April 1976.

During the early 1950's Mexborough was still a small town with rows and rows of terraced housing and a population of around 13,000 people, it had with six pits surrounding it from a number of other small towns like Barnborough, Denaby Main, Manvers Main, Thurnscough, Goldthorpe, Kilnhurst and a few others, the mines being the major employer of the area, a number of workers were also employed in steel, the power station, and on the railways. (Today, all the mines have closed, together with the closing and dismantling of its power station during the 1980's).

My father was a coal miner and he worked at Wath Main Colliery, he was a miner for approximately forty-two years. His only break - if you call it that!! - was when he went into the Army for four years and served in both India and Burma fighting against the Japanese (*Interesting therefore that my son Michael is married and lives in Japan with their three children*). My father died in 2000, after spending a number of years in a Nursing Home.

My mum had a few jobs, initially working in a peanut factory and then as a Dinner Lady. She also worked, as a nursing assistant at a hospital near Doncaster and then became a home help working with elderly people and those with disabilities. She died during early March 2005.

I was born at 2 St. George Place just of Herbert Street, the houses in these streets have all been knocked down now. We moved to 54 Sycamore Road and stayed there for about five years until we moved again to 90 Maple Road and we lived there until I was eighteen.

I have two sisters and one brother. My older sister Rita was born on 30 September 1946 and brother Gordon was born on 6 May 1948, both born in the same house as me. My younger sister Janice Dawn was born on 8 August 1961 at the Mexborough Montague Hospital.

As we grew up Gordon and Rita, played together a lot. The age difference was such that we seemed to grow up in different eras and with different sets of friends, so we all went our separate ways during our younger days and as I grew older and got more involved in football, so I never really noticed what they were doing. (*Although I'm very happy to say that we have grown much closer as we have reached middle age*).

My mother and father were very hard working parents who were very committed to their family. They were also quite liberal and they allowed us to do very much what we wanted but they had a 'code of conduct' where we were regularly warned against getting into trouble and having the police come to our house. My father was a lovely man and when he wasn't down the mines, he would often take us for long walks in the surrounding countryside.

90 Maple Road, Mexborough - taken in 2005

Although an industrialised area, there was lots of agricultural land and many woods and fields surrounding the area. He never learned to drive and would either walk or cycle the two miles to Wath Main Colliery, eventually he bought a small Honda motor bike to get to and from work but never progressed to driving a car.

At the age of three and a half, I contracted polio, it was in September 1955, and I think I was the twentieth reported case in Mexborough District after an epidemic hit the town. I spent three weeks in the Kendary Fever Hospital in Barnsley. My parents were informed that I might end up disabled and that I may never be able to walk properly again, in the end I was one of the nine cases of non-paralytic poliomyelitis, so it was quite amazing that I went onto become a professional footballer.

Like most people in the area, we were quite a poor family and we didn't have a lot of money. I remember once as a small boy, having butter put on my hair because we didn't have any Brylcreem and when we got out into the countryside, I was chased by a swarm of flies.

I first attended the infant school near Sycamore Road and I started kicking a football around in that same road, kicking the ball against a high wall of the local corner shop and a house, the wall having had two goals posts painted onto it.

We never went on family holidays and the farthest I had ever travelled as a youngster was on day trips to Cleethorpes with my Mum to go on the annual Miners Welfare outing.

The only other trip we did with Mum was to go onto a red double-decker bus to visit her sisters Joyce and Muriel, who lived in Bradford. We had to change buses in Barnsley and I always wanted to sit up top on the front seats so I could look out of the windows.

We always went passed the Wakefield Trinity Rugby Stadium and I used to imagine what is would be like one day to play in such a stadium.

My earliest memories of playing were as a three year old on various wooden contraptions and carts that my Dad, he was a very practical man, he made for us from old wooden boxes and pram wheels. I also used to love wearing old brown leather football boots with the strap across the front, I loved them so much, that my Dad would take out the studs so that I could wear these boots all the time.

When we lived in Sycamore Road, I recall playing football with my brother and his friends. Having played with kids three and four years older than me certainly helped me develop my football skills much quicker.

Then at the age of six, I attended Roman Terrace Junior School, which now has also been knocked down and today stands a Nursing Home on the site.

Almost immediately after going to the school I was able to get into the school team, which was mainly made up of boys who were already ten years of age, whilst I had just turned seven. I was able to play football for a further two years with older boys, which had a significant impact on my football and educational development.

I had an idyllic childhood in that I was able to play in the countryside and because I had an older brother, I was able to do and try things that a boy of my age wouldn't have normally been able to do. I was really able to get back to nature.

We made bows and arrows and went hunting rabbits, I also collected birds' eggs and we built dams in the local stream. We made our own fishing rods and went fishing in local lakes and went swimming in the rivers Don and the Dearne and the canal that ran through and close by Mexborough (these rivers were highly polluted with waste from the steelworks and coal mines that dumped this without any restrictions, as there are today).

We went "scragging" apples and pears from the local orchards and we made dens from the freshly cut hay in autumn time and lit campfires and on occasions were allowed to camp out if my brother was with us. We had pet rabbits and pet mice in the shed and always had a family dog, which my Dad would take for daily walks.

I used to go every week to the Saturday morning pictures, and I remember watching Laurel and Hardy movies, Tarzan movies with Johnny Weismuller and also Flash Gordon with Buster Crabbe in the starring role as well as seeing the Looney Tunes cartoons.

Around the age of eight, I started getting into music and I remember buying my first 45 single which was 'Only the Lonely' by co-incidentally The Big 'O' Roy Orbison. I also really liked Cliff Richard and I remember my renditions to a mirror of the song 'A voice in the Wilderness' from the film starring Cliff called Expresso Bongo. I also used to go to the Saturday afternoon discos at the Empress Ballrooms in Mexborough and used to dance to 'Glad all over' by the Dave Clark 5 and 'I wanna hold your hand' by the Beatles, who I was really into in the early sixties and the Rolling Stones. I still think Elvis Presley was absolutely brilliant.

I also, as a young lad, used to go train spotting and I would get up really early and get onto a train to Doncaster with a packed lunch that I made myself. I would stay there all day and I remember how everyone looked for the 'Streaks' to come through. This was to do with the speed and also because of the whistling noise they made as they sped through the station. These were a special train examples of which were 'The Flying Scotsman' and 'The Mallard' that were green and had a long sloping front. They would go very fast at around 120 miles per hour, which was a speed record at the time. They were either going from London Kings Cross to Glasgow or Edinburgh or vice versa and only occasionally stopped at one of the platforms.

When I played football for the Roman Terrace Junior School, my Dad would come and watch me, he would give me a half crown for every time I scored a goal, he soon changed this to three goals, as I always scored for the school and he really

Roman Terrace Junior School 1961 — Peter on the front row with the ball. Derrick Skirrow on extreme right front row

Roman Terrace Junior School 1963 — Peter holding the cup. Robert `Lobby` Lee and Paul Marshall are on back row, last two on the right.

53

I loved playing football as a young kid and it always felt totally natural for me to play with a football and score goals. As I got more and more into it I would take a ball on my own and if no one could come out and play then I would play 'wall ball', a game where I had to hit a nominated garage door from wherever the ball rebounded to and I also allowed myself only one or at most two touches.

Sometimes when it was freezing and there was about six inches of snow on the ground, the only mate I could find to come and play was a Graham Pilling (nicknamed Plug), who was one of a family of thirteen children, so he wasn't spoilt like all my other friends. We would go out in the snow and play on a local pitch for hours, just the two of us.

We would have an FA or European competition, which involved sixteen teams like, Manchester United, Arsenal, Sheffield Wednesday, Sheffield United etc. Sometimes we would toss a coin to see who got to be the local team as neither of us wanted to be one of the others, support your local teams we always thought, unlike today where the top clubs have support from all over the country and even the world.

Some times though we picked foreign teams like Inter Milan or Real Madrid etc. as we were becoming increasingly aware of European clubs at that time. We would play each other on a knockout basis round by round. One of us would go in goal, while the other would dribble around and shoot and also make up their own commentary whilst representing one of the teams. Each had ten minutes to score as many goals as possible but you couldn't score from within the six-yard box. We would have a pen and paper and a watch and drew each round as teams got knocked out.

We never worried the whole day about eating and only drank water from a tap that was provided for the allotments that backed on to the field.

Now as you have read, I hated staying indoors and I was always out playing and if I wasn't playing football then it would be cricket or rounders or any game that involved running around or going on long bike rides. The only indoor games I played were Subbuteo table soccer, Howzat, the cricket game or Football Manager the board game, although I did eventually progress on from these to Monopoly and Cluedo. I also collected everything from the Lesney/Corgi toy cars (which incidentally I later found out were made in Leyton/Hackney), toy soldiers and Army vehicles, stamps, cigarette and match boxes and I eventually started to collect football programmes along with writing to Football League clubs for autographs.

I really enjoyed going to school and at playtime a group of us would play football with a tennis ball, not to the liking of my parents, as I was always in need of new shoes or plimsolls. At the age of ten, I frequently watched Rotherham United at Millmoor, but I really supported Sheffield United.

I remember one match at Mexborough Town stadium when Rotherham

United played in a charity football match versus a Yorkshire County Cricket Se-lect Xl. After the match I waited with some other lads for the players to come out of the dressing rooms to get their autographs.

After getting most of these I was still waiting for Freddy Trueman to come out, as he was a big star in Yorkshire at the time.

As he came out, I said "Can I have your autograph please Freddy " but to my utter dismay he pushed me out of the way and said "It's Mister Trueman to you son" and walked away without signing for anyone. It was quite a devastating experience for a ten year old and I have never forgotten this experience. When I became a professional footballer myself, I always vowed that I would always sign autographs however many and however long I was kept back.

I have never liked Freddy Trueman to this day since and other people in the media have confirmed to me that is typical of the man.

Frederick Sewards Trueman was a great Yorkshire and England bowler, fast and frightening with a classical bowling action and a mop on unruly jet-black hair. He made his Test debut in June 1952 and by 1964 at the Oval against Australia, he had taken his 300th test wicket, being the first bowler to achieve this feat, he went onto to take 307 test wickets from just 67 tests. Trueman sadly died on 1 July 2006 after battling with lung cancer.

My Dad always used to say to me that I should study at school and get a good education and I can still hear him saying that in his very broad Yorkshire accent *'Thar not going darn't pit, thar can stay on at school and get thissen a good edyercation'.*

I then attended the Secondary Modern School in College Road, in the old Grammar School building, and stayed there until I was sixteen. My class teacher for 2 years was Peter Hardy. I remember him well because after I complained to him about my end of year school report, in which he described me as "promising but spends too much time dreaming about playing football" he called me to the front of the class and actually underlined this statement in the report. At least he was against corporal punishment in schools.

Hardy was born in Wath upon Dearne on 16 July 1931 into a mining fam-ily, the men of the family all went down the pit, but he did not join them, after teaching in a number of Yorkshire schools, he moved into politics and was elect-ed as the Labour MP for Rother Valley, South Yorkshire until 1993 and then was elected MP for Wentworth, serving until his retirement in 1997 and became a keen campaigner for the preservation of wildlife and natural habitats.

He was created a life peer as Lord Hardy of Wath. His life was marked by trag-edy, his eldest son Stuart died from cancer, aged 12, and his adopted son Martin died aged nine. My former teacher, Peter Hardy sadly died during December 2003, aged seventy-two.

The other teacher there who had an influence on me during those years was my football team manager Des Parks, he later moved to live in Northampton. Today, he is most probably retired. Although, I can't remember very much about him, I can recall that he was a great motivator and made you want to play for him and I was selected for the Don and Dearne district schools team at Under-11.

I became very involved in school football between the ages of eleven and fourteen, unfortunately from about 14-years of age, the leagues were disbanded due to a dispute between the Teachers about payment for this extracurricular work outside of school hours.

We did continue to play in organised school matches although there were no leagues, but I did get selected for the District Under-15 team.

Secondary School in College Road

During this whole period of my school football days, I was never coached once in the skills of the game, but I did attend a training session when I was fifteen whilst with Don and Dearne schools U 15's at Barnburgh College and being coached by a John Adams who was a teacher and also a Regional Coach for the Football Association. He later become involved with Anton Johnson who was a Director of Southend United and later chairman of Rotherham United (*He was their chairman in 1980, when I rejected a move to join them*).

From about fourteen years of age I lost a lot of interest in football and started going out at nights a lot more, chasing after girls of course, with one or more of my friends at that time. There was Paul Marshall, (*Paul's older sister later married Peter Middleton who was a very promising footballer, he was born in Rawmarsh on*

13 September 1948, he started off as a junior with Sheffield Wednesday in 1965, before moving onto Bradford City in July 1968 and during a four-year stay the inside forward, made 127(4) League appearances with 25 goals and he played a further 20 Cup games and scored 9 goals. In February 1972, he joined Plymouth Argyle in a swap-deal, which he was unhappy about, making a scoring debut, but just days later he was struck by a passing car, receiving serious injuries which ended his playing career, despite several come-back attempts). Middleton committed suicide in 1977), Derrick Skirrow (He was the best man at my wedding to Susan), Mick Griffin (I was later the best man at his wedding) and Robert (Lobby) Lee.

Derrick, Paul and Lobby Lee were in the same Roman Terrace Junior football team with me for a couple of years. We would regularly buy bottles of Bulmers or Merrydown cider to get drunk or try and get served in one of a number of local pubs. Mick Griffin and I also started a rock band about this time with him on the drums and me as lead singer. We recruited a couple of guitarists and played a couple of school charity events and I remember that two of the songs we sang were the Who's 'My generation' and Wayne Fontana's 'The Game of Love'. We were never going to get very far as my voice wasn't the best in the world and I couldn't play any instruments but it gave me a taste of being a 'front man'.

Robert Lee was the biggest of us all and he looked by far the oldest, at thirteen he already had sideburns, so we used to send him in to the off-license to buy us the drinks.

I can still remember the first time I ever got drunk in a pub, which was called the Red Lion in Mexborough and drank about six pints of bitter, when I was only about fifteen, needless to say that when I got home and went to bed, the room was spinning and I was sick all over the bed, which my Mum had to clean up. She once told me that she gave me a severe belting that night, I was so drunk, to this day, I can't remember it. I also tried smoking at this time, but I never got hooked, Thank God, and I have never smoked since.

At Secondary School, I achieved 6 GCE 'O' levels, which were English Language, English Literature, Mathematics, History, Geography and General Science and 5 CSE Grade 1's in English, Maths, History, Geography and also Art and Crafts.

The reason for the duplication was that it was the first year that GCE 'O' Levels were introduced in the Secondary School and so as a back up the school put the 'A' stream kids into both sets of examinations, so that if any of the class failed at GCE, they would still have an opportunity of gaining academic qualifications.

When I was just turning sixteen, I played for Mexborough Youth Club football team, but this usually involved going to a pub before hand and sinking two or three pints before the match. We didn't take it too seriously, but we were still successful and won the Youth League Championship and Cup on a couple of occasions. It was at this time I moved to the Grammar School.

As I was growing older I noticed that certain members of my family were a fairly 'off the wall' bunch.

My sister Rita became a 'Hippy' and went hitch hiking around the country on many occasions and later became a Jehovah's Witness and still is to this day, she lives in Southport and nursed our Mum for her last six years on earth before her death. My sister Rita and her husband Martyn, have since relocated to Hastings in East Sussex when Martyn retired in 2008. They live on the seafront very close to the Pier, which burned down quite recently but is currently being rebuilt. They are very happy and settled down South.

My brother Gordon was a 'Teddy Boy' for a while and I remember him in his long suit jackets with velvet collars and 'Beatle Crusher' shoes. He had a lot of tattoos, which he now always regretted having had done and has since had many of them lasered off. I remember, he once converted an old ambulance and drove overland to Australia, having to sell off his blood, don't ask me how, in Turkey when he ran out of money. He eventually made it there and after living in Brisbane for five years, he got dual nationality.

Gordon came back to England, studied a lot to gain several qualifications, and today he is a Social Worker and lives and works in Rotherham. (Although he always talks about going to live back in Oz) I always thought that it was a coincidence that I ended up playing at Brisbane Road for Orient, whilst Gordon actually lived in Brisbane, Australia . Gordon retired in 2013 and like myself is really enjoying his retirement and also his hobby as a potter and he also likes to travel as often as he can.

My sister Janice works as an IT Services Manager and lives in Sheffield. She travels a lot down to London, where I meet up regularly with her. My sister Janice has since taken early retirement from the IT Company she used to work for and in a complete career change, is now working as an Asylum and Refugee Integration Manager in Sheffield.

As a teenager, I was in my own little world at times and was a bit of a dreamer with a vivid imagination. I watched every Hammer horror film ever made, usually Dracula and Frankenstein movies with Christopher Lee and Peter Cushing and If I wasn't dreaming of playing football for England, I was either a pop star or a secret agent. I always watched programmes like the Avengers and The Saint and then became an avid fan of the James Bond 007 films.

Whilst at the O's I remember doing a photo shoot at Brisbane Road in the White Aston Martin used by Roger Moore in the 1977 film 'The Spy who Loved Me'. I adored Diana Rigg as Emma Peel in the Avengers (who incidentally came from Doncaster) and I have since always been attracted to feisty, independent women.

Peter with a family friend (on left), his mother and father, brother Gordon (next to Peter) and sister Janice.

Thank you, Mr. Bennett

In 1968, I first attended the new 6th Form College at the Grammar School in Maple Road and stayed for two-years. This is when I started taking football more seriously. The teacher there who had a great influence on me becoming a pro footballer was Bob Bennett, my PE teacher, I remember at the time, he was a good looking man, who had a thick head of blonde hair and a permanent tan, looking very fit. He was a terrific person and I had tremendous respect for him. He also had a beautiful blonde girlfriend who he later married. They are still together. I met them in 1997 when I went to a Grammar School football reunion and were able to talk briefly about old times.

Through the work on this book, I have since established contact again with Bob and so I hope to meet up with him again in the not too distant future. He retired in December 2005, when he reached his sixtieth birthday, which was a sad loss for the school after his many years of service.

He has been an inspiration to many other pupils over the years as well as myself and I can't speak highly enough of his contribution to the development and success I enjoyed in my career. He helped me tremendously and was terrific at putting the game over to us boys. He used to encourage players like myself and Alan Sunderland and he stressed the importance of our education to us.

When I think of my time at the Grammar School the similarities between Bob and the schoolmaster Mr. Chipping, from a 1930s British made film starring Robert Donat called *'Goodbye, Mr. Chips'* always comes to mind, as Bob was similarly held in such high esteem by his former pupils. The film was nominated for seven academy awards, Donat was the only victor for best actor, but the film was up against another great film that year, in *'Gone with the Wind'*.

I won school Colours and Honours and whilst playing for the schools First XI I represented Yorkshire Schools for two years between 1968 and 1970. In the 1969-70 season I was selected for the Northern Counties U-19's select XI against a Southern Counties XI, in the final of an English Schools U-19's trials match.

I also played on 7 April 1970 for the England 'B' team at the sixth English Schools Football Association's Festival of Football held at Skegness Town's Football Ground against the Derby County FC youth team and I scored twice in our 2-0 victory.

The local paper reported that the depth of talent in English schools football was shown at the annual festival.

The England Schools 'B' side was impressive in their 2-0 victory of the youth team of Derby County, the first goal came when Revill crossed from the wing for Kitchen representing Yorkshire to head home. Kitchen had always been a threat and he gained just reward with another goal in the closing minutes. He dribbled, side-stepped and evaded

English Schools Festival XI v Derby County Youth, April 1970.
Peter, third from right on front row.

Mexborough Secondary School Team, League and Cup Winners 1964-65
Peter third from left on front row. Back Row, the teacher (right) Des Parks
and middle row Paul Marshall

Mexborough Grammar School, April 1969
(Peter second from left on front row, next to Bob Bennett).

Peter Kitchen (Yorkshire), N. LePage (Channel Islands), T. Hughes (Stafford-shire), I. Revill (Derbyshire).Reserves: J. Hodge (Leicestershire), S. Elliott (York-shire), R. Higginbotham (Yorkshire), R. Milhaly (Derbyshire) and D. Vincent (London). also remember playing with Londoner John Delve who had a good League career in midfield with Queens Park Rangers, Plymouth Argyle and Exeter City between 1971 and 1980, making over 260 appearances and scoring 18 goals. There was also Dave Alexander who played in the Northern Counties XI and as full back for the England youth XI, I played in later life, many years with him for the Corinthian Casuals Schools Vets team.

I also played alongside Alan Sunderland several times. He was a fast running right-winger with bags of skill.

We did well during my time at the school and twice we got into the Yorkshire Schools final, but we lost to Thomas Aquinas of Leeds, who beat us one year and St. Michael's School the following year, but we were a strong side playing in a strong schools football area. My memories of Yorkshire schooling have not been withered by time. I have not seen my school colleagues for a number of years, but I did receive a telegram from Alan wishing me well, just before one of Orient's big FA Cup games in 1978.

Robert William Bennett was born on 3 December 1945 in Wath, the next village to Mexborough, he trained to be a PE teacher between 1964 to 1967 and started teaching at Mexborough Grammar School in September 1967, he was a former footballer, he first played for Doncaster Rovers between 1961 and 1963, captaining the youth team and playing in a few reserve games, he was offered a contract by the manager Oscar Hold, but his mother thought he should become a PE teacher and so went to college instead.

At Mexborough Grammar they were very proud of the number of footballers they have produced who have gone into League football. Other than Alan and myself the school has seen the following boys play in the Football League:

Geoff Salmons, another Mexborough-born lad who played for Sheffield United and Stoke City, he is featured in earlier in this chapter.

Frank Barlow, Sheffield United, *Ian Banks*, Barnsley and Leicester City, also featured earlier in this chapter, *Peter Hart*, Huddersfield Town and Walsall, with over 600 appearances.

Dylan Kerr, although born in Valletta in Malta in 1967, he was brought up in Mexborough and had a long career with Sheffield Wednesday, Arcadia Shepherds in South Africa, Leeds United, Doncaster Rovers, and Kilmarnock and too many other clubs to list, more recently he was coaching in Arizona, USA, and he made approximately 250 senior appearances.

Kevin Eley, Rotherham United, Chesterfield and Gainsborough Trinity, *Dean Whitehouse* a youth player with both, Barnsley and Torquay United and finally *Steve Kulic* a player on Rotherham United's books.

We also had at the School, *Richard Graham Lumb* from Doncaster who played first class cricket for Yorkshire between 1970 and 1984, he had 529 first- class and 'A' class innings, making a total of 14 507 runs, his highest innings being 165 not out.

Chapter 2
A successful junior career and seven happy years with Doncaster Rovers

I started playing as a young lad for Don & Dearne School teams at U-11's and U-15's and for Yorks Senior Schools and at national schools level.

Bob Bennett played for Denaby United in the old Midland League and he was responsible in my early playing career for me receiving my first ever payment in football.

My Yorkshire County game against Lancashire had been called off in the morning and so he asked me to come along to Denaby's match against Farsley Celtic. I remember the game very well, I started as a substitute and I came on with about twenty minutes to go and scored with literally my first touch of the game, and I received a cheque for the princely sum of £1.50.

Around this time I left the Mexborough Youth club team to join Denaby Youth Club I found the club better organized and a lot more serious about the game and they used to enter into the National Youth Club competitions, although in the season I played with them, we didn't progress that far. It was during my time there that I went on trial with Sheffield United with about three or four of the Denaby players. We attended the Ball Inn training ground and played in a mixed team trial game against the United youth side under floodlights.

I thought I'd played well, scoring a hat trick but no one from the club made any attempt to talk to any of us, the coaches from United only appeared to be interested in their own youth players.

(*When I scored a hat trick against them for Orient in March 1978, I did an interview with Radio Hallam and I recalled this same story to the reporter because I had been a United supporter as a boy and that I wanted to play for them at the time, I scored a few goals against them in my career, as if it was some sort of retribution against them for rejecting me or never signing me*).

First spotted by the great George S. Raynor, a former manager of the Swedish national side

Local journalist Peter Catt in his tribute to me, mentioned earlier in the Tributes section of this book, said that it was George Raynor who first spotted me. He was quite correct, Raynor saw me playing for Yorkshire Grammar Schools on a number of occasions between 1969 and 1970.

George watched me quite a few times and I remember him always shouting from the sidelines 'Up the line, up the line' to our players when taking throw-ins.

Thus was quite a simple instruction in that he always advocated throwing the ball forward in order to gain ground.

He would also shout 'Come on you Lilywhites' which was a reference to our all-white kit and the white rose of Yorkshire. He had been manager of Doncaster Rovers between 1967 and 1968 for 69 League games, with 30 wins and 19 draws, but he stepped down due to ill health and later he was scouting for the club. He had a remarkable record in the game.

Raynor was born in Hoyland, near Barnsley, Yorkshire on 13 January 1907, he attended Barnsley Grammar School and played local football with Elsecar Bible Class, Mexborough Athletic and Wombwell Athletic before moving to Sheffield United in 1930. The little 5ft 6ins right-winger made his League debut with Mansfield Town in 1932, making 9 appearances with one goal. In 1933 he was with Rotherham United and during a two-year stay, he played 59 League games, scoring 17 goals. In 1934 he was with Bury and during a three-year spell me made 54 League appearances and scored 4 goals, he ended his League career with Aldershot and in the 1938-39 season he appeared in 35 games with 4 goals.

During the war years, he guested for Charlton Athletic, Bury, Bournemouth, Hull City and Crystal Palace.

In 1943 he was the coach of Iraqi national side and also coached British troops in Baghdad. He was appointed coach of AIK in Sweden and after being recommended by the secretary of the FA Stanley Rous, he was appointed as coach to the Swedish national side. In 1947 he team gave England a fright pulling back from 3-0 down to a score line of 3-2 before Stan Mortensen scored for the English and a year later his team were crowned Olympic champions.

In 1949 his side did beat England 3-1 in Stockholm and the next year they finished third in the World Cup Finals in Brazil. In 1953 on their way to meet the great Hungarian side in Budapest, the team coach passed a statue of Stalin and he told his players. 'If we win I'll paint Stalin's moustache red'. He was spared the job when achieving a 2-2 draw, just two-weeks later the Hungarians went to Wembley to thrash the English team 6-3, England's first ever defeat on the hallowed turf.

He held a coaching position with both Roma from 1951(In 1952, his Swedish national team gained bronze in the Olympics) and in 1953 he was with Lazio and in June 1955, held was appointed coach with Coventry City, in January 1956, he a brief stint for a few months as manager of the City, with a record of: Played 16, Won 6 Drawn 5 and Lost 6, after starting the season as Coach under Jesse Carver and took over when had resigned but failed to gain promotion. He was demoted to coach again when Harry Warren took charge but Raynor soon left in August 1956 because of boardroom interference for a position with Lincolnshire Education Committee as a football coach, he returned to Sweden during December 1956.

In 1958 the Swedes hosted the World Cup Finals, his team lost to Brazil and a 17-year old Pele by 5-2 in the Final. His record as coach of Sweden was in charge for 89 games, won 51, Drew 16 and lost 22.

In 1960, he returned to England and became manager of Midland League side Skegness Town and signed the great Alick Jeffrey when he gave up football for a while after breaking his leg, helped him back to fitness and sold him back to Doncaster Rovers in 1963.

Raynor was a great coach who put his faith in skill, who was also a brilliant tactician and motivator and seemed to be appreciated more in Europe than in England. Yet, I felt very honoured that he was the man who first spotted me playing and recommended me to Lawrie McMenemy at Rovers in 1970. Sadly, George Raynor died in the early 1990s.

The Yorkshire team manager at the time was a Schoolteacher in Doncaster named Eddie Beaglehole who was very prominent in local schools football and his son Steve later became Doncaster Rovers youth coach.

At the age of eighteen I was watched by the Doncaster Rovers boss Lawrie McMenemy and he came to visit me and my parents at home and after I signed the contract and as he had left a scout from Leeds United turned up at the house and asked if I would be interested in signing for them. But I quickly told him I had just signed for Doncaster Rovers, he apologised for the inconvenience and left.

The local Doncaster Evening Post newspaper reported on 31 July 1970.

Mike Sinclair reports:

ROVERS BEAT OFF LEEDS UNITED TO SIGN UP KITCHEN

Doncaster Rovers manager Lawrie McMenemy beat Leeds United by minutes when he signed 18-year old Mexborough boy Peter Kitchen on professional forms. Kitchen is the centre forward who scored a hat trick for Yorkshire Senior Schools against Rovers Juniors at Belle Vue last season.

The former Mexborough Grammar School boy Kitchen, who has attracted the interest of a number of other clubs, could be the boy to watch next season. Although he is still young enough to play for the junior side, Mr. McMenemy said: "I hope he will be challenging for a first team place by the end of the season."

Kitchen was one of the young players taken to Lilleshall and McMenemy added: "when the others clubs found out he hadn't been signed by anyone I had to move quickly. A few minutes after I went and signed him a scout from Leeds United arrived at his house."

Also signing with me on the same day were two 19-year old defenders from Durham City, Roy Young (The full back went to make just 6(1) League appearances for Rovers) and David Adamson (The full back played 28 League appearances for Rovers).

The story ended with the comment:

The former Mexborough Grammar School boy Peter Kitchen, who has attracted the interest of a number of big clubs, could be the new boy to watch next season.

I was joining a long established club, having been formed in September 1879 by a worker who was the same age as me when I joined Rovers, at eighteen Albert Jenkins a fitter at the Doncaster LNER works, who got together some fellow workers and formed a team, in October, they played their first match against Rawmarsh, who later formed themselves into what is today's Doncaster Rovers.

As I was just about to finish school, I was continually being watched by Doncaster Rovers, I played for Yorkshire Schools against the Navy and a Doncaster Rovers XI and I scored a hat trick in both games.

My first professional game for Doncaster Rovers was in a pre-season friendly at Boston United's York Street Ground on 1 August 1970 and I played up front with veteran striker Laurie Sheffield. I scored our goal in a 3-1 defeat. In the

**First day of training at Doncaster Rovers, July 1970.
Peter fourth from left, next to boss Lawrie McMenemy.**

Boston defence that day was Jim Smith, the long-serving manager who was assistant to Harry Redknapp at Portsmouth, and he was manager of Oxford United when they were relegated into the Nationwide Conference in May 2006.

This game was followed with my appearance on the subs' bench against the great Leeds United team of this era with the likes of Bremner, Giles, Clarke, Jones, Charlton, Hunter and co.

I didn't get on the pitch in this game but whilst at Rovers we did repeat this fixture on several occasions at both Belle Vue and at Elland Road. Needless to say I can't recall ever winning any of the games but I do remember a few hard tackles from 'Big Jack' Charlton and Norman 'bite your legs' Hunter.

I remember even before I signed for Rovers, while I was still an amateur that I was on the bench for a Rovers friendly game against the Italian giants Lazio, it was a warm-up game for them before they played at Sunderland and Wolves in Anglo-Italian Cup matches, in which they lost 3-1 and 1-0 respectively. The match was played on 5 May 1970, the attendance was 3090, Rovers were expecting a crowd in an excess of 6000.

After a goalless first half, the Italians scored four times without reply, the fans were rather disappointed with the result, until they remembered it

Peter with wife Susan in 1977

was like us playing a top First Division side, like Leeds United, in those days.

In the end I never got onto the field, Lawrie McMenemy not using any substitutes with only the Italians using a few subs. I was desperate to get on the pitch but also terrified that 'Lawrie Mac' would actually bring me on.

It was in this year that I also got married to my girlfriend Susan on 11th July 1970 at Doncaster registry office followed by a reception at the Conisborough Working Men's Club where her father George was a steward. Initially we lived in a Rovers clubhouse that we rented in Dublin Road in Intake, Doncaster. We stayed there for about a year before returning to Mexborough where we rented a house from Ben Bailey, who was the Rovers chairman at the time. The house was at 10 Hampden Road, which was opposite the football ground of Mexborough Town.

I signed a professional contract with Rovers, at the start of the 1970-71, after I had completed my A Levels so I was never an apprentice at the club. I wasn't sure what I wanted to do in terms of a career and I had applied for two jobs, both of which were offered to me. One was as a junior reporter with the South Yorkshire Times newspaper and the other was with the Royal insurance Co. I was about to go to Lilleshall with the Rovers on a Coaching course for Managers so I told them both I would make a decision on my return. On the coach back from Lilleshall was when Lawrie McMenemy called me up to the front seat and asked me if I would like to sign as a professional for the club.

Within the Doncaster Rovers official handbook for the 1970-71 season, it stated that there have been few changes in personnel during the summer. Peter Kitchen, a Mexborough-born lad who has been prominent in schoolboy football was signed in July 1970, he has played for Don and Dearne Boys, and represented both Yorkshire Senior Schools and England Schoolboys, he is 5ft 8 and a half inches tall and weighs 10st 5lbs.

It appeared to be a good move for me. They had been promoted as Fourth Division champions in the 1969-70, incidentally the same season Orient were promoted to Division Two as champions.

So in July 1970, I signed for Rovers and received a £250 signing-on fee (this was a standard Football League ruling) and I was paid £125 in July and £125 the following June. I was on £15 per week basic plus £10 First team appearance money, £4 for a win and £2 for a draw. There were also enhancements for league positions and crowds, but as we got relegated during my season at the club, I can't remember ever receiving any such payments. (As the seasons went by I received an increase of £5 per week every year and by 1975 I was on £40 per week, plus the bonuses had improved a lot by then).

It was during this time that I bought my first car for £50, using some of my signing-on fee and then I had the car re-sprayed white for £5. Professional foot-ballers are renowned practical jokers and one day while I was out training some of the Rovers players got a white plastic cup, stuck it upside down on top of a blue box, taped it to the roof and wrote *POLICE* on the side of the box. (At this time Morris 1000's were being used as police cars).

I made quick progress as a raw talent through both the youth and reserve sides and I scored 15 goals for the youth side playing in the Northern Interme-diate League, being second top scorer behind Bernard Coley, who incidentally never played for the first team.

On 17 October 1970, I scored my first hat trick, in an 8-0 victory over Hud-dersfield Town juniors in the Northern Intermediate League cup, we reached the semi final of the competition, losing to Sheffield Wednesday Juniors.

During my first season at Belle Vue, I made 20(1) appearances for the reserve side, which played in the North Midland League, scoring 8 goals and was the second top goal scorer behind Tony Marsden, an experienced player who was in and out of the first team. My first goal came on 8 September 1970 in a 2-1 win over Hull City Reserves at home and I also scored twice in our 5-1 home victory over York City Reserves. The club was battling financially and manager McMenemy was forced to blood youngsters into the first team.

In this Rovers team at the time was a John Flowers who was one of the senior professionals, having joined Rovers for a five-figure fee from Stoke City in August 1966, he was born in Edlington, near Doncaster on 26 August 1944, he was the brother of the more famous Ron, who played for Wolves and Northampton Town, making over 500 career League appearances, he also won 49 England caps and their uncle was George Flowers who played more than 150 times for Rovers between 1929 and 1935.

John was married to Maureen Flowers who went on to become the Ladies woman's UK pairs darts champion. After splitting up with John, she became the wife of World darts champion between 1983 to 1989, Eric Bristow, she also later divorced him. Today, she runs the Sneyd Arms Hotel in Tunstall, Stoke-on-Trent.

John and Maureen were the parents of Tim Flowers the former England goalkeeper who played for clubs like Southampton, Blackburn Rovers who paid £2.4m for his services, Leicester City and Coventry City with over 520 League appearances and a Premiership championship medal to his name, with Blackburn in 1995. He also won 11 caps for England, he retired in the 2002-2003 season, and more recently was goalkeeping coach with Manchester City.

It was a bit of a strange situation as John Flowers, a hard tackling midfielder, lived in the Midlands and he was allowed by manager Lawrie McMenemy to train with Port Vale on a daily basis and just come up to Doncaster for the matches. He was also, I think, one of the first players I have met who wore a false teeth plate for his top teeth, and he used to take them out during games, this was a new experience to me...

John was a fine player who went on to make 162 (2) league appearances for the club, before moving onto Port Vale as a part-timer in August 1971, with a further 34 League games under his belt, he left football in 1971 to become a licensee.

At this time I was chosen in the Northern Intermediate League Select team, which played against the Youth League Champions, Middlesbrough at Ayresome Park on 17 November 1970.

It was this performance, and the fact that Rovers had crashed out of the FA Cup to Crewe Alexandra, and with a very poor start to the League campaign that elevated me quickly to my first team debut in a Third Division fixture at Shrewsbury Town on Friday 27 November 1970 before 5,215 spectators. The season also saw the departure of some of the squad members that took Rovers to the Fourth Division Championship in 1968-69, with John Bird being sold to Preston North End, Rod Johnson joining Bradford City and John Regan emigrating to South Africa. McMenemy had no money for new players, his only signing was Glenn Johnson from Arsenal, so he was forced to use youngsters like me.

Fairy Tale Start For Peter Kitchen -
A Diamond Up Manager McMenemy's Sleeve

It was a fine Shrewsbury evening, and I made a dream League debut with a goal on ninety seconds and we won 3-0, our first away win of the season.

Mike Sinclair in the Doncaster Evening Post wrote:

18-year old Peter Kitchen marked a fairy-tale first team debut with a fine opportune goal. Ian Branfoot floated the ball over, John Regan drew a defender and Kitchen flashed in to flick the ball past Town goalkeeper Bob Tooze. Eight minutes later Rovers went two ahead through a header from Stuart Robertson.

The points were secured on 69 minutes when after a Graham Watson shot was fumbled by goalie Tooze, in came Kitchen to hit the ball against his body, on hand was Archie Irvine, who made no mistake for the third goal.

Apart from scoring one and having a hand in the third young Kitchen made an extremely promising debut, he twice had shots smothered by Tooze and just wide with another effort.

Manager McMenamy described Kitchen as a 'diamond up my sleeve' and although I didn't want to play the youngster so early into the season, I was pleased at the way he performed after a call to replace the injured Rodney Johnson.

It gave us a new option upfront and enabled us to play a more attacking brand of football, which paid dividends to secure our best result of the season.

The following week against a high-ride Swansea City side, who were unbeaten in seven games, the boss gave me another chance and the 4174 crowd at Belle Vue gave me a special cheer as I ran on to the field for my home debut, it felt good and I needed just ninety-five seconds to notch my first 'home' goal, but we fell away to lose 2-1.

My goal came from a long goal-kick from goalie Glen Johnson, Watson picked up the ball just inside the Welshmen's half, he slipped to the ball to me, I wrong footed their keeper Davies before pushing the ball inside the post.

I should have made it two a few minutes later, when after a Regan left wing cross, I dived full-length and Davies made a flying save to stop a certain looking goal. I was then given a rest after two further defeats.

I was recalled on Friday 26 March 1971 for the home match against league leaders Aston Villa on a cold and rainy Yorkshire day before a nice 7879 crowd.

We seemed to revel in the big match atmosphere and turned on some excellent attacking football, although the visitors took the lead after just ten minutes after a cross from Willie Anderson, which gave the former Orient favourite Gordon 'Harry' Gregory an easy chance to score.

We equalised some seventeen minutes later through Stuart Robertson and three minutes later I was on hand to head home a Brian Usher high cross. I had another effort saved, but in the end we ran out good 2-1 winners to the delight of the boss, so I got a chance in the next game.

However as the season progressed, I was only given a decent run in the final eight games of the season, we lost the final four games and Rovers were relegated back down to the Fourth Division again.

I didn't really socialise with many of the players in the early days, because I was a young father and spent a lot of time with my son Michael, who was born on 6 December 1970.

We usually finished training at about 1pm most days, so I was able to be with my son and play with him, I really enjoyed being a father, and it was a special time for me.

In the end it was a highly successful season for me, if not for the club, having also played in 13(1) League games and scoring 6 Third Division goals.

During the Whitsun weekend at the end of May 1971, I played in the Barone Tournament in Breda, Holland, my first ever trip overseas, this was a competition for Under-21 players and I scored twice for Rovers in the competition and played

with players like Glen Johnson, Stan Brookes, Steve Uzelac, David Adamson, Bernard Coley and Kevin Gallagher who topped scored with 5 goals (Gallagher was not the same player who once played for Chelsea and Scotland).

**Peter with sons
Darren, 3 and Michael, 7**

We played against R.B.C. Holland, we lost 1-0, Akedemisk Boldklub of Denmark, won 1-0, who were the eventual winners of the competition defeating Rotherham United in the final, N.A.C. of Holland, won 2-0, Jeunesses d'Esch, won 3-0, Kon Lierse Sp of Belgium, won 6-0 and we draw 1-1 with FC Tournhout of Belgium. We lost 1-0 to hosts Barone of Holland in the third place game with their goalkeeper making some great saves, but we did receive a nice cup for our efforts, having scored 13 goals and conceding just 2 goals.

During the following season of 1971-72, I was too old to play in the Northern Intermediate League but I did top score for the reserves with 11 goals from 25 appearances, including a hat trick in a 5-0 defeat of Bradford City Reserves, although I was not a regular in the first team, making just 6(3) starts and netting once.

In the early seasons with Rovers, I used to work every summer for between four to six weeks at a yogurt factory in Kilnhurst. This was between 1972 to 1975, depending upon the length of the pre-season break because during this time I didn't earn any appearance or win bonus money.

I had a young family then, and I was only earning between £25 and £40 per week during these years. My second son Darren Paul had been born on 19 October 1974. I did a variety of jobs at the factory over those years from preparing orders to be dispatched, mixing the yogurts with fruit, working on the production line and cleaning down the refrigeration stores and I often worked on the night shift from 6pm to 6am.

One of the bonuses was that I could bring home lots of yogurts which were free to employees, which my kids loved and my son Michael would often bring round several young friends who would be queuing up at the door for yogurt.

It was also during this time that I played in Charity games on a regular basis and on several occasions I played for the Charlie Williams XI around the Doncaster area. Charlie was a real character, who had played many years for Rovers, making a total of 157 League appearances between 1954 and 1958 in the Alick Jeffrey days. When Charlie got tackled he would lie down on the ground as if he was dead.

He would proudly announce with regards his playing days, 'I couldn't play, flower, but I could stop them that could'. Another former O's player, Tommy Johnston makes reference to old Charlie Williams in his biography. After a very successful career as a comedian, he later became a Director of Barnsley Football Club.

At the end of the season manager Lawrie McMenemy had been dismissed and he took over as manager at Grimsby Town, with Maurice Setters, the former Manchester United, West Ham United, Coventry City and England U-23 former midfielder, replacing him as our new boss. The new manager had arrived and so as a relatively unknown young player, I was having to impress a new man all over again.

After McMenemy got the sack, my career at Rovers came to a bit of a halt and I hardly played in the first season under Setters. I was very much a fringe player and I felt that he never really rated me that highly. He always pushed both Mike Elwiss and Terry Curran before myself and I always thought this was because he had signed them both, whilst I had been signed by Lawrie Mac.

We experienced another poor start with just one win from the first six games but ended the season in twelfth position. Setters played a number of young players and I sometimes I played alongside another good find in Michael Walter Elwiss, who ended the season on 15 League goals and he was attracting attention from a number of big clubs. Micky Elwiss was a very good player and was expected to achieve great things. He had later moved to Preston North End for £70,000 and was later with Crystal Palace, West Ham and Preston for a second spell but his career was ended prematurely through injury. He netted exactly 100 League goals from 314 league games, I remember he married the daughter of the Chairman whilst at Preston. More recently he ran a dairy just outside of Doncaster.

There was also another good youngster in defender Steven Uzelac, who stayed at Belle Vue for six seasons, making over 180 appearances before moving to Preston North End.

I only played in 6(3) League game, scoring once and that was at Southend United, who were pushing for promotion, during March 1972, a match that attracted 16,073 spectators, the largest I had played before in my short League career.

We gave them a good run for their money in the second half, after being 1-0 down at half time through a Bill Garner header. We seem to come to life and two minutes after the re-start, when I hooked a left wing pass round three Southend defenders and into the net. I was so excited that I fetched the ball from the netting and kicked it straight into the crowd for which referee Gordon Hill booked me for dissent.

It looked as if the game would end in a draw, but to their credit Southend fought back and scored through Billy Best.

We ended the season with two good wins, although I didn't play, we beat, champions–elect Grimsby Town by 2-1, with McMenemy retuning for the first time to Belle Vue as the Mariners manager. This was our first win from ten matches, followed up with a 4-1 thrashing of Bury. The worrying factor for the club and new boss Setters, was that average home attendances had been the second lowest ever since records were kept.

On 29 July 1972 we played a home pre-season friendly against Stoke City in front of a crowd of 6,214, we lost 2-1, but I did score a goal against the great 35-year old goalkeeper Gordon Banks. Stoke were League Cup holders at the time, so it wasn't a bad result.

It was a great moment for me scoring against the great Banks, who had won 73 England caps and played over 500 League appearances and best remembered for the wonderful save he made from Pele's header at the 1970 World Cup finals.

I was put through with just him to beat and I dribbled past the great man to slot the ball home. In the Stoke side that day was Geoff Hurst, George Eastham and Geoff Salmons.

Having just dribbled past the great Stoke goalkeeper Gordon Banks, Peter shoots into an empty net. The other Rovers player is Mike Elwiss

On a sad note it was only a few months later that Banks' League career came to an abrupt end after a car crash, which resulted in him losing his sight in his right eye. He later went to play in the States with Fort Lauderdale Strikers in NASL, I read that the showmanship of the American game wasn't quite up to his liking. After a couple of defeats, he was driven onto the pitch in a hearse, he then helped to carry a coffin onto the pitch when the team manager jumped out of the coffin as Dracula and the announcer informed the fans that the Strikers were on their way back from the dead.

That season I played much more regularly for the first team with 37(1) appearances and I netted six goals and I also netted two goals in the FA Cup, one in a tricky away tie at Conference side Scarborough, who attracted the second largest crowd in our season of 7,109. I also made 5 appearances for the reserves with 3 goals, and it was in that reserve side that I first partnered big Brendan O'Callaghan, who also worked his way up through the junior side, and in later seasons we formed a lethal partnership in the first team.

In September, Alick Jeffrey, who had made another comeback, decided to call it day - a pity, as we could have done with his experience, because in the League we were bottom of the Fourth Division and without a point. We thought victory was ours in the home game against Stockport County when in the 89th minute Ian Branfoot ran up the right wing and from his centre I managed to nod it home for a 2-1 lead, the young fans went wild and ran onto the field and the play was held up for a while.

The lads seem to lose concentration and instead of just holding out for the points, we still attacked them looking for a third goal, but the ball was lost in midfield, Eddie Garbett streaked away and lobbed our goalie Johnson for the equaliser, still it was our first point of the season.

Gateshead-born Ian Grant Branfoot was a stylish right back who joined Rovers from Sheffield Wednesday in a player exchange deal with Archie Irvine for Harold Wilcockson in December 1969 and he became a fixture in the Rovers side until joining Lincoln City's manager Graham Taylor. He went into football management after he retired, most notably with Southampton.

During the 1973-74 season, I was more successful in the goals department with 15 League and Cup goals, I also netted 6 goals from eleven starts for the reserves, ending as their top scorer. In the League Cup I scored a hat trick in our surprise 4-3 win at Notts County, although a 6-0 defeat at Newcastle United before 16,065 soon brought us down to earth. In that Newcastle team were Bobby Moncur, Frank Clarke (later the Orient manager) and Malcolm Macdonald, but although we lost it was a terrific experience to play at St James Park, something I did on several occasions later in my career.

Two week later we were at home to second from top Southport, who were undefeated in six. The local press had written us off the night before, which fired us up and on 63 minutes I got away from my marker and ran down the wing. I slipped the ball to Archie Irvine who smashed it home from fully 25 yards and near the end Elwiss scored for our first win of the season.

I scored one of my best solo effort goals thus far for Rovers, it was at the end of November at home to Bury, we were already 1-0 up through Irvine, when on 22 minutes I picked the ball up on the centre circle, and waltzed passed both Heslop and Holt ran towards the edge of the penalty area, to smash the ball past their goalie Forrest. We eventually ran out easy winners by 4-1, but I should have made it five when two chances were blocked on the line.

In December we had a tough cup match at non-league Scarborough. It wasn't such a great journey to the ground, the driver having to encounter fog for most of the way. We were in a new all-blue strip. It was a pretty close affair but on 27 minutes, we had a corner taken by Irvine, it came over and I scored with a rare header, out jumping their defence for the lead. In the second half the home team came at us and on 55 minutes Colin Appleton blasted home a free kick for the equaliser.

But we had the last laugh when Mick Elwiss forced home from close range for the winner. In the Third Round we went out of the Cup, 2-0 at Reading.

We ended the 1972-73 season in 17th position and so ended another season best forgotten about.

Notts County hit by great Kitchen super show, with a brilliant hat trick

The following season manager Setters used a more attacking policy with a 4-2-4 formation in a number of matches. It certainly paid dividends for me in the 4-3 League Cup victory over Notts County at Meadow Lane, to end their nine-month unbeaten home record, they had just come off a great 4-1 win over Malcolm Allison's Crystal Palace.

It was a great game for me as I was going through a lean spell in the goals department, having not scored in the League since the previous December.

It was Brendan O'Callaghan's first-team debut, which gave us more scope up-front taking some of the weight off Elwiss and myself.

On seven minutes the ball was swung into County's area, up jumped Brendan to beat Brian Stubbs to the ball, it fell to me and I gleefully smashed it into the roof of the net, which certainly appeared to rock the home side, but a string of fine saves by Kim Book gave us that single goal lead at half-time. Kim was the brother of the more famous Tony of Manchester City fame.

The 7,735 fans were certainly in for some excitement in the second half. Only a minute played and we had scored a second goal. It was a beauty from Elwiss: he ran fully fifty yards, drew their keeper Brown and calmly placed the ball into the corner of the net.

County upped the pace and Kevin Randall pulled one back on 65 minutes, but we kept going forward and I picked up a great pass from Peter Woods, I left their full-back Worthington for pace, cut into the box to score.

We were now under real pressure from County and Randall headed in their equaliser on 76 minutes, we had lost a 3-1 lead, but their was no change in the tactics, we were looking for a winner, but it looked odds-on a replay

With just seconds remaining we forced a corner. Irvine took a short kick to Woods who crossed it over, to my surprise I was left unmarked, with their defenders following both Elwiss and O'Callaghan, and I tucked the ball away for a sweet victory, it was a match to remember for the Rovers fans who travelled to Nottingham. So ended a personal nightmare for me, I last hit a first team goal way back on 9 December last year. I hit the uprights, the crossbar and had efforts scrambled off the line by defenders, but I could not get the ball into the net, until the County match. It had been a long time coming, but the goals were worth waiting for.

During mid-September we were thumped 5-1 at Peterborough United, but the following week at home, we came back with a vengeance. Unfortunately, only 1517 were there to see it, due, I'm sure, to the pouring rain.

The first half against Workington was a close affair, we fell behind early, but on 29 minutes Woods, deep in the visitors own half, sent me away I ran towards their goal passed to O'Callaghan, who returned the ball for me to ram the ball past goalie Rogan.

Big Brendan and I were still celebrating when they were already taking a corner and Rowlands headed past goalie Kim Book for the lead. In the second half we turned on the magic to win 5-2, with a couple of spectacular goals from O'Callaghan.

The following week at Gillingham, I scored with a rare long distance shot with a swerving 25-yarder, it didn't make much difference, we lost 5-1, one of their goals came from David Peach, of course it was a penalty.

In December, I scored the first goal in our 3 -0 win over Tranmere Rovers in the Second Round of the FA Cup, a rare win indeed, Having lost five League games that month and still bottom of the Fourth Division. Not much of a Christmas celebration for those connected to the club and with a prospect of facing Liverpool at Anfield on 5 January in the FA Cup with many predicting a record defeat for 'Donny'.

The FA Cup, a draw at Anfield

I remember very clearly what is today described in my profile on the Rovers website as a 'nearly' goal. The scene was the famous Anfield stadium on 5 January 1974 in a Third Round Tie in the FA Cup. Here we were, little Doncaster Rovers bottom of the Fourth Division, up against the might of Liverpool who were leaders of the 'old' First Division before a large crowd of 31,483 and I still have the local press article on the match headed:

'LIVERPOOL IN THE SOUP KITCHEN'
Liverpool is nearly smashed by ace Peter

Doncaster-born Kevin Keegan was in the Pool team and scored with a brilliant header on just four minutes. Steve Highway ran powerfully into the box, he passed to Ian Callaghan who centred for the little striker to open the scoring. Seconds latter Keegan missed a golden opportunity to extend the lead when blazing over from close range.

I then scored our first two minutes later, it was my 13th of the season and was rather a 'gift' goal, but I'll take it. We forced a corner on the left, I pushed Storton, the ball ran to Murray whose shot was parried by Ray Clemence, who was put under pressure by O'Callaghan could only parry his kick, the ball ran to Woods who passed to me and I managed to sneak the ball under his body but I had thought my half-hit shot was saved by Clemence, but he somehow he allowed the ball to trickle through his hands and it rolled gently into the net.

Then twelve minutes later Emlyn Hughes failed to clear a cross from Alan Murray and 17-year old Brendan O'Callaghan volleyed it past Clemence to silence the Kop.

Elwiss flicked the ball onto Woods and big Bren ran in to volley it home. Liverpool came roaring forward and Phil Thompson crashed a thirty-yard shot against the crossbar and they forced corner after corner, but somehow we survived to lead 2-1 at half-time.

In the second half Keegan scored when rising high above the Rovers defenders to meet another Callaghan right wing cross for another great header against the side he had supported as a youngster, for Liverpool's equaliser on 58 minutes.

In the closing seconds, I was chasing a long ball through and as Pool's Emlyn Hughes and goalkeeper Ray Clemence dithered, I toe poked the ball over Clemence from the edge of the goal area and the ball sailed, oh so slowly on towards the gaping goal, the ball seemed to take forever to drop down and when it did it dropped onto the crossbar and then was cleared for a corner kick, that's when the final whistle went to our disappointment and to the Kop's relief.

After the match Maurice Setters, our boss, informed the press 'I am disappointed that we didn't win because I thought we deserved it. All of our players were tremendous, this was the day the young Rovers players came of age.'

The Liverpool boss Bill Shankly said: 'Full marks to Maurice and his Doncaster team for holding us at Anfield, we know it would not be easy, it's these kind of upsets which makes the FA Cup so special.'

However, then came the sting from the famous Scotsman: 'Yes, I suppose they deserved a draw, but both their goals were gifts.'

We lost the replay at home by 2-0, their goals coming from Steve Highway and Peter Cormack, but we were not disgraced, the match was played during a midweek afternoon, it was the time of the electrical workers national strike and a three-day week due to the many enforced power cuts. It was one of our biggest crowds for many years: 22,499.

We had our chances but this time Ray Clemence was not giving us any late New Year gifts. He saved an O'Callaghan header with his fingertips, due to a number of injuries I had to play in a deeper role, which I suppose robbed us of taking advantage of any half chances going on the day.

We lost, but we matched the mighty Liverpool over two games, the thought on all Rovers fans minds was, how can we play like this against one of the best teams in the land, yet are still bottom of the Fourth Division?

I read Kevin Keegan's comments later in the season in the national press, he was reported as saying that the matches against us were the hardest they had on route to the final in which they eventually beat Newcastle United at Wembley.

I heard that most kids in Doncaster bunked off school to watch the match, as did a number of teachers. I finished the season as top scorer with 15 League and Cup goals and Elwiss was sold to Preston North End for £70,000 to make ends meet because crowds were dwindling, with an average of 2,297 for the season.

On 20 January 1974, we played at Stockport County, which was one of twelve games to be played on a Sunday due to various strikes and the three-day working week, when Saturday was counted as a one of the working days. Admission was by programme, which was priced at 65 pence. We drew 0-0, the match drew a crowd of 4050, which turned out to be our best gate of the season and which may have heralded the start of Sunday matches. We finished the season in twenty-second place and Stockport were two places below us.

During the 1974-75 season I missed just three League matches and was top scorer on 24 League and Cup goals. However it was not a great season, by mid-November 1974, Setters was sacked and John Quigley, the coach, was put in charge. We lost our first match with John in charge at Mansfield Town by 5-2, we only improved once Stan Anderson, the former Middlesbrough manager took charge in February 1975.

I remember on the day of Setters' sacking, he got the players together and informed them of the club's decision. He was in tears, which I found rather

In action for Rovers v Reading.

strange at the time, given that he always projected an image of being an aggressive character as a player and manager both on and off the field. He was typical of a player who had played at the highest level and, as with many good players, he couldn't understand why some players couldn't pass the ball ten yards, so he would pass his frustrations onto his players.

Other great players who spring to mind who weren't able to make a successful transition to management were Bobby Charlton and Bobby Moore. We tend to judge people by our own standards so when the basics come naturally to a player, it is hard to understand why everyone else can't do the simple things.

During the managerial years of Setters, I don't think we were ever out of the bottom end of the table.

Quigley, or 'Quigs' as he was known, was in charge for the match against Barnsley, I was chosen as a substitute and was brought on with twenty-five to go and scored our equalising goal.

Setters was at the game, and when I saw him a few weeks later, he appeared to be a bit aggressive and called me a cheat and said I had never played for him with the same energy and enthusiasm. I didn't respond, but it was clear to me it was because he didn't inspire any confidence in the players, as I explain in a later chapter on the managers I have played for.

I was on the transfer list at my own request at the time as I needed more money and had been quite unhappy at the club under Maurice Setters. The first thing Stan did was to call me into his office and he immediately asked me to sign a new contract. He offered me a one-year deal plus a one-year option on the contract and also included a £1500 loyalty payment. At last I felt wanted and appreciated.

Anderson's appointment made a huge difference to the team and to me personally. He rarely shouted and had a calm personality, which enabled him to be rational during matches and to deal better with the pressures of a football manager. He certainly instilled me with confidence and I scored 12 goals from the next 20 games.

His training techniques revolved much more around ball work and passing rather than the 'Kick, Bollock and Bite' mentality that Maurice Setters had preached. The team gained confidence and we went on a winning run under the new boss.

On 1 February we went to Shrewsbury Town and lost by the remarkable score line of 7-4. I bagged a couple, then we went on a winning run of five games, in which I netted five goals, we ended the season, firstly with a fine 4-1 win over Bradford City, I netted twice, and then we came back well at home to Exeter City on 22 April, we were 2-0 down, but we fought back despite losing our goalie Graham Brown with concussion and having Steve Brookes between the sticks. I scored, and then further goals from Terry Curran and Les Chappell earned us a 3-3 to the delight of the 4,251 fans.

I ended up on 24 League and cup goals and was voted the Supporters Club player of the year for the first time I was at Belle Vue, something I'm still very proud of. We finished in a relatively safe position, seventeenth spot in Division Four.

During August, Terry Curran left us in a £60,000 deal to join up with the great Brian Clough at Nottingham Forest. I had become good friends with Terry, who was was a big gambler, he came from South Elmsall, near Pontefract, so he was a regular at the horse and dog racetrack. He tried to teach me about the weights and form in relation to the horses, but I couldn't afford to risk losing money at the time, so I never really got into it.

Terry Curran, a right winger, was another of Donny's greats, having progressed through the youth ranks. He went on to have a great career with a number of big clubs at the time like Derby County, Southampton, the two Sheffield clubs and Everton, making 394 appearances with 72 goals. Nowadays, he works as a salesman in Yorkshire.

He was one of the supply lines for both myself and Brendan (O'Callaghan) at the time, but as part of the deal in came Ian Miller and Denis Peacock plus £50,000, Miller went onto play a vital part in my career at Belle Vue. Terry had some big money transfers during his career, but probably his best spell was with Sheffield Wednesday between 1978 and 1981. He was a very tricky and skilful player but never knew when to release the ball.

I also made friends with Salford-born Brian William 'Bundle' Joy, who Setters had signed. The versatile player – having played in eight different positions in his 34 games for Rovers – midfielder came from Tranmere Rovers, having started his playing career with Coventry City and was then with Torquay United. He rented a house in Mexborough from Ben Bailey, the Rovers Chairman, and we shared lifts to go to training in Doncaster. He used to drive an MGB roadster and I used to love it when he had the roof down in the summer. (I have since that

Peter with Brian Joy at the National Railway Museum, York - 2014

experience always loved convertible cars and have driven one since 1993). Old 'Bundle' left Rovers for Exeter City in July 1973, after a spell in San Diego, USA. He ended his league career with York City in 1977. I have since lost touch with him having moved to Bo'ness in Scotland.

I managed to make contact with my old team mate Brian Joy, who lives in Bo'ness, near Edinburgh and who had himself just retired as a Sales Director for a Media company and we arranged a 40th reunion in May 2014 in York, with our other halves, Katherine and Sylvia.

It was really good to catch up with Brian on what we had both been doing for the last 40 years and we spent a very enjoyable day and evening together and Brian and I were even able to fit in a visit to the National Railway Museum.

Brian and Sylvia have 2 daughters and a son Ian, who also had a career as a professional footballer. In addition, they have a number of grandchildren and Ian is now a TV Sports presenter for BEIN sport, living and working in Miami, USA.

Outside of football, my other good friends at the time were Stan Smith, who was a Geordie and also a team manager with one of the Mexborough and Swinton Junior teams and Wilf Pugh, who was and still is a Doncaster Rovers season ticket holder. I was Best man at the wedding of Wilf to his wife Sue in 1978 and they are regular visitors to our house as we often go away on short breaks together. Wilf and I also attend a few Rovers away games when they are playing in and around the London area. Wilf had a kidney transplant in 2013 and I'm pleased to say he has made a remarkable recovery. In July this year, we will be celebrating Wilf's 70th Birthday with him and Sue and their family, over a whole weekend away in North Yorkshire

The 1974-75 season got off to its usual start, near the bottom. We travelled to Swansea City in September and were leading 3-1, but up popped their 17-year old striker Geoff Thomas with two goals in three minutes for his hat trick to share the points.

I scored on 30 minutes. Murray made the running on the right and from his centre I poked the ball into the net, while the whole of the Swansea defence just stood still and watched. Our third came when Curran raced away and from his cross I made no mistake.

It was an exiting match, just a pity there were only 1532 there to witness it. The following week, we made amends and crushed Rochdale 4-1, I bagged one but it was Alan Murray who did the damage with a hat trick.

In the First Round of the FA Cup, we had an easy 3-1 win at non-league Oswestry Town. I bagged a brace, but we lost 1-0 at Chesterfield in the next round.

In action for Rovers v Cambridge Utd.

One match I remember very well, it was at second from top Shrewsbury Town on Saturday 1 February 1975, we lost by 7-4, yet at one stage we were 5-4 down with what looked a good penalty shout turned down for a shirt pulling incident on Terry Curran, who was causing havoc in their defence.

I netted a couple that day but in the end the Evening Post reporter Joe Slater voted our man of the match to be goalkeeper Graham Brown, making many vital saves to keep us in the game. The men who destroyed us were two players signed by Shrewsbury from non-league Stourbridge namely Ray Haywood and Phil Bates, who scored five of the goals between them, which cost their club £250, as part of their transfer deal, Shrewsbury had to pay £50.00 a goal, which I suppose cost them most of their gate money?

The defeat gave us a bit of a wake-up call and we recorded 7 wins from 8 League games, including 5 goals from me, I netted two in the 4-3 win over Mansfield Town, the first time we had won more than two wins on the trot in three years. It was a pleasing feeling to have scored the winner with just a couple of minutes remaining, with what Joe Slater described in the Evening Post, as the best goal of the day (Joe was a great admirer of mine and I was sad to hear of his death in 2003) before our highest League crowd in many years of 7,278 against the League leaders, who had lost only two games in twenty-nine.

I ended the season as top goal scorer with 21 League and 3 Cup goals, followed by Brendan with 12 goals.

The following season – 1975/1976, I had signed a new one-year deal and I had a tremendous season.

We played a pre-season home friendly against a Manchester United XI, even though half of their team were made of Central League players, manager Tommy Docherty and his assistant Pat Crerand were in attendance.

We took the lead after 11 minutes when big Bren nodded down to me and I made no mistake when shooting past Mexborough-born goalie Ray Mountford (he never made any first team appearances for Manchester United, but did spend a few season with Rotherham United).

The visitors equalised two minutes before half-time through John Lowey. But in the end, we won 2-1 when Terry Curran popped in the second to the delight of the locals in the 2,874 crowd.

The League campaign opened with a 2-0 home defeat against Cambridge United, our first win came against Crewe Alexandra, by 3-1. It was the League debut of Ian Miller, replacing Terry Curran who by then had moved to Nottingham Forest, and it took him less than a minute to become a crowd favourite. Also it was the only goal for the club by Martin Alesinoye an amateur from Barnsley, the first black player to appear in the Rovers first team since the days of Charlie

Williams. Martin was eventually released by the club and drifted into non-league football.

Joe Slater wrote in *The Evening Post*:

Peter Kitchen deserves much of the credit for Rovers second goal after 49 minutes. He snapped up on a bad Crewe pass, beat two defenders and pushed the ball to O'Callaghan, who made no mistake which cheered the 2,467 crowd.

Towards the end of September we had a good 1-0 win at Barnsley and the following week we thrashed bottom of the table Southport 5-2, whose manager Jimmy Melia, had resigned only a few days earlier.

It was pleasing to see over 5,000 fans in attendance on a wet and windy day, it was also pleasing for me with another hat trick, my third coming from a gem of a cross from Ian Miller. I thought to myself, I had better do something, as big Brenden had already scored 8 goals during the early part of the season and I was only on three.

In October 1975, we were at Stockport County, I scored our first goal and big Bren scored in the last seconds to snatch the points for a 2-1 victory, I remember all the players after the match, sang in the bath 'You can't stop the Cal-Callaghan' - to the tune of Alan Price's hit song at the time 'No don't stop the carnival'.

We had a good run in the League Cup, we knocked out two Third Division sides in the early rounds - namely Grimsby Town and Crystal Palace, who were managed by Malcolm Allison and they also had Terry Venables as coach. We had a pretty strong side, with Miller, O'Callaghan and myself, we formed a pretty

lethal strike force and were supported from midfield by Alan Murray (was Graham Souness's assistant manager when at Newcastle United), Les Chappell and the England cricketer Chris Balderstone. In the Third round we knocked out Torquay United in a replay.

In Round Four, we were at home to Hull City, which attracted a wonderful crowd of 20,476, and record gate receipts of over £13,000. The Second Division side were playing very well but missed a number of good chances that we seemed to hand to them on a plate, because we went for goal and left space at the back.

Once again Brendan's aerial power caused the visitors problems and from one of his great knockdowns, I prodded the ball home for the opener.

I think we got overexcited and made many mistakes and on 29 minutes we were punished, when from a John Hawley cross the burly Alf Wood scored.

We pressed for the winner, once again Big Bren provided the opening for Ray Tennent to head home off a post. On a sad note there was some violence on the terraces but overall a wonderful day for Doncaster Rovers.

Four days later a pumped-up side thrashed Newport County 5-1. Although I didn't score, I had a rather pleasing moment in the match as shown by the words of Joe Slater in the Evening Post:

"There was Peter Kitchen giving another superb performance in the 'background' making goals this time, rather than scoring them. In the final minutes of the match, he left defender after defending trailing to present O'Callaghan with his 17th goal of the season, he then set up Miller's second goal. The hero of the day though was Ian Miller who completed his hat trick with a tremendous 25-yarder and O'Callaghan with his second goal of the game and 18th of the season in the final seconds for an emphatic victory."

It was nice for Big Bren, both Don Revie, the England team boss and Johnny Giles the Eire boss were watching him, he had dual qualification, his father having been born in the Republic of Ireland.

Rovers player John Christopher Balderstone was a really nice guy and a very elegant and creative midfielder who joined us from Carlisle United. One day in September 1975, he spent the early part of the day playing cricket for Leicestershire against Derbyshire and helping to win the County Championship and in the evening he made his way to Doncaster to play against Brentford, the match ending 1-1. He made a total of 556 League appearances with 93 goals. He also played in 2 Cricket Test matches against the West Indies in 1976 and stood as an Umpire in 2 ODI's both against South Africa in 1978. Sadly this great man died of cancer in March 2000, aged just fifty-nine.

So we had made it to the Quarter Finals of the League Cup and a trip to London to face the mighty Tottenham Hotspur. I suppose our run had to end sometime and it did with a bang at White Hart Lane, but in the early stages we gave Spurs a scare when Alan Murray opened the scoring on seven minutes to the delight of the 4,000 travelling Donny fans. Stephen Reed had centred, there was Brendan to knock it down and Murray headed powerfully past Pat Jennings. John Pratt equalised on seventeen minutes, with our defence all stood still thinking Martin Chivers would be blown up for off-side and they scored a second after Jimmy Neighbour burst away on the right and John Duncan slotted home on thirty.

I scored an equaliser to make it 2-2 in the fifty-second minute. Brendan intercepted a pass from Willie Young, Jennings couldn't stop his shot and I was on hand to rifle the ball home.

For almost an hour we were a match for Spurs but then Les Chappell gave away a silly own goal just two minutes later, his back pass to goalie Peacock, was missed by the keeper and the ball slowly trickled into the net. It was all downhill from then on in, and we lost 7-2 with Martin Chivers bagging a brace and John Duncan a hat trick, before a crowd of 25,702.

In the end Spurs ran out convincing winners, even though the London morning papers headlines read 'Lucky Lucky Spurs. '

We then lost a few league games in a row, including a 4-2 home defeat against the league leaders Lincoln City.

On 14 February we had a home match against Hartlepool United and we needed just ten minutes to end a nine-week run of home failures, yet we still attracted a healthy crowd of over 5,000. I opened the scoring on three minutes, my eleventh goal from ten matches and then O'Callaghan netted a second and I lobbed in a third for an easy victory.

"Kitchen scores the best goal I have ever seen"

Doncaster fan Bob Gilbert informed the Author about a goal Peter Kitchen scored at Newport County on 21 February 1976 and to back up his memories we have used some of Joe Slater's match report in the Doncaster Evening Post of the following Monday.

Gilbert stated:

Rovers were 2-0 up through O'Callaghan, but as usual we let it slip and were pegged back to 2-2. The final seconds were approaching and a draw seemed inevitable. Then,

Doncaster Rovers FC: Peter on 2nd row, 5th from left, Brendan O'Callaghan is on the top row 5th from left.

The Goal Gourmet

Peter took the ball up from the half way circle, he went onto dribble the ball through the whole of the County defence, past the goalie and smacked the ball into the empty net, I'm sure it gave him as much pleasure as it gave us few Rovers fans amongst the small crowd that witnessed the game. It was sublime. It was a pity only 1,543 fans were there to witness it. Thank you Peter for your wonderful goals and so many great memories!

Joe Slater wrote:

Kitchen Scores A Goal To Remember

Doncaster Rovers threw away a two goal lead in the end they forced their fourth consecutive away victory.

The goal, which clinched the points, is one, which will remain in the minds of those who saw it for a long, long time.

Match of the Day would have revelled in it. Slow motion replays would have revealed the artistry and coolness of a goal in a thousand.

It was just that. Difficult to describe, because Peter Kitchen simply picked up the ball, waltzed and dribbled his way through the Newport defence, drew goalkeeper John Macey and tapped the ball into the empty net before turning in triumph to receive the congratulations of his colleagues and the cheers of the few Doncaster fans who had made the long trip to Wales, giving Newport only their second home defeat of the season and secure Rovers a seventh spot in Division Four.

Sheer Magic From Kitchen

Now I was on a roll and in another home match at the end of February against Darlington I bagged two more goals and we won 3-2, and as Mike Sinclair in the Evening Post wrote:

The prolific scoring partnership of Kitchen and O'Callaghan – they have scored 48 goals between them so far this season - kept Doncaster Rovers hopes of promotion alive. Kitchen seems to get better with every game and there's a buzz of anticipation every time he get the ball near the opposing penalty area. Some of his play is sheer magic and it can only be a matter of time before some big club makes Rovers a giant offer for him. It is remarkable to me that former Rovers players like Curran, Elwiss and Gilchrist have all been snapped up, yet Kitchen, in my opinion, is a far better player than all of them, yet he has been overlooked.

I must mention one memorable moment in the game, even though no goal resulted, it was when Kitchen brilliantly beat two men in hardly any space along the by-line, he squared to ball back in to the area only to see both Alan Murray and Les Chappell having their shots blocked. I'm sure if he had the chance himself, he would have tucked it away with ease.

With the win we moved into sixth spot just three points behind fourth-placed Tranmere Rovers but like in other seasons, we lost our way in the final run-in with three draws and three defeats in the final six games.

Two goals against Sheffield United in the Final of the Sheffield County Cup

Later in the season, I netted the two goals against the club that I had supported as a boy that won us the Sheffield County Cup, defeating Sheffield United, who had just been relegated from Division One. They had finished bottom, but they had a strong side out that night for the Final at Bramall Lane with players like Tony Currie (a wonderful creative midfield player), Eddie Colquhoun and Simon Stainrod on Friday 7 May 1976. The competition has a rather anomalous status and is not even counted by some football historians as a senior competition. The competition was for the five Football League sides that were members of the Sheffield & Hallamshire FA and for one thing it was not always completed due to fixture congestion.

We had a bye in the First Round and in the Semi Final at Oakwell, we defeated Barnsley by 3-2. I played but didn't score, the goals coming from O'Callaghan, Miller and Mark Jones.

The Final took place before a Bramall Lane crowd of 4,502. It was Chris Guthrie, a player I later played with at Fulham, who scored the Blades opener but I scored the equaliser. In the second half I bagged the winner to secure Rovers first piece of silverware since the 1968-69 season, when they won the Division Four Championship.

Our team that night was: Peacock, Reed, Brookes, Ternent, Uzelac, Taylor, Miller, Wignall, O'Callaghan, Kitchen, Robinson Sub: Creamer.

Even though it was not considered a major match (outside of Doncaster), I was quite excited, every player from the winning side was awarded a crystal decanter each, it was the first thing I had ever won as a professional footballer.

The season ended with us still in the Fourth Division, but finishing in a decent tenth spot and Brendan (O'Callaghan) ended on 28 League and Cup goals and I finished on 24 goals, but I was voted the Rovers player of the year for the 1975-76 season.

The crowds improved, a tribute to the entertaining style of play by Anderson's team, with a home average attendance of 6,083.

We had a very good team and played some excellent attacking football but couldn't get the balance right between attack and defence and this stopped us from progressing out of this division.

At this time we had at the club Glynn Snodin, who was an apprentice, and his younger brother Ian, who was also an associate schoolboy and another gifted player. Glynn was noted for his great free-kicks, he could swerve the ball both ways. He was called up for Bobby Robson's 1986 World Cup squad of forty but never made the final twenty-two.

They both played between them over 500 League games and scored 86 goals. Both of them were terrific lads and very good players who went onto to have successful playing careers and even enjoyed a spell in management at Doncaster. Glynn was the reserve team manager at Charlton Athletic, and I occasionally bump into him at a match. In March 2006, after six-years at the Valley, he was appointed first team coach with Southampton.

The Great Brendan Richard O'Callaghan

After many months of searching, we managed to locate big Bren living in Woore, Cheshire where he has lived with his wife Janice and family since 1983.

I built up a wonderful partnership with Brendan, the 6ft 3ins centre forward. He was a strong target man, who would knock the ball down for me and I would anticipate his flick-on's and score the goals, he was a big factor in my success at Rovers and he was a very good finisher himself, especially in the air.

Brendan O'Callaghan was born on 23 July 1955 in Bradford and joined Doncaster Rovers as a junior and during his five seasons at Belle Vue, he made 212 appearances and scored 79 goals, he joined Stoke City for £45,000 in March 1978, scored after just 10 seconds of his debut. Proved to be a good strike partner for Garth Crooks and in later years played more in the centre of defence, he stayed for eight seasons scoring 49 goals from 294 appearances (Nearly half at centre half), he also won 7 Republic of Ireland caps whist with Stoke. He joined Oldham Athletic in February 1985, before retiring through injury in 1986.

He then worked at Dudson UK from 1986 to 1989 selling commercial ceramics and then he worked for the PFA, where he took a Diploma in Management Studies (DMS) at Staffordshire University and then a Masters in Business Administration (MBA) at Trinity College, both funded by the PFA. In 1991, he passed his Advanced Coaching Award (full badge) at Lilleshall.
Brendan then joined Save the Children Fund in 1994 as their funding manager and stayed for ten years until deciding to look for a new challenge.

Brendan was a very good player as well as a great player to play alongside. He was unselfish and always knew when to go for goal himself or to head down to me or another team mate. His obvious abilities were in the air although for a big man he wasn't ungainly and he was skilful and an excellent finisher. He was a good striker and scored a lot of goals himself in his career. He was different from

Joe Mayo, my Orient strike partner, in that he wasn't as mobile and so he tended to get in the box more and therefore he did score more goals than big Joe.

People used to say that we seemed to know what the other was thinking or going to do, but I believe that we were so successful as a partnership because we had such confidence in each other to do our respective jobs. I always felt that big Bren would win the ball or make the right decision or vice versa, so anticipating this became second nature.

Another player who played a big part in my success at Belle Vue was the fast and tricky 20-year old winger Ian Miller, who on his day could be just brilliant; he was the main source of supply to Brendan for his knockdowns to me.

The Exciting Ian Miller

Ian 'Windy' Miller, born on Friday 13 May 1955, was one of the best player I ever played with, yet he didn't make it during his career into the 'old' First Division, he should have played at the highest level. He was the quickest thing on two legs when belting down the right wing, I recall that he took part in the Scottish sprint championships whilst at Rovers.

He was a typical Scottish winger, although he was very much more direct that some other Scottish wingers I played with, like Archie Irvine and Peter Marinello, Ian was a more intelligent player.

Ian had a long career, which started off with Bury, then onto Nottingham Forest. He moved to Swindon Town on 17 July 1978 and then played many years for Blackburn Rovers, Port Vale and Scunthorpe United. He was a successful coach with both Wolverhampton Wanderers and Blackburn Rovers. In July 2005, he was appointed assistant manager to Colin Hendry at Blackpool, this after a spell as Head Coach. In November both Hendry and Miller were asked to leave Blackpool. In December 2005, Miller was named as assistant manager to the youngest manager in the Football League, Chris Casper at League Two side Bury.

Miller was very skilful and had great ability to go past defenders and leave them standing. He was like Brendan, a very unselfish player, and more often than not he was able to get the crosses in for both of us at either the near or the far post, consequently we both knew mostly what he was going to do. This was so unlike Terry Curran who was also a very good player, he also had great skill and a terrific dribbler, but who was a bit of an enigma in that we never knew what he was going to do (I don't think Terry ever did either). He would only give you the ball when it suited him and not the strikers waiting for his cross, whereas Ian saw his role as a pure winger, yet he still managed 8 to 10 goals a season for us. During his career he netted 40 goals in 530 league games.

It has been said by many Rovers fans that the three of us - Kitchen, O'Callaghan and Miller formed the most memorable forward line in Rover's history since WW2. Miller was appointed in July 2006 first team coach with Leicester City.

Back On The Transfer List With Doncaster

At the start of the 1976-77 season, I made my intentions very clear about wanting to leave Belle Vue and I asked to be placed on the transfer list. I was twenty-four years old, scoring lots of goals, one of the top strikers in the Fourth Division, and I wanted to play at a higher level and to prove to myself that I could achieve in a higher division. I remember telling my wife Susan that I would move anywhere except London, as I didn't really want to leave Yorkshire and so I always hoped it might be Leeds United or Sheffield United who would come in for me.

I started off the season slowly but I then hit seven League goals from six games. We played Lincoln City in the League Cup and in a second replay tie, the match was played at the City Ground, Nottingham after the first two games finished 1-1, so a neutral ground was required for the third tie before a smallish crowd of 3,726,

The game finished 2-2 at the end of extra time and Brendan O'Callaghan scored both our goals and so the match went into a penalty shootout, this was the first time that a penalty shootout competition was used to decide a tie in a major cup competition in England. Shootouts were used in minor tournaments such as the Watney Cup, but never before in the League Cup and they were still a way off in the FA Cup.

I knocked in our first spot-kick and eventually Brendan scored, what was the winning kick to see us home by 3-2 on penalties, in this nerve-racking exercise, but I was impressed at playing at Forest's ground, who were in the 'old' Division One.

We went out at home to League Champions Derby County in the next round 2-1, I scored our only goal before nearly 15,000 fans. The Derby team was managed by Brian Clough and his Assistant Peter Taylor and contained several household names at the time, like Terry Hennessey, Dave Mackay, David Nish and the great striker Kevin Hector.

At the end of September 1976, we had Tony Woodcock on loan from Nottingham Forest and he was played on the wing because Brendan and I were playing so well. He made his debut in our 4-0 win over Darlington, he scored the opener and I scored a brace. Woodcock made just six League appearances, scoring twice but he returned to Forest because Rovers could not find the £12,000 needed to sign him. We all know just how well Anthony Stewart Woodcock did and just two years later, he moved to Germany, signing for Cologne for £500,000. In 1982, he came back to England and joined Arsenal before returning to Germany in 1986 and finally made a career total of 351 appearances scoring 123 goals and he also played 42 times for England, scoring 16 goals. Today, he still lives in Germany acting as a successful players agent.

We always jokingly said that it was because he spent a few weeks at Belle Vue playing alongside players like Brendan and myself, that he later achieved so much, or was it really because he played with us in Division Four, and it was so dire in the lower divisions that he had the impetus to become more focused and motivated to do better in his career!

On 2 November we were thrashed at Halifax Town 6-0, but bounced back to lose only two from twenty League games and we enjoyed a run of seven wins from eight games

A few days after the Halifax defeat, I had a home game to remember against Hartlepool United who had a new manager – Bill Horner. I scored both goals, then in one of my very rare excursions to help out in defence, I sliced my clearance straight into the path of their Paul Bielby who scored easily. Then I had a fight in the second half with their defender Bob Scott and we were both booked. In the end, with eighteen minutes to go, I picked up the ball beat a couple of defenders and cheekily slipped the ball through keeper Eddie Edgar's legs for my eleventh goal of the season for a 2-1 win, it was the fourth highest goals total throughout the League, not bad considering the team was once again near the bottom of the Fourth Division

In November we battled Third Division promotion contenders Shrewsbury Town in the FA Cup, we drew 2-2 at home and I netted twice. I was on top of my game during the time and Joe Slater in the Evening Post wrote:

Peter the Great Keeps Rovers in the Cup.

Peter Kitchen had a great game, he scored twice, could easily have doubled that total, and displayed some of the finest touches I've ever seen from any player. Time after time, he left defenders trailing with real pace and a swerve and he was always in the right spot creating chances for himself.

In the replay we fought hard but went down 4-3.

The week after our Cup exploits we faced Crewe Alexandra and my number one fan, Joe Slater in *The Evening Post* wrote:

Peter The Great Has Done It Again!

With just 18 seconds after the re-start Kitchen picked up the ball beat a few defenders, ran into the penalty box to smash a left footer in the net past Crewe keeper Geoff Cuddington.

I netted a second seventeen minutes later, made for me by new boy Ian Bailey on loan from Middlesbrough, and we ran out 3-0 winners. It was my sixteenth goal of the season to become the Fourth Divisions joint-top goal scorer.

On 11 April, I scored two goals against Scunthorpe United, the second, I remember very clearly, it was a spectacular overhead kick to record my 100th goal for the club, it was a Miller cross a little nod on from O'Callaghan and I beat Richard Money to the ball to bang it into the net, and we won 3-0.

A week later I netted a hat trick in a 6-3 win over Workington Town. Alan Burkinshaw in the Evening Post wrote:

Kitchen Cooks Up New Joy

Peter Kitchen breathed new life into Doncaster Rovers promotion bid by scoring a hat trick and providing the inspiration for the demolition of bottom-of-the-table Workington, who had the worst defence in the League, and he has now scored 7 goals from the last five games. His third coming from a stunning 15-yard volley past Mike Rogan in goal.

At the end of the month, on 30 April 1977, I scored the winner in a 2-1 win at Crewe Alexandra before 2,259 fans, which turned out to be my final appearance for Rovers, and so ending, what was a wonderful chapter in my career, which saw Rovers end in one of their highest League positions in years, eighth spot.

I had great success at Belle Vue, but it was the right time for me to move on, I was out of contract and as mentioned, I had wanted to get away for some time but manager Stan Anderson had turned down several offers, including a number from Orient's George Petchey.

It was over my final three seasons that I hit the headlines for Rovers with 75 first team goals, including 27 League and Cup goals in the 1976-77 season. In the end I netted 89 League and 16 Cup goals for Rovers, but I was still 91 goals short of the club's all-time League goal scoring record holder, Tom Keetley (1922-29), yet today I'm still their fourth all-time leading goal scorer with just Keetley and Alick Jeffrey with 129 League goals and Bert Tindall ahead of me. If I had stayed, I'm sure I would have been much closer to the top.

Rawmarsh-born Alick James Jeffrey was recently voted the most popular ever player for Rovers. His son, also named Alick, was a reserve player for Rovers and today works for the club in their commercial department.

Jeffrey had a long career that spanned more than sixteen years until ending his career with Worksop Town in the early seventies. He made a total of 211(4) League appearances with 132 goals. He actually retired because of leg that was

The Peter Kitchen Story

badly broken in two places, during October 1957 whilst playing for England U-23s against France in Bristol.

He went to play in Australia in 1962 with the Auburn club, came back to England to play non-league football with Skegness and broke his leg again. He decided to return to Belle Vue in December1963 at the age of twenty-four, and bagged 95 League goals from 190(1) appearances. The final turning point in his career during 1966 when club captain John Nicholson and himself were involved in a car accident in the early hours on Sheffield Road, Warmsworth.

Nicholson was killed and Jeffrey was out for several months, he was never quite the same again. He died in Benidorm, Spain in November 2000, at the time he was the President of the club.

Things appeared to be happening on the transfer front, I was allowed in May 1977 to miss Rovers final three League games of the season, incidentally all defeats, to go on trial with Ipswich Town.

Voted A Fourth Division Award Winner Twice In A Row

During my final two seasons at Belle Vue, I was voted a PFA Divisional Award winner for the Division Four team and very proud at being honoured in this way by my fellow professionals having gained the most votes from all the players from Division Four.

When I met up with Ian Miller recently we jokingly recalled one of trips to the PFA awards in 1977 and our pre-meet with John Robertson, the Nottingham Forest and Scotland winger.

Ian had been a friend and team-mate of Robbo's at Forest before his transfer to Doncaster and he had arranged for us to meet John before the dinner for a drink. John had been nominated for a place in the 2nd Division PFA team when Forest won promotion to Division one under Brian Clough.

Robbo, who Ian told me always had a scruffy and unkempt appearance, had to hire a suit from Moss Bros and it clearly didn't fit him. The jacket was too small, the trousers were too tight, and the material was shiny and worn and he clearly didn't look like a successful and talented footballer. He had now realized how badly he was dressed but it was too late to do anything about it and he was mortified of meeting and sitting with the other members of the 2nd division team, which included Ray Wilkins of Chelsea, Mick Channon of Southampton and George Best of Fulham.

John did not look comfortable at all throughout the whole evening and when we caught his eye, we couldn't help but laugh at him.

In The 1976 Award Winning Team There Was:

In goal, *Peter Grotier* (Lincoln City), born in Stratford, London on 18 October 1950, he started as a youth player with West Ham United, after a loan spell with Cardiff City, he moved to Lincoln City, after being on loan, in 1974 for £16,666 the fee was raised by the City fans. He joined Cardiff City in December 1979 and played alongside me. Grotier made 314 career appearances between 1968-1980.

The left back was: *Ian Branfoot* (Lincoln City) was born in Gateshead on 26 January 1947, he started his career with Redhugh Boys and then played for Gateshead. Sheffield Wednesday in 1965, before moving in December 1969 to Doncaster Rovers with Archie Irvine in exchange for Harold Wilcockson.

He played with me until he moved on to Lincoln City in 1973, when he retired from playing, making a career total of 355(3) League appearances with 16 goals and was appointed assistant manager at Reading.

He later had a successful managerial career with Reading for five years. Taking them to promotion from Division Four as well as Wembley glory in the Simod Cup. He also had spells as coach with Crystal Palace, scout, and then assistant manager for Swansea City and also manager with Southampton and Fulham and was Academy Director at Sunderland until leaving in May 2002, and is now scouting for a few clubs.

Right back was *Kenneth Leslie Sandercock* (Torquay United), he was born in Plymouth on 31 January 1951. He started of with Torquay in 1968 after a short spell with Leicester City, he returned to Torquay. He made 160(14) League appearances with 6 goals.

Number 4 was *Geoff Hutt* (Huddersfield Town), Ken was born in Duffield on 28 September 1949. The ginger haired player started off a youth player with Huddersfield and also played for Blackburn Rovers (loan), York City and Halifax Town, making a total of 393(1) league appearances with 6 goals.

Centre half was *Sam Ellis* (Lincoln City), was born in Ashton-under-Lyme on 12 September 1946 and he also played for Snipe Wanderers, and W.H. Smith before joining Sheffield Wednesday, and he made a surprise FA Cup Final appearance in 1966, after just 11 senior games for the club. In 1970 he moved to Mansfield Town and Watford. He eventually hung up his boots in May 1979, having played a total of 422(6) league appearances, scoring 45 goals. He was appointed manager with Bury and then number two at Manchester City, he moved to Lincoln City as coach and then manager and later returned as coach with Bury.

He was later head coach with Sheffield Wednesday. As a young player, he won 3 England U-23 caps.

Number 6 was *Terry Cooper* (Lincoln City) who was born in Croesyceiliog, near Cwmbran, Wales on 11 March 1950 and started as a junior with Newport County in 1968, he moved on a free transfer to Notts. County in 1970 and later he also played for Scunthorpe United and Bradford City in June 1979 for £10,000 and Rochdale in 1981. He made over 400 League appearances.\

My Doncaster Rovers colleague *Ian Miller* was on the left wing, and *John Ward* (Lincoln City) was inside left, born in Lincoln on 7 April 1951, he started with local amateur side Adelaide Park before signing for Lincoln in 1970. He played with Workington (loan), Watford, and Grimsby Town before joining the Watford coaching staff in 1982. He made a total of 282 League appearances with 100 goals.

At centre forward it was not as as I would have expected Brendan O'Callaghan but rather *Ronnie Moore* (Tranmere Rovers) who was born in Liverpool on 29 January 1953, starting his career with Tranmere Rovers, he later had spells with Cardiff City, Rotherham United, Charlton Athletic and Rochdale. He made a career total of over 350 League appearances, with over 100 goals. He later had successful managerial post with Rotherham United, after a brief spell in charge with Tranmere. He was in charge with Rotherham for 398 matches with 143 wins 121 draws and 134 losses. In 2005, he was manager of Oldham Athletic.

Ronnie Moore is currently managing Hartlepool United and has done such a good job this season, that Jeff Stelling, the Sky TV sports pundit and Hartlepool supporter is always singing his praises on his Saturday sports programme and rightly so after the remarkable job 'Mooro' has done in maintaining their place in the Football league this season

I was at number 10 and on the right wing was the exciting *Tony Whelan* of Rochdale. He was born in Salford on 20 November 1952 and he started off as a youth player with Manchester United before moving to Manchester City and later playing out his career with Rochdale and was one of only a handful of the first black footballers playing in the League. After Rochdale, he played in the States for Fort Lauderdale Strikers and after six happy years he returned to England in November 1983 when his playing career ended with Witton Albion when he suffered a double fracture of his right leg.

He made a career total of just 127(3) League appearances with 20 goals. He has worked for over eight years at the Manchester City Centre of Excellence and more recently in the same capacity with Manchester United. In 1994, he graduated from the Open University and has also written a book on United's youth policy entitled *The Birth of the Babes 1950-57*.

The 1977 Team comprised of:

Goalkeeper *Terry Poole* (Huddersfield Town) was born in Chesterfield on 16 December 1949, another who started in the youth team at Old Trafford before joining Huddersfield in 1968. He later played for Bolton Wanderers and Sheffield United on loan, making over 250 first team appearances.

Left Back was *Brendan Batson* (Cambridge united) was born in St. George's in Grenada on I February 1953. He became one of the first high profile pioneering black footballers.

He moved to England when he was nine years of age having never seen a game of football and a teacher at his school watching his early efforts on the field, remarked 'perhaps cricket is more your game'. He joined Arsenal as a school boy, after four years at Highbury learning his trade, he moved to Cambridge United and in 1978 to become a cultured defender. He joined up again with the former United boss Ron Atkinson at West Bromwich Albion to team with fellow black players Laurie Cunningham and Cyril Regis.

Batson's playing career was cut short by injury in October 1982 after more than 300 League appearances to become a very able and active administrator at the Professional Footballers Association rising to become a senior executive.

In December 2000, he was awarded in the New Years Honours List an MBE for his services to football and a couple of years later he also acted as the Managing Director of his old club - West Bromwich Albion.

The Right back was *Andy Ford* (Southend United), the muscular tough-tackling defender was born in Minehead on Tuesday 4 May 1954, he started with his local side before moving to AFC Bournemouth in 1972 but he never made any first team appearances after the club wound up its reserve side, he moved to Southend United in May 1976, and became their Player of the Year. He moved to Swindon Town stayed at the County Ground for three season before moving to Gillingham for £30,000 in June 1980. After retiring, with nearly 300 League outings under his belt, he set up a local business and returned to play with Dartford and was then with Gravesend & Northfleet and stayed as manager for eight years until resigning in January 2005 to become manager of Stevenage Borough in March 2005 but he left at the end of the season.

In midfielder was *Dennis Bond* (Watford), born in Walthamstow on 17 March 1953, he joined Woodford Town and then onto Watford as an apprentice, making his League debut at the age of seventeen. Being very slender and just 5ft 7ins, he had to work hard to make his mark in the game, which revolved around subtle passing rather than strength and tackling ability. In 1967 he moved to Tottenham Hotspur for £30,000 whilst suffering from chicken pox. He only made 27 League appearances before leaving White Hart Lane in 1970, moving to Charlton Athletic. In 1973, he returned to Vicarage Road and six-years later he joined Dagenham, then played for Highfield Sports, Boreham Wood in 1982 and then Waltham Abbey. In 1986, he was assistant manager with Potters Bar football club.

At centre half was *Lindsay Smith* (Colchester United), born in Enfield on 18 September 1954, he started as an apprentice with Colchester, early in the 1977-78 season he went on loan with both Charlton Athletic and Millwall. He joined Cambridge United in October 1977 and later played for Plymouth Argyle and Cambridge again for £5000, making over 400 career League appearances.

At right half was *Barry Dominey* (Colchester United), born in Edmonton, London on 21 October 1955, he started his career with Enfield WMC before moving to Colchester United in 1973, he made 53(15) league appearances with 3 goals before moving out of the League in July 1977 with Yeovil Town, a club that his Father had also played for in earlier years. In recent years he worked as a scout for Colchester's Centre of Excellence, in March 2005, it was reported by that club that Dominey had just died.

On the wing was the great Ian Miller again, and at inside forward a well known player, *Alan Curtis* (Swansea City). Born in Ton Pentre, Wales on 16 April 1954, he had a long and distinguished career, having started with Swansea in 1971, he joined Leeds United for a then record fee for a Third Division player of £350,000 during June 1979 and was then sold to Southampton for £180,000 three years later. After spells with Sunderland and Cardiff City, he ended his League career back with Swansea before hanging up his boots due to an injury in 1991, V
During his long career he won 35 Welsh caps and made 577 League appearances, scoring 117 goals, Curtis has filled various roles with Swansea including coach and assistant manager and the Football in the Community Officer and also managed the youth team.
In July 2005, he was rewarded with a Testimonial against Fulham held in the club's Liberty Sadium a 20,000 all-seater in which he played in the final ten minutes before a 12,000 crowd. He will continue to work at the club in the Hospitality section, but has since rejoined the club's coaching staff and is current-

ly Assistant Manager. Swansea City have achieved their best ever league position in the Premier league this season.

At centre forward was Brian Joicey (Barnsley) born in Winlaton, on 19 December 1945, he started off with North Shields, scoring in the 1969 Amateur Cup Final at Wembley, before joining Coventry City in June 1969, he later had four-years with Sheffield Wednesday before moving onto Barnsley in July 1976. In March 1974, there was talk of move to Orient to cement their challenge to Division One, but the deal fell-through, as did Orient's promotion challenge. His finest moment in football was scoring a hat trick against Crystal Palace in February 1974 to help Wednesday reach the 5th Round of the FA Cup. He got into the 1977 Divisional awards with his 25 League goals. His football career ended after damaging his kidney in 1979 whilst playing for Barnsley at York City, he later collapsed after suffering a stroke, but he came back to play non league football two-years later. Joicey made a total of 252(24) League appearances with 100 goals. More recently he was the sales manager in Sheffield for GT cars Fiat.

I was at number Ten and on the right wing was *Don Hutchins* (Bradford City) born in Middlesbrough on 8 May 1948, a skilful, speedy wingman who leant his trade with North Riding, Stockton and Middlesbrough Boys before Raich Carter signed him for Boro' on junior terms. He later played for Leicester City, Plymouth Argyle for £6000, where he was their top scorer in 1970-71 and then with Blackburn Rovers.

He moved to Bradford City in part-exchange for Graham Oates plus £10,000 in July 1974. It was his thrilling wing play, he was brilliant at out swinging crosses and his flowing locks when flying down the wing, which made him the darling of the Valley Parade fans. When voted into the top Division Four side by his fellow professionals it was the first such honour for the club. He left City in 1981 to play a few games for Scarborough, he retired soon after ending a long career, which spanned some fifteen years and 388(9) League appearances with 74 goals. He still lives in Baildon and is a regular at Valley Parade.

Brendan O'Callaghan got into the Fourth Divisional awards side in 1978, the year after I left and to prove his great consistency Ian Miller also made the same team, his third award in a row.

Chapter 3
Down To London,
Successful Times With Orient

On trial with Ipswich Town then down to London to meet O's chairman Brian Winston

To force the issue I exercised the option on my contract the previous summer so as to speed-up a move. Bobby Robson at Ipswich Town took me on a month's trial during May 1977, but the Ipswich first team by this time had already gone on tour to Israel for ten days so I didn't get much of a chance to play until they had returned.

I played in one reserve game against Cardiff City at Portman Road and then a friendly game and a Testimonial game with the first team at Chelmsford City and Colchester United, scoring in both games. The Ipswich side was their full first team including Paul Mariner, Trevor Whymark, Mick Mills, Alan Hunter, Roger Osborne etc and also some up and coming young players like Russell Osman, Terry Butcher, Alan Brazil and Eric Gates. In the Chelmsford City team was an ageing Jimmy Greaves.

On the very last day of my stay at Portman Road, I meet with Bobby Robson who indicated to me that I had done very well and that he was interested in signing me and he asked me how much did Doncaster want.

I told him that they were asking £75,000, but would probably accept about £50,000, he said that he would speak to Stan Anderson to see if they could do a deal, but he was thinking of £25,000. He also said that he could not promise me even a game in the reserves as he had Trevor Whymark, Paul Mariner and Clive Woods in the first team and Alan Brazil, Eric Gates, Robin Turner and David Geddes (who was on loan to Aston Villa at the time) in the reserves.

I received a call from Ron Gray the chief scout on the Monday to say that they couldn't agree a fee for me with Doncaster Rovers and therefore Bobby Robson would not be signing me.

(To Robson's credit I met up with him when I was with at Orient. It was after our FA Cup victory at Norwich City in January 1978 and after the match he complemented me on my game and said that he had made a mistake and that he should have signed me for Ipswich).

Orient boss George Petchey had also followed my goal scoring exploits with Rovers and was on the look out for a decent striker to partner their big centre forward Joe Mayo. Having heard I had returned to Belle Vue, he phoned Stan Anderson and asked if I was still available. Anderson asked "How much are you offering?", an offer of around £30,000 was made (the exact amount was never made known to me, but fees of £40,000 and £45,000 were often quoted in the press) and the deal was verbally agreed between them, however before I put pen to paper, I made two visits to London to discuss the move.

The first visit was on my own and I met up with the Orient chairman Brian Winston at Kings Cross Station and I was taken to Brisbane Road to meet George Petchey. I then went with Winston who took me around the district and we had lunch at a restaurant in Woodford.

At the ground we obviously discussed financial and personal terms and I remember they were laying new turf, which was to prove a really good investment. I must confess, when I first saw the stadium without any grass I was not particularly impressed and Brian Winston must have picked up on this as he made a comment to this effect.

Orient offered me a three-year deal which I was reluctant to accept, as I did still wanted to try and get into the First Division and therefore wanted to keep my options open. I said that I would discuss the offer with my wife and so I returned home. I very much saw this move as a stepping stone and hoped that if I was successful in Division 2 then surely I would get a move to a First Division team so didn't want to commit myself to a three-year deal.

I returned to Leyton a few days later with my wife Susan, to look around the district specifically at houses and compare prices. I had bought a three-bed semi about a year before for £7,500 and so it was quite important for us to make the right decision. My wife did not really want to come down south to London, she was a girl who would have been happy to stay in Conisborough all her life and she did not have a very outgoing personality.

(I suppose one of the most famous people from the town was singer Tony Christie, born Anthony Fitzgerald on 25 April 1943, in Conisborough, he had two top twenty hits in 1971 "I did what I did for Maria" and "Is this the way to Amarillo" and in latter life moved to Spain.

The Amarillo song was re-released in March 2005 for comic relief and reached number one in the charts again with the biggest single sales for the year and was seven weeks at number one).

We looked at houses in and around Epping, which we quite liked and eventually ended up moving there. After the two meetings I still wasn't convinced about signing so I asked for an increase on the basic salary and a two-year deal only which in the end Brian Winston agreed to.

I then gave my word on this and said I would return a signed contract in due course, once I had the offer in writing.

I read that evening a quote from Doncaster boss Stan Anderson in the local paper that they were not considering any other offer other than the one from Orient, but there were other clubs in the wings waiting to pounce should the Orient deal fall through.

Anderson further stated: 'We have set up a deal with Orient and until such time as it is no longer on we will not be listening to any other offers from other clubs. Everything is down to Peter now, he has to decide on whether to sign for Orient. That's the only offer under consideration.'

When I got back home, Stan Anderson phoned to ask how things went and he informed me that another club had made a firm offer for me but he couldn't tell me who it was until I had made a decision on Orient, but in the end he felt obligated to let me know that it was from Keith Burkinshaw, the manager and Bill Nicholson the chief scout of Tottenham Hotspur.

Also Mansfield Town, newly promoted to the Second Division had put in an offer for me of £20,000 plus a recognized striker, but the offer did not prove attractive enough to Rovers who wanted cash and the Mansfield offer did not match that of Orient.

I was gutted about the Spurs offer, but I had given my word to Brian Winston and therefore I signed for the O's in June 1977, and I did not talk to Spurs, a side I had always dreamt about playing for. I suppose it is an example of the old fashioned values of integrity that my parents had somehow instilled in me and which I mostly still carry with me to this day.

At Orient I received a £4,000 signing-on fee, plus £1,500 as a tax free resettlement allowance and I was on a basic of £150 for the two years I was in Leyton, plus various bonuses. I came down in June 1977 to find some digs until I was able to buy a house. I was initially staying with Colin Church's mum (he was and I believe still is the club's electrician) before moving in with Maurice Newman (he was a scout for the club) and his family.

Sad To Leave The Lads From Swinton Junior Football Team

Prior to moving to Orient I was still coaching and managing one of the junior teams at Mexborough and Swinton junior football teams, a position I held from 1972 until going to London in 1977. In that team I brought on a young

Mexborough-born lad named Ian Banks and as I left for London, he had signed for Barnsley.

I was so happy that the midfielder went onto have a great playing career, with more than 600 career games and 90 odd goals, until his retirement in 1995.

My love of being involved with junior football was not widely known, I managed the Swinton Junior U-15's in the Doncaster Sunday Football League. It all began for me when they asked me to come down and help with a bit of coaching. I couldn't stand back and see them being given the wrong ideas, so I ended up as manager.

Swinton ran three teams: Harold Whitehouse looked after the U-14's, Stan Smith the U-16's and me the U-15's. Up until I joined, my team had not won anything but I had some useful players and they played some good attacking football.

When I first took over I just wanted them to win, but in the end I was just happy and got more satisfaction to see them play some good football. Whenever we weren't playing away, I would go down Friday night to my old Mexborough School organising training and coaching.

As a manager of a junior team, one had to be realistic about the prospects of boys making a career in the professional game. There are millions of footballers playing every Saturday, but only a very few have the balance of skill, dedication and attitude to enable them to go on and become a professional footballer. Even so, I enjoyed coaching and training with the lads and was just happy to be able to put back in to the game many of the benefits the game gave me.

I was very sad on leaving Doncaster Rovers, as we did have some very good players and it was a shame that we weren't ever able to get promoted as this might have enabled me to achieve my professional ambitions with them. I also had a wonderful rapport with the Rovers fans and I still get goose bumps when I recall them singing "There's only one Peter Kitchen" and "Peter Kitchen walks on water " La La La La La!! It was a wonderful and very rewarding time in my career, and I always enjoy going back to Belle Vue and I look forward to visiting their new ground in 2007.

First Day At Training With The O's Lads And My Meeting With Den, A Sparky

I joined the O's squad in training for pre-season on 1 July 1977 at Highams Park. I remember being made to feel very at home by the players who were all very friendly. It was something I became used to as this friendliness seemed to be endemic throughout the club from the Directors to the office staff to the ground staff who all seemed not only to be employees but supporters as well.

On that first day at Highams Park I recall Alan Whittle and Bill Roffey asking me if I wanted to go to the local café, next to the railway crossing for a sandwich. Afterwards I was walking back when a white van with Waltham Forest Borough Council pulled up alongside me and the window wound down. A small round-faced man said in a broad cockney accent

"Orright mate, you the new signing from up norf? Welcome to the Orient mate, I'm Den, a sparky. If you need any jobs done give me a bell " and thrust his telephone number into my hand. I later became friends with Dennis Barefield and his wife Margaret who helped Susan and I settle in the area and we still keep in contact. He is still an Orient season ticket holder and he often reminds me that I might be an 'Orient Legend' but he is an Orient 'Leg End'.

(Peter and Neil met up with Dennis at the Orient Supporters Club in October 2005, when he still fondly recalled the story).

I scored on my first team debut for O's in a 2-0 League Cup victory at Fulham on 13 August 1977(although I played a few games away in the Anglo Scottish Cup). I made my League debut seven days later at Luton Town; even though we lost 1-0, I thought I had quite a good game. Then on 23 August, a disastrous 4-1 home defeat was inflicted by Blackpool and that was the end of George Petchey's six-year reign as boss, Brian Winston sacked him straight after the game.

Then we had to go and play at Sunderland and Peter Angell acted as caretaker-manager, I netted my first League goal for the O's in a 1-1 draw before 28,261 Roker fans.

Then came the visit of Oldham Athletic on 3 September and under Peter Angell we played a more attacking style and it was certainly an exciting game, we won 5-3 and I bagged a brace, but the match ball was presented to the former O's player Vic Halom, having scored his 100th League career goal.

The talk around the club was who was to be the new manager, it was clear that Angell did want to be considered and in the end it was the experienced Jimmy Bloomfield who returned to the O's for his second spell in charge.

Peter Angell was a very nice guy and a very genuine man, and whilst I was on my own in digs, he invited me around a few times to his house in Southgate for lunch, which was a very nice gesture. He didn't want the manager's job, he was always happy to be number two.

Bloomfield's appointment seemed to be a popular move with the fans, as the crowd almost doubled to 8,751 for the home match against Bristol Rovers on 17 September. Bobby Fisher hit a rare goal and I netted my first penalty for the club to secure a 2-1 win, it was a good start for the new boss.

First hat trick for the O's against Mansfield Town

I had a good little spell during October, bagging four goals from three League games and my partnership upfront with Joe Mayo was beginning to pay dividends. After a dry spell in November, we picked up in the following month and I notched my first hat trick for the O's in the 4-2 win over Mansfield Town, it was also the first hat trick by an O's player in six years.

The local *Newham Express* reported:

Scoring for Orient v Cardiff City, October 1977

Peter Kitchen returned to form in devastating fashion cracking in his first hat trick for the O's the to bring his season's tally to 12 goals. It was John Chiedozie, who made his England Youth debut last week, who opened the scoring on just thirty-five seconds from twelve yards, his first goal for the first team. Twelve minutes later Kitchen opened his account and scored two more in fine style.

The return of Joe Mayo to the side after an absence of three matches was highly significant in Orient's play and Kitchen looked much more relaxed which Mayo back in the side.

Awarded a Crate of J & B Rare Scotch Whisky

Before the match with Brighton & Hove Albion, I was awarded a crate of J&B Scotch in recognition of my hat trick against Mansfield. The whisky was shared amongst the players who took part in the game and a crate was also presented to the club, it seemed to go to our heads, as we didn't perform against the Seasiders and we lost 1-0 before nearly 9,500 fans.

The Great FA Cup Run - 'Kitchen Sinks 'Em'

In January 1978, saw the start of our FA Cup campaign and when I started to hit the headlines in the National press with some lovely captions like:

Sun: **Killer KITCHEN**

Daily Express: **Chelsea dished by KITCHEN**

Daily Mirror: **On the Boil! KITCHEN whistles in to score Orient Cup stunner**

Sun: **O! KITCHEN sinks Norwich**

Daily Express: **KITCHEN SINKER: Boro' Knocked out**

We knocked out Norwich City in a Third Round replay at Carrow Road and I hit the winner which stunned the 20,421 crowd.

The Daily Mirror reported:

Orient's Kitchen strikes late to put our Norwich

Orient, badly placed in the Second Division, qualified for a home tie against Blackburn Rovers in the Fourth Round of the FA Cup with a Peter Kitchen goal in the 87th minute at last night's Third Round replay at Carrow Road.

With indomitable spirit Orient often matched their First Division opponents and inflicted their first home defeat of the season. The architect of the goal was 17-year old tiny Nigerian-born John Chiedozie who outpaced defender Sullivan – as he did frequently – and centred for Kitchen to sweep the ball past Kevin Keelan in goal.

When Norwich was on target there was the veteran John Jackson in goal, who produced some cat-like saves to make him a candidate for an England cap. The Norwich team trailed off the pitch with their heads down.

Some of the other press reports stated:

Kitchen pounced onto a great cross from Chiedozie to rap in his 18th goal of the season. Orient were robbed of victory when Norwich scored in injury-time in the first game after Kitchen hit O's opener, in this game they hustled and closed them down and caused them all sorts of problems and at the back they had the great John Jackson in goal with four majestic saves.

A jubilant Kitchen said afterwards: "I wanted to prove I was capable of playing in a higher grade – and this was a great way to do it."
O's manager Jimmy Bloomfield said: "What pleased me most of all was that we won it deservedly over two matches. The lads were heartbroken at being robbed in the last match. But none thought we would lose this time."

The Sun Newspaper reported:

Peter Kitchen a bargain buy at just £30,000, once again displayed his incredible goal-getting ability. From a Bobby Fisher throw-in, the ball reached Joe Mayo who tried to shied the ball from two Norwich players, the ball broke to young winger Chiedozie, his cross curled in and Kitchen moved like a white flash to knock in an unstoppable volley.

Although Orient were on the defensive for long periods, the quality of their football on the break was splendid, there was one move, after half an hour that left Norwich gasping. Magnificent control from Chiedozie, left Colin Sullivan floundering, his pass to Mayo was inch perfect, when the cross-arrived that man Kitchen was there again with a fine side-footed volley when Kevin Keelan did well to turn away.

David Miller in *The Daily Express* reported:

Glory night for Orient and Kitchen

Nigerian John Chiedozie, aged just 17, gave the pass for the winning goal, which put even the ageless elegance of Martin Peters from Norwich momentarily in the shade. He sliced past Sullivan and curled in an early, low cross, in came the burly looking Peter Kitchen to brush past two defenders and lash the ball past the veteran Keelan for the winner.

KILLER KITCHEN knocks out Blackburn Rovers

In the Fourth Round, we started off poorly against Blackburn Rovers, who completely outplayed us with some smooth football, and took a deserved lead on 68 minutes through Stuart Metcalf and they must have thought to themselves that they had done enough.

However, in the final twelve minutes we came alive, I latched onto a long ball from Phil Hoadley cut in on the right to beat their goalie John Butcher with a curling shot, which I enjoyed. I then took my goal tally to twenty for the season on 86 minutes, I put Joe Mayo through and when his shot was blocked on the line by John Waddington, I followed up to rip the ball home. Big Joe rounded off a great fight-back in the final seconds knocking in a cross from young 17-year old Kevin Godfrey to secure a great 3-1 victory before 9,547 fans.

Their manager Jim Smith was not overly impressed with his team losing to a team like Orient, he told the Daily Express: "I can't believe the result. They hardly had a kick and beat us."

Mr. Smith, what can I say? We had three kicks and it was enough to secure our victory.

Peter in action against Chelsea
n the FA Cup at Brisbane Road

Sun
SOCCERCARDS
DEFENDERS
407
BOBBY FISHER
(Orient)

Bobby was one of five Orient players who were ever-presents in the 1977-78 season. Began his career as a midfielder having signed professional for Orient in August, 1973. Now Bobby is one of the top defenders in the Second Division. Bobby has now played over 150 League games for the East London Club whom he joined as a youth.

B. FISHER (Orient)

Sun
SOCCERCARDS
STRIKERS
870
JOE MAYO
(Orient)

Joe formed a great scoring partnership with Peter Kitchen as Orient reached the Semi-Finals of the 1977-78 F.A. Cup competition. Began League career with Walsall, then went to West Bromwich for four seasons before joining Orient in March, 1977. Scored on his League debut at Blackburn for Orient on 12th March, 1977.

J. MAYO (Orient)

Sun
SOCCERCARDS
STRIKERS
849
PETER KITCHEN
(Orient)

Peter shot to fame in the 1977-78 season when his seven F.A. Cup goals took Orient to the Semi-Finals of the competition. He also scored 21 League goals in the same season. Joined Doncaster Rovers from school and hit over 100 goals in first-team matches for the Yorkshire club before joining Orient in June, 1977.

P. KITCHEN (Orient)

SOCCERCARDS
DEFENDERS
432
JOHN JACKSON
(Orient)

Goalkeeper John had played 346 League games for Crystal Palace when he was transferred to Orient and is now on the way to his 200th League appearance for them too! Moved in October, 1973 and is still performing brilliantly between the sticks. Has played soccer in the United States in the summer for St. Louis Stars.

J. JACKSON (Orient)

Sun
SOCCERCARDS
MIDFIELDERS
614
TONY GREALISH
(Orient)

A full Republic of Ireland international. Tony is a fine midfielder, who joined Orient straight from school. Graduated through the Youth teams to make his League debut v Sheffield Wednesday in September, 1974 as a substitute. Given his first full game v Forest in November, 1974 and scored a goal. Still a youngster he has already played 150 League games.

T. GREALISH (Orient)

Cig Cards - Five Stars of the 1977-78 Season: Top Row: Bobby Fisher (L), and Joe Mayo (R), Center: Peter Kitchen, Bottom Row: John Jackson (L) and Tony Grealish (R)

Bring on Chelsea

So then came the visit of Chelsea to Brisbane Road in the Fifth Round on 18 February. They played quite well and were marginally the better team with Ray Wilkins controlling the midfield. I scored during the match but it was ruled offside, although it looked a good one to me. This was followed by a wall collapsing, fortunately no one was injured and the game was able to restart. John Jackson made a tremendous save near the end. We were well deserving of a replay, and this match at the Bridge turned out to be one of the finest moments in my footballing career.

I loved living in London and soon become quite famous with the O's and I was out and about a lot, whereas my wife Susan found it hard to settle down south and in making any new friends. I think the fame started to go to my head a bit, I was regularly in the national newspapers and doing several TV inteviews and was even opening pubs and presenting prizes at various functions and fetes. I was being featured in the national newspapers and in Football magazines, offered a contract for my picture to be featured in a set of cigarette cards and even Kenneth Wolstenholme, the famous football commentator, invited me to a championship boxing event.

London Evening Standard's Footballer of the Month for January 1978

I was now the talk of the Town, and I remember the *London Evening Standard's* Peter Blackman came to Brisbane Road on 3 February for an interview and to present me with an inscribed silver salver and two magnums of Louis Kremer White Label Champagne.

Kitchen's big dream leads to another

Blackman wrote:

Orient's Peter Kitchen was talking about life in the often bleak, lower regions of the Football League as he said: "To survive down there a player needs to have something special inside him"

He was recalling fixtures against clubs like Hartlepool, Workington and Newport. " That's the world of packed lunches, all-night coach rides and grounds where players can hear every word on the terraces, "he said.

But Kitchen, now an Orient star striker, had the inner strength to keep going. He dreamed constantly of making the big time, even though the bruises from being 'whacked' from behind from Fourth Division defenders spread wider each weekend.

His credentials were sound: after a quite start with Doncaster his goal-rate in successive seasons read 15, 24, 25 and 27. Slowly, the transfer drum beat the message and from time the leading clubs watching him included Ipswich Town.

Finally, George Petchey who was then Orient's manager paid £30,000 for him last summer. The explosion came last month when his four FA Cup goals which took him to 20 goals for a season and wins him the Evening Standard Footballer of the Month award. Petchey, now with Millwall, believes that Kitchen has rocketed into the £150,000 class.

Kitchen with his slightly curved shoulders, straight hair and moustache, resembles Jimmy Greaves in appearance. His slight build contrasts sharply with the accepted image of a husky striker patrolling the opportunity in the Fourth Division.

Kitchen did well at Mexborough Grammar School and now he is top of the class among London strikers. But he still remembers the "frustration" at Doncaster. "I often thought of packing it in," he said. "The one thing that kept me going was the conviction that I could score goals. In the season before Orient bought me I'd gee myself up for a game when I was told so-and-so from another club was watching. I don't know all the clubs that watched me by they included Ipswich Town, Orient, West Bromwich Albion, Crystal Palace and Spurs."

"Our build up is to make sure that I am always on the end of our moves, but credit too must be given to Joe Mayo who forms an effective partnership with me."

Kitchen continued: "Strikers should always hunt in pairs, I seem to be getting all the attention, but Joe and the rest of the lads are making it easy for me. I just feed off Joe, poaching if you like."

As Kitchen left for a TV interview, he was taken to the studio in a chauffeur-driven car, I asked him if there was a secret about goal scoring.

"I'm asked that question at least once a week," he said. "My reply is always the same ....a striker must, at all times be an optimist."

Important match at Spurs then the Chelsea replay

In between the FA Cup exploits with Chelsea, we had an important League game at White Hart Lane against Tottenham Hotspur and when Joe (Mayo) headed us into the lead, we looked a good bet for a win, but Spurs fought back with a goal from Colin Lee and we drew 1-1 in front of a large 32,869 crowd. Although, I almost scored our winner with a spectacular volley that required an outstanding save from Barry Daines in the Spurs goal to save a point. Spurs who had Glenn Hoddle and Peter Taylor in their team won promotion back to the 'old' Division One that season.

The next game was our replay at Stamford Bridge and 36,379 packed into the Bridge to watch the encounter. We were playing well, but then Bill Roffey lobbed the ball over John Jackson and into the net and the first half ended with us 1-0 down. I, like most others at the ground, thought the match was over, but we had something special in store for the boys in blue and our loyal fans.

Chelsea dished by Kitchen

Kitchen double sinks Chelsea and sends Orient on their way.

The Daily Express reported:

An Oriental Yorkshireman scored a goal fit for the folklore of the FA Cup which sent Orient bubbling to a shock win at Stamford Bridge. One of the best goals ever scored in the history of the famous FA Cup.

Kitchen first levelled the scores with a marvellous effort – then got a great winner Chelsea were leading after Billy Roffey's first half own goal, but Kitchen soon got into the act in the second half and he struck magnificently.

He first sped onto a Kevin Godfrey through ball, twisted past Ron Harris, cut inside Micky Droy like he wasn't there and danced around Ian Britton before scoring past Bonetti from six yards, it was pure magic and probably one of the best goals ever scored in the history of the competition.

**Peter in full flight against Chelsea,
being watched by Ron 'Chopper.' Harris.**

115

One of the great highlights in Peter Kitchen's career,
scoring the 2 goals that knocked out the mighty Chelsea from the FA Cup
at Stamford Bridge on 27 February 1978 before a crowd of 36,379.

His second, and the winner, came when Glenn Roeder broke out of defence, set big Joe Mayo away, he slipped the ball to Kitchen who scored from eight yards to silence the Chelsea fans.

That was enough to ensure pie and mash celebrations in London's East End and Kitchen covered in lager and light ale poured over him by his delirious team mates in the dressing room after the match.

Kitchen told me straight aft the match: "That first goal was one of the best I have ever scored, it was just instinctive. It was also the first time in the match I managed to get free from Ron Harris. I had played terrible up to that point, till then I hadn't had a kick all match. I have never been past the Third Round before, now we all feel Orient can go on and on."

O's Acting Manager Peter Angell said: "It was a great performance and Peter's first great goal decided it all, our Chairman slipped away from the dressing room celebrations to phone boss Jimmy Bloomfield who was in hospital for observations and tests."

Peter the Pearly King!

"At Chelsea, a better side and a Yorkshireman named Peter Kitchen beat them." I remember the great journalist Brian Glanville remarked that my goals against Chelsea were the best he'd seen for many a season, and he often spoke about it.

Kitchen: The Pearly King of Leyton

Just after the Chelsea win I did a photo shoot at Brisbane Road dressed up ad the Pearly King. I remember doing that as it was excruciating for me at the time because I have an immense dislike of buttons (strange the hang-up's we have!). I met the Pearly King and Queen of Leyton at the ground, and I borrowed his suit for the photo shoot.

Ken Gorman of *The Daily Express* reported:

Orient, so long London's forgotten club, have won themselves a place against Arsenal in the FA Cup Semi Final.

After holding Middlesbrough to a goalless draw at Ayresome Park, the impudent O's bundled First Division Boro' out of the FA Cup in the Brisbane Road replay.

The first Orient goal was a real gem from Peter Kitchen in the fifth minute, he controlled a pass from Phil Hoadley with his left thigh, swivelled and struck a stunning 25-yard half volley, the ball crashing into the net via a post.

It was a brilliant piece of opportunism from Kitchen, his seventh Cup goal and his 23rd of the season, from a man who cost just £30,000 eight months ago.

The second goal came from his striking partner Joe Mayo, taking a pass from David Payne, his half hit shot from fully 20 yards, but Boro goalkeeper Jim Platt dived too soon and the ball bounced over him into the net.

Kitchen was posing all sorts of problems to the Boro defence, almost snatched a third, but the first half ended with Hoadley and Billy Ashcroft cautioned for a brawl.

Boro's nine-match unbeaten run and dreams of a semi final spot for the first time in 102 years were beginning to vanish as the minutes slipped by, but five minutes from the end they pulled a goal back when David Armstrong scrambled the ball home, then Mills headed wide with only Jackson to beat but it proved too late and it was a night of jubilation for East London and a wonderful tonic for O's boss Jimmy Bloomfield in hospital after a serious operation.

The Boro manager John Neal said: " We just didn't play well. In fact, we didn't perform as we can in either match against them."

It was during this period that I netted my second hat trick for the club against Sheffield United.

The local *Walthamstow Guardian* newspaper reported:

Kitchen's Cold Steel

Peter Kitchen the man with the goalscoring Midas touch, unravelled three more gems on Monday to ease Orient's relegation worries.

The most lethal striker in Division Two carved Sheffield with a stainless steel hat trick, which boosts his goal tally for the season to 27.

It was the boys from Yorkshire who took an early lead on ten minutes when John Jackson parried a Bobby Campbell header into the air, but Campbell was on hand to nod in, despite a brave attempt to clear from Bill Roffey.

It took Kitchen just fifty seconds to put O's back on terms after Roffey planted the ball into the box, the bounce caught Cutbush flat footed and there was Kitchen to score with a glancing header.

Peter Kitchen in 1978, during his salad days at Orient.

On fifty-five minutes, Phil Hoadley cracked a twelve yarder, which was well stopped by Jim Brown, but in steamed Derek Clarke with a blockbuster which was destined for the net but it was stopped on the line by Colin Franks with his hands and up stepped Kitchen who made no mistake with his spot-kick.

Kitchen put the game beyond doubt for the home side with his third, and best goal of the game. Joe Mayo was disposed of the ball just outside the box, Kitchen picked up the loose ball and started on a run towards goal, he left defenders for dead and cracked the ball under Brown from just inside the box.

007 photo shoot and our unreleased record

I remember we had a photoshoot at Brisbane Road just before the Arsenal semi final from one of the James Bond cars, a white Aston Martin, as the O's were quite high profile at the time. I sat inside the car and some of the other players sat on the bonnet.

During the Cup run the players recorded a record called 'Fantastic O's' which unfortunately (or fortunately) was never formally released due to our exit in the semi final.

The FA Cup Semi Final against 'lucky' Arsenal

On reflection, during the route to the semi final the whole team had a 'cavalier' approach to the games in that we never really expected to win against First Division opponents and so had nothing to fear.

The semi final was a different ball game for two reasons, I think in that we all suddenly realised we were just one game away from a Wembley final. There had been all the publicity in the build up and we had signed a deal with Admiral Boots for the Semi and the Final if we got there, the importance of the day seemed to get to us, as we were quite an inexperienced team when it came to such big games.

During the week all of Bloomfield's team talks were not about going out and attacking the Arsenal defence at the start, but rather about stopping Arsenal playing (this was typical of Jimmy's team talks, which was one of the reasons for my disagreements with him) and on the day with Jimmy back in hospital, Peter (Angell) reminded us of the jobs that Jimmy wanted us to do to stop the Gunners from playing.

We never really got going against the Gunners because we were so obsessed with stopping them playing and so we were never able to recreate the form of the previous rounds and when the two deflected goals from Malcolm MacDonald went in, there was no way back for us.

I know we certainly missed the creative flair of John Chiedozie, who broke his leg playing in a junior cup game a day after our success at Norwich City, in which he laid on the pass for my goal. In the semi final Bloomfield and Angell decided to drop another young winger, Kevin Godfrey, who was most disappointed at being left out of the big game and replaced him with the more experienced Derek Clarke – a good friend of mine – but that plan didn't work.

Both Joe (Mayo) and myself got very little decent service upfront during the game and we didn't have enough options to worry the Gunners defence, which was renowned for being very organised.

Consequently, I felt the whole game was an anti-climax and a huge disappointment to me, the rest of the players and the fans. We were so close to a Cup Final, which is every player's dream. I was very disappointed, and so I just wanted to get off the park as quickly as possible and into the dressing room. The game could never be described as a 'classic' or a spectacle.

When one looks back we did really well to get so far in the competition and I felt very satisfied with my contribution, which gave me immense satisfaction and so much affection from the O's fans, they nicknamed me 'The Goal Gourmet'.

All the goals in the FA Cup run gave me great satisfaction, the Middlesbrough goal, I think was my best *(the Author disagrees and thinks the first goal against Chelsea was better, although admittedly, the Middlesbrough goal was brilliantly executed)*.

Every game in the Cup campaign seemed like a Cup Final to us, we had great support from the fans and the spirit among the players was terrific. We were always underdogs, yet every one of the players really played above themselves. Everyone ran and chased for each other, which was something I had never experienced before (or since). 'Jacko' (goalie John Jackson) and Joe's (Mayo) performances were out of this world.

There was talk on how the hospitalisation of manager Jimmy Bloomfield would affect the team. We were all surprised as he had never said anything about his illness to us. I don't think it affected me too much because I was always so focused on the games in hand and I did have some differences of opinion with Jimmy about the formation that we played, however I can't speak for the rest of the team, they may have been affected by him being away, in different ways.

In truth, none of the players really knew how serious his condition was and he didn't say anything at the time which is why this didn't have as much an impact on the team initially. It was not until much later that we were told that he had a colostomy bag and later still that he had bowel cancer.

Another fact that I have just touched upon was Jimmy Bloomfield's likeness for a defensive pattern of play. Although we did very well in the FA Cup by playing the extra man at the back (Nigel Gray) our League form certainly suffered. Jimmy's team talks and tactics mostly involved discussions about how to stop the other team from playing and he would spend a lot of time talking about the opposition. I felt we had the basis of a very good side and if we had gone out and attacked teams we would have won a lot more games. I felt Jimmy just wasn't ambitious enough and always opted for a safe option.

Consequently, I believe our league form nosedived and we started to draw at home and lose by the odd goal away.

The Second Division at the time was a strong one with some very good teams. Spurs, who won promotion, had Glen Hoddle, Gerry Armstrong John Pratt and a number of other players with First Division experience. Bolton had Peter Reid, Frank Worthington and Sam Allardyce, Brighton had Peter Ward, Brian Horton and Mark Lawrenson. Southampton, who were managed by my old boss at Doncaster Lawrie MacMenemy, had Alan Ball and Mick Channon and Crystal Palace had a very strong young side who also were promoted the following season

We should never had been in the position of having to win at Cardiff City in the final game of the season to avoid relegation, we should have been on the edge of the promotion chasing group. We had a terrific squad of players and with perhaps one or two more and a bit more ambition we could have got close to promotion.

We went to Cardiff City on Tuesday 9 May 1978 having to win to avoid a drop into the Third Division, the task was daunting with City unbeaten in 11 home games and the O's with just one away League win in 13-months.

The turning point came on 36 minutes, after a long throw-in near the corner flag from Paddy Grealish which was nodded on by Joe Mayo into the patch of Derek Clarke whose shot took a deflection to send the ball spinning in the air where Phil Hoadley connected with his head and there I was to toe-poke it past the Cardiff goalie Ron Healey from just a few yards for the eventual winner.

I think a corner count of 16 to 3 in O's favour reflected or do-or-die effort that night, the win lifted us to a mid-table position.

Jacko was a terrific keeper, Phil Hoadley and Glen Roeder were excellent defenders who were comfortable on the ball and could also play a bit, and Bobby Fisher and Bill Roffey were really good full backs who weren't afraid to get forward. In midfield Peter Allen and Paddy Grealish were very intelligent players, worked very hard and were good passers of the ball with John Chiedozie and Kevin Godfrey very quick and creative players on the flanks. Up front Joe andmyself were an effective and successful combination and we also had good squad players like Nigel Gray, Derek Clarke, David Payne, Peter Bennett, Alan Glover and also Henry Houghton amongst a crop of good young players.

My tribute to Joe Mayo

It would be fitting at this point to pay special tribute to big Joe Mayo who I would rate as the best team player I ever played with. Joe was unselfish and worked harder than any other player I know for his team mates. Although he was tall he was not ungainly in any way and had great skill and mobility, which sometimes worked against him. Because he chased back so much he didn't get in the box enough to score as many goals as he was capable of but his unselfish approach and his strength certainly helped me to focus on applying the final touch to a lot of good moves. We were a perfect combination and Joe also used to say that having someone like me playing off him gave him the encouragement to work so hard. He is a really nice guy and I am sad that he moved away from London and that I don't see very much of him anymore. Big Joe ran a hotel in Cricceith in North Wales for thirteen years but sold it in 2002, he now works for the Imperial Tobacco Company based in Bristol.

Joseph Mayo was born in Tipton on 25 May 1952. He started his career with Dudley Town and then went onto a 10-year career in the Football League with Walsall, West Bromwich Albion, Orient, Cambridge United, Blackpool before going like I did to and play for the Happy Valley Club in Hong Kong. Big Joe made 259+ (16) career League appearances, scoring 68 goals.

One of the reasons for O's decline, I felt was the continuation of playing Nigel Gray in the back-line. (Its no reflection on Nigel, who I felt was a very sound player and a really nice guy and I have seen him several times since, including at a supporters Club meet the players evening at the end of 2005) but when Phil Hoadley got injured Bloomfield brought in Gray who deputised very well, however when Phil came back, instead of reverting back to the 4-4-2 formation, he tried to accommodate both Nigel and Phil and that's when he switched to the five at the back with Glenn Roeder sweeping behind those two.

Although, I must say, it worked during our Cup run, he kept the same formation for league games and that's when I felt the results started to go against us, and instead of changing we kept this formation right through the campaign and as a result we very rapidly dropped down the league table.

At the end of the season with the league win at Cardiff City, from a threat of relegation we jumped to finish in fourteenth spot in Division Two and I ended as the top goal scorer in Division Two, I'm told that not since the days of the O's legend Tommy Johnston have the club had someone on top of the goal scoring charts.

Missed out on the Adidas Division Two Golden Boot Award by a single goal

One disappointment for me was not winning the Adidas Golden Boot award for Division Two because I only scored 21 League goals, where Bob Hatton at Blackpool notched one more than me in the League. Unfortunately for me, they did not take into account the 8 Cup goals I netted that season, a total of 29 League and Cup goals versus Hatton's total of 24 (22 in the League, one in the FA Cup and one in the League Cup), which I felt was a bit unfair. But, on the other hand I did miss a penalty that season, it was against Luton Town on 2 January 1978, I must have had two much champers over new year, I remember that my foot slipped on the turf as I connected with the ball and it went past Milija Aleksic's left hand post and we only drew the game 1-1.

Authors Note:

(Milija Aleksec was a good goalkeeper and interesting character, the son of a Yugoslav Father, who was born in Newcastle-under-Lyme on 14 April 1951 and starting his career with Stafford Rangers after being rejected by the Port Vale manager Sir Stanley Matthews, he then played for Plymouth Arygle, Luton Town, Tottenham Hotspur. The highlight of his career was playing for Spurs in the 1981 FA Cup Final at Wembley, which they won after a replay by 3-2.

Milija has spent a number of years in Johannesburg, South Africa and the Author, who had worked with Milija at Panasonic back in the mid-nineties, caught up with him again in September 2005 at the Golfers Club retail outlet, where he now works.

He stated, "Yes I do remember Peter Kitchen, he had a good season with Orient in 1977-78." When I reminded him of Peter's penalty miss, he quickly modestly stated, "It must have been a fluke, big man, because I never got any-where near any of the penalty kicks I faced".

This was only the second penalty I had ever missed in my career, the first miss was for Doncaster Rovers in a Fourth Division match against Bournemouth on 18 December 1976, I hit a weak shot and Keiron Baker saved it easily to his left, the match ended 0-0. I remember these two games very well, because I lost out on win bonuses, and the miss against Luton, and I wish I could have at least taken home half an Adidas Golden boot.

Division Two leading goalscorers 1977-78

(Bob Hatton was a football nomad, who served nine clubs during two decades as a professional. Born in Hull on 10 April 1947, after leaving school at fifteen years of age, he joined Wath Wanderers, the nursery club of Wolverhampton Wanderers. He joined the Molineux ground staff, which began a long career with Bolton Wanderers, Northampton Town, Carlisle United, Birmingham City, Blackpool, Luton Town, Sheffield United, and finally with Cardiff City in 1982. He netted 217 goals from 620 appearances during his nineteen years as a professional player. In 1984 he started work in the insurance industry. Hatton himself said: 'They used to say Bob Hatton moves looked like a British Rail timetable'.

	League	FA Cup	FL Cup	Total Goal
Peter Kitchen – Orient	21	7	1	29
Bob Hatton – Blackpool ***	22	1	1	24
Paul Randall – Bristol Rovers	20	2	0	22
Mick Vinter – Notts. County	18	4	0	22
Stuart Taylor – Oldham Athletic	20	1	0	21
Neil Whatmore – Bolton Wanderer	19	1	1	21
John Duncan – Tottenham Hotspur	16	1	3	20
Garth Crooks – Stoke City	18	0	1	19
Phil Boyer – Southampton	17	1	1	19
Gary Rowell – Sunderland	17	1	1	19

*** Hatton also scored one goal in the Anglo Scottish Cup

My apologies to Jimmy Bloomfield

I had several arguments with Jimmy and one occasion I walked out of his office after telling him to f*** off.

Sometime later, when I was with Fulham, I went to visit him and I apologised for my behaviour, which looking back was totally out of order and out of character. I was very sorry to read of Jimmy's death in April 1983, aged just forty-nine, I went to his funeral and remember feeling very sad that we never got on very well.

I had a great first season with the O's in 1977-78, and I recorded 29 League and

Cup goals and during the season. In January 1978, I won the Daily Mirror Footballers of the Month award. Also, during the following March, I was voted by the London Evening Standard as their Footballer of the Month. But there was one award that gave me even greater satisfaction and pleasure as I was honoured with the Orient Player of the Year award. It was a great climax to what was a wonderful season for me with the O's.

I also won the Supporters club's away goal of the season award, for the goal I scored at Hull City on 10 December 1977, but I think was more of a 'team goal', rather than an individual effort, we had a really good build up involv-

Evening Standard Player
of the Month March 1978, with
manager Jimmy Bloomfield.

ing a number of players and when the ball was crossed I volleyed in from about waist height.

On reflection, a reason for our poor league form was the reliance on me for the goals, out of a total of just 59 League goals scored, I bagged twenty-one of them and big Joe, 9 goals and in the FA and League Cup I hit eight of the thirteen goals and big Joe 2 of our goals, if only we had someone else to take the pressure off of us in the goal scoring arena.

Trip to Orlando

Because of our success in the FA Cup and for a reward of staying in Division Two the team and their wives went on a trip to Disneyland in Florida. It was just unbelievable and made possible by the club and its chairman Brian Winston. We left Heathrow on 1 June 1778 via National Airlines to Miami and then onto Orlando.

It was just a dream of a holiday and we stayed in the actual Disneyworld resort

**Peter with friend and team mate
Derek Clarke in Florida, 1978.**

and the wonderful Magic Kingdom and River Country going down water slides that were over 260 feet long.

We played one exhibition match on the Saturday against a Central Florida Xl, which we won 4-2 at the Tangerine Bowl in Orlando, but before the game we gave a coaching practice to over 500 youngsters from the area for two-and-a-half hours in the burning sun, but we enjoyed it. We returned to the hotel for a light meal and freshen up and returned to the Bowl for the match.

The next day we were at Sea World, and an evening visit to Rosie O'Grady's a real Dixieland saloon. We departed for Heathrow, the end of what was a memorable trip for us all. I have since been many times to Florida and liked it so much that I bought a two-week timeshare in Cocoa Beach (the nearest Beach resort to Disney) that I still have today.

1978-79

The 1978-79 season started off with two wins, I scored in the opener in our 2-1 win at Sheffield United before 19,012 fans. It was the Sheffield debut of Alejandro Sabella an Argentinean midfield player signed for £160,000 from River Plate. Argentina had just won the World Cup and following the signings of Ossie Ardilles and Ricky Villa at Spurs, foreign players were beginning to become fashionable. I'm sure the United manager and the former Orient player of 1948, Harry Haslam, was hoping for a similar success against us.

Alex Sabella showed some silky skills and was a big hit with the Sheffield United fans, making 76 League appearances with 8 goals before his move to Leeds United in June 1980 for £400,000, but in a struggling side, he battled and returned to Argentina in January 1982 to play for Estudiantes, later picking up

4 International caps for his country. He made just 27 appearances for Leeds with 2 goals. He later spent time with Gremio in Brazil before returning home. In the 2014 FIFA World Cup Finals in Brazil, Alex Sabella was the manager of Argentina, who reached the World Cup semi finals before losing to the eventual winners Germany. He resigned immediately after the tournament

It was a nice return back to Yorkshire for me, because before the match I was presented with an embroidered tracksuit top and also made Honorary Vice President of the Mexborough and Swinton Juniors Football club. The game was televised on Yorkshire Television and Martin Tyler was the commentator.

We then dumped Sunderland 3-0 at home, but then we went through a terrible slump, with just a single point from six games and without a goal to show for our efforts. I suppose a bit of panic set in and Jimmy Bloomfield brought in Ian Moores and Ralph Coates during October from Tottenham Hotspur and Moores netted a brace on his debut in an excellent 2-0 win at Charlton Athletic's Valley, to stop the rot, although we also missed a hatful of chances that night.

I scored a couple, my first since the opening day of the season in our 3-2 win over Luton Town on 28 October but I found goals more difficult to come by because I was playing in a slightly withdrawn deeper role behind the front two of Joe and Ian. I played my final game for the O's, scoring once, in a 5-3 defeat at Leicester City.

At this point in my career I was desperate and ambitious to play in the First Division. I really felt I was good enough to do so and I could see it wasn't going to happen this season with Orient.

I thought to myself, having been with Doncaster for seven years and now with Orient for one and half years I wanted to prove my doubters wrong that I could make it in the First Division.

I did make certain comments in the press for which I was fined by the club £50 for speaking to them without permission, it was about the team selection. This was not a criticism of the club, its players or supporters. In hindsight, I was too impatient to wait for the right move to come, I was worried the same thing would happen to me as had happened at Doncaster Rovers, like asking too much for me and then pricing me out of the market to a bigger club.

Orient had already turned down decent offers for me from both Crystal Palace and Norwich City. The first offer was of £100,000 + Neil Smillie (Jimmy is reputed to have asked for Vince Hillaire as well as the £100,000 which Palace wouldn't agree to) and the second a straight cash offer of £140,000 from Norwich, managed at the time by John Bond.

Always in the back of my mind was that Jimmy Bloomfield was just not ambitious enough to get the Orient any higher, so I had to force the issue and I put in a transfer request.

I got on well with most of the Orient players but especially with Derek Clarke who lived in Loughton whilst with the O's and we shared lifts to training along with going out socially with our wives. In May 2012, I met up with Derek Clarke again, when Katherine and I celebrated with Derek and his wife, Veronica and family at their 40th wedding anniversary in the Midlands where they now live.

(Born in Willenhall, Staffs on 19 February 1950, Clarke was a member of a unique footballing family, with all his five brothers – Frank, Kelvin, Wayne, and the most famous of them all, Allan of Leeds United and England fame. Remarkably the five brothers scored a total of 589 League goals between them, from 1555(85) League appearances. During his playing career, which spanned some eleven years, Derek scored 43 League goals from over 200 appearances. After his retirement in 1980, he spent five years in London running his own Builders Merchants Company, before moving back to the Midlands).

My spell with the O's was certainly a happy one and my Dad, who had always watched me at Doncaster, tried to get down to London as often as possible if he could get a lift. Harry Zussman used to give me one of his special Havana cigars if I scored a couple of goals which I then always gave to my dad. He loved smoking

```
889077 PO FD G
299992 PO TS G
K 35 AP8 0855 LONDON T 22


GREETING


PETER KITCHEN FULHAM FOOTBALL CLUB
..CRAVEN COTTAGE
FULHAMSW6


EVERY GOOD WISH AND THE VERY BEST OF LUCK
     HARRY ZUSSMAN AND DELIA


COL 5W6,
```

**Telegram from Orient director Harry Zussman
and daughter Delia to Peter on his joining Fulham.**

them as it gave him a sense of satisfaction and to have a ten-inch cigar to puff was great for him. I can still see him after matches in the players' bar at Brisbane Road puffing away on the cigar to the dismay of everyone else in the room.

I really liked Harry and his daughter Delia, they were really both lovely people and along with Brian Winston, they were one of the main reasons for the friendliness of the club at that time. I can remember when my wife Susan and I moved into our home in Epping, they sent us flowers and Brian gave me a bottle of whisky.

Also during the 1977 / 78 season, the Club arranged for all the players and their wives to have tickets for the Royal Variety performance which was attended by the Queen. Afterwards we were taken for dinner to a Nightclub in Berkeley Square where I recall dancing later with Susan alongside the late comedian Les Dawson. This was a far cry from my days with Doncaster Rovers, where every year I would have to have a confrontation with the club directors to get between £5 and £8 a week rise each year. I soon realised I had to ask for a lot more knowing that they would never offer this, but at least I would get more than they expected to pay me.

Harry and Delia sent me a telegram when I made my debut for Fulham, I thought, here I am having left the club and they still send me a goodwill telegram, it was a really nice gesture.

I was very sad when I leaned of Harry's death in July 1981, he was a true Orient gentleman.

Of Hair and Moustaches...

I recently stumbled across an Internet article by Tony Nash (www.cardiffcity. rivals.net) that gave me the number 5 spot on a list of footballer fashion *faux pas* entitled, "*Haircuts from Hell.*" Under my picture it states: "Peter Kitchen - never mind the hair, what about the Mexican moustache - started a subculture that still grips parts of West Wales. Peter played in the early 80s for City."

This brought back memories of another near hair disaster. Footballers, then as now, are always concerned about their appearance and the need to be fashionable. During the late 70's whilst at the O's, the latest hair fashion was a long haired perm, examples of this style were worn by Kevin Keegen and Glen Hoddle. However I was very self conscious and once you have a perm - it takes awhile to get rid of it. Being very aware of the P*** talking that goes on amongst footballers in the dressing room, I decided to first try a trial run. I got my wife Susan to buy a batch of small curlers that women usually use, and she proceeded to wind them tightly into my hair. I then sat on the couch waiting for my hair to dry. After a couple of hours, I unveiled my new look, and found to my horror - I looked like a younger, less pretty version of my Mother. Needless to say I never had a real perm done.

Chapter 4
No great impressions at Fulham, thanks to manager Bobby Campbell

A move did eventually come, in February 1979 when Fulham's manager Bobby Campbell came in with a £150,000 cash offer, plus a young 19-year old Welsh-born striker named Mark Gray as part of the deal, who hadn't really shown much at Craven Cottage or earlier in his career with Swansea City as a Welsh school boy international.

Peter signs for Fulham, February 1979, with manager Bobby Campbell.

However, before I put pen to paper I told Campbell I wanted £50 a week more, the clubs had agreed the fee, at my age, now twenty-seven, I had to get some sort of financial security, which he agreed to pay. Brian Winston, the O's chairman must have been a happy man, the deal represented a 400% profit for the club. It's incredible to think now, that a mere £50 a week could possibly be a stumbling block to agreeing to a transfer, when compared to the salaries and signing on fees that players are paid today, even in the lower divisions.

This was Fulham's record transfer deal at the time, which remained until Kevin Keegan took over as their boss some twenty years later. I felt I had a good chance of promotion at Craven Cottage, they were lying in sixth position in Division Two at the time.

I received a £20,000 singing-on fee which included a brand new Toyota Celica car and I was on a basic of £275 in year one and £300 in the second year

On Debut for Fulham v Brighton 1979, being tracked by Mark Lawrenson.

and £325 in year three, plus various bonuses.

I made my debut at home against Brighton & Hove Albion but we lost 1-0 in front of a good crowd of 18,464. It was a difficult debut as Brighton were top of the table and had a very good team with Mark Lawrenson at the heart of their defence. I did score the following week in a 2-2 draw at Preston North End. I returned to Brisbane Road on 27 March, but the O's beat us 1-0 with Paul Went scoring a penalty to secure the points. I scored four further goals by the end of the season, a tally of 5 goals in 17 games but we finished the season in a disappointed tenth position, being only one place above Orient in the final League table.

I soon realised I may have made a mistake by moving to Craven Cottage, I could see that the side I left at Brisbane Road were a much better side than the Fulham team I had joined and as for Campbell, I soon lost all respect for the man. The least said the better!

The following season I hardly got a run in the side, I twisted my ankle during pre-season and missed the start of the campaign, a visit to Birmingham City on 18 August 1979, Gordon 'Ivor' Davies deputised for me and scored a hat trick in a 4-3 victory, so quite rightly Bobby Campbell kept him in the team. He did exceptionally well for Fulham and during his two stays at Craven Cottage (1977-85 and 1986-1991) scored a record 159 League goals from 394 games, he also won 16 Welsh caps, scoring twice.

My first game that season, in September, was as a substitute in the 3-1 win over Burnley, but Campbell did not like playing me alongside Davies, as he only wanted to use one striker to partner the target man, Chris Guthrie up front. Chris was a nice guy and I got on well with him, he was an avid fisherman and used to regularly bring in trout to give to the lads, even today, he loves his fishing. He was not a particularly good player and not in the same league as Brendan or Big Joe.

I always suspected that there was always more to the situation than this because it was obvious that I loathed the man (Campbell) and I made no secret of the fact.

I felt I was also resented by some of the Fulham players because it was no secret that I had done well financially from the move from Orient, which included the new car. I remember on the day I had signed, I was in Campbell's office, and in came Les Strong, the only Fulham player to survive right through the Campbell reign. When he was introduced to me, his first question to Campbell was how much money had they given me and if I was on more money than him.

Unlike the friendliness of Orient from the top, Brian Winston to all the players and fans, at Fulham I never really felt welcome. The atmosphere at Craven Cottage was reflected by the personalities in charge at the club, from their manager Campbell and chairman Ernie Clay.

A good player doesn't become a poor one overnight and having scored well over 100 goals in five seasons, to being left out of the team, unable even to get a place on the subs bench didn't happen by chance or coincidence.

My experience with Fulham was the worst I had in my long career.

I started the 1979-80 season in the first team, with two home appearances in the Anglo Scottish Cup against Plymouth Argyle on 4 August, we won 1-0 with a goal from Peter Marinello, but I got injured in the next match four days later and when we went down 5-0 at the Cottage to Birmingham City before 2,889 fans. This was not one of favourite competitions, having played six games in the competition for the O's, without finding the net.

I made just 4(3) League appearances during the whole of the season, scoring once in the final match of the season, a 5-2 defeat at Shrewsbury Town. The whole season was a total disaster for me personally and for the club. We were bottom of the table by November and stayed there for most of the season and were eventually relegated into the Third Division for the third time in their history, this after Campbell had taken over a side from Alec Stock who were highly fancied for promotion into the First Division.

As the 1979-80 season progressed, Campbell became very unpopular with the fans, so much so that I noticed he would never sit in the dugout during matches at Craven Cottage to avoid the fans' abuse.

I spent most of the season in the reserves and scored about 30 goals in the Combination. Campbell didn't like me and he hardly ever said two words to me and never mentioned the fact that the club had received offers for me from a number of clubs. Fortunately, I had established some reliable press contacts so I always heard about these offers.

During one week at the end of August and early September1979, I played in three games for the reserves against Arsenal, West Ham United and Queens Park Rangers, I scored hat tricks against the Gunners and the Hammers, and a brace against QPR, they played strong teams, yet even with the first team battling near the bottom of the table, I couldn't even make the subs' bench, thanks to Mr. Campbell.

It just amazed me that as their record signing at the time, I was never picked for the first team. The reserve coach at the time was the former Orient and Arsenal favourite Terry Mancini, and at least I got on well with him, which meant I had one friend on the management side.

It was during my time in the reserves that I played several times with George

Best. He was living in Putney at the time having been on the books of San Jose in the States, so he used to train at Roehampton with the Fulham reserve players. I remember, he usually had his Alsatian dog with him and a young Swedish beauty around him named Mary Anne Stavin, who was Miss World in 1977. I was very sad about the death of Bestie on 25 November 2005, aged just fifty-nine.

The whole experience really affected me, and also my marriage, I became increasingly unhappy, and it was a difficult time for my marriage with Susan, and in 1980, we separated and I moved into a flat in Enfield.

Separating from my children was the hardest decision I have ever had to make in my life. (Susan and I eventually got divorced in 1982) and yes I also missed being at Orient, the chairman Brian Winston was certainly more charismatic than his counterpart at Craven Cottage, and this rubbed off on everyone at Orient.

I played in the final game of the season for Fulham at Shrewsbury Town on 3 May 1980, this was only because the Cardiff City management team were watching me, we lost 5-2 and I scored the first goal before a crowd of 6,328.

It was only four wins in April that helped Fulham to avoid relegation and they finished in a dismal 20th position in Division Two, even Orient finished higher in 14th spot, so much for a career move to south west London.

When I was at Craven Cottage the first team players were assigned an apprentice, who was responsible for cleaning our boots and getting the training kit ready for the start of each day and mine was a small West Ham-born lad named Paul Parker, who had been at the Cottage since he was eleven. He was a really nice lad and I was very pleased that he went onto have a very successful career at Fulham. He then got himself a dream move to Manchester United in 1991 for £2m and the speedy quick tackling full-back went on to play for England. Parker made over 400 League appearances for a number of top clubs, before going into management with non-league side Welling United.

I did not make a great impression at Craven Cottage and it is a period of my life I would rather forget and instead of fulfilling my dream of playing in the 'old' First Division, I started to lose some belief in my ability and motivation for the game.

The move to Craven Cottage proved to be catastrophic to my career, from being on a rising path to much higher achievements, my time at Fulham put to an end to all that, and certainly Mr. Campbell did me no favours.

In retrospect, it was my own fault because I was so determined to progress that I rushed into the move to Fulham, I only needed to wait another four months and I would have been out of contract at Orient.

I'm sure that if I had waited until my Orient contract had expired I would have got the move I was seeking, as I had, off the record, already spoken to Terry

Venables at Crystal Palace about a move to Selhurst Park.

In July 1980, I was involved in discussions with Rotherham United about a possible move back up North, they offered Fulham £150,000, which would have been a club record fee for them, but in the end I rejected the offer. Both Rotherham and Fulham had agreed terms, It was a brilliant offer that was made by their manager Ian Porterfield and their chairman Anton Johnson and Secretary Jim Bennison, who was a friend from my days with Doncaster Rovers. They offered to buy me a house for £25,000, the ownership of which they would have signed over to me at the end of a three-year contract or before if I was transferred. I was also to receive £350 per week and a sponsored car.

In the local Rotherham press, reporter Jim Ferguson stated:

Rotherham make record bid to buy Kitchen

Jim Bennison stated that "Both clubs had agreed on a fee, our manager will meet Peter over the weekend to discuss the players' terms, he concluded by saying: Personally I hope the deal goes through, Peter is a good player and a friend."

I rejected this wonderful offer, because I didn't want to drop down a league into the Third Division, I was in the middle of a divorce proceedings from my wife Susan and I wasn't sure what her plans were in terms of house moves and the children. I was also unsure whether I wanted to move back up North.

I also heard that Martin Peters, the new Sheffield United manager had also made an offer to Fulham in excess of £140,000 for me, but I decided against talking to them for mostly the same reasons.

It's a funny game, because Rotherham then turned their attentions towards Ronnie Moore at Cardiff City, and after they signed him, it gave Cardiff City the money to sign me from Fulham. Rotherham also won promotion from the Third Division the following season.

Chapter 5
Cardiff City gets their Man

On 20 August 1980, I signed for Cardiff City and the fee was £120,000. Their manager at the time, and a former player of nine years was Richie Morgan, he was elevated to manager after working in the commercial side of the club. I received a £20,000 signing-on fee and the deal I was on wasn't bad with a basic of £350 in year one, £375 in year two and should I still be at the club, £400 in year three, plus the normal bonuses.

City's General Manager Ron Jones, a miner's son from the Aberdare Valley, told the local press that I was not a gamble, as some people had suggested, 'I believe he can score goals with us and his personal problems with the Fulham Manager Bobby Campbell were not enough to deter us from signing him'.

I had not forgotten how his Midas touch helped Orient to the Semi Finals of the FA Cup but his joining Fulham turned out to be the wrong move for him, when he was dropped, yet his scoring for their reserves was quite prolific and there is not a tremendous difference between Reserve and first team football, as there is an overlap of first-team players'.

A Fulham fan, Terry Chalk who worked at the Headquarters of the Coal Board told a local Cardiff newspaper: 'Cardiff City have signed an exciting player, he was not used properly at Fulham.'

Arriving at Cardiff City for the first day of training, 1980.

When I arrived, I soon learned that Ronnie Moore had been the butt of the Cardiff fans anger as he had hardly scored for them during his spell at the club and some fans were even wearing T-shirts with slogans on which said 'I once saw Ronnie Moore score'. In all fairness, he scored quite a few goals for Rotherham as they went onto win promotion and we all know how well he has done in management at the club. (As previously mentioned in the section on the PFA Divisional award winners).

I made my debut seven days later in a 1-0 win over Chelsea in the League Cup. The second leg at Stamford Bridge on 3 September took place when they were busy with ground impr o v e ments and I scored our goal in a 1-1 draw, with about ten minutes remaining

I remember rushing towards the stand behind the goal, what is now I think the Matthew Harding Stand with my hand raised in celebration, to receive the acclaim of the fans, only to find a giant hoarding along the whole length of the pitch blocking off the terraces with lots of painted people and faces in blue and white colours but no sound or movement!!

I'm sure the fans in the Shed must have thought me mad, but who cared, I scored again at Stamford Bridge and we had knocked them out of the League Cup. Unfortunately we lost to Barnsley in the Third Round and my young prodigy from Doncaster, Ian Banks, scored one of the Barnsley goals.

Also in their side was a young rugged defender named Mick McCarthy, who I would describe as the dirtiest player I played against. I recall throughout the whole game he kept stamping on my foot or studding at the back of my ankles at every opportunity whilst the referee was following play in the other half of the pitch. (*This youngster went on to have a wonderful career both as a player and manager.*

Born in Barnsley to Irish parents on 7 February 1959, he started off with Barnsley as an18-year old in 1977 before playing with Manchester City, Celtic, Lyon in France and Millwall until being appointed in March 1991 as player-manager with the Lions. McCarthy won 57 caps for the Republic of Ireland before being appointed their manager in February 1996, taking over from Jack Charlton, resigning his post in November 1992 having lifted them from 54th to 13th position in the FIFA world rankings. In March 2003 he took over as manager of Sunderland, taking them to promotion back to the Premiership in May 2005), but after a disappointing season he was sacked by Sunderland on 6 March 2006.

Mick Macarthy is currently manager of championship side Ipswich Town who finished 6th in the Championship and were in the Play off semi finals, but missed the chance to go to Wembley, losing to rivals Norwich City on aggregate over the two legs

Five goals in the Welsh Cup

I had a day to remember in the Third Round of the Welsh Cup at Ninian Park on 3 December 1980, before just 1080 fans, when I bagged five goals in the 6-0 thrashing of Welsh amateur side Cardiff Corinthians. Corries, as they are known, were one of the oldest Welsh amateur clubs around.

Playing in my first Welsh Cup game, I gave City the lead on twelve minutes from a corner, the ball came over into the near post and I nodded in from knee height from a few yards out, giving their thirty-four year-old goalie Malcolm Colville, who also worked as a handbag salesman, no chance.

After going close with a twelve-yard drive, my second came on forty-one minutes from a Paul Giles cross. In the second half we overran the amateur side. Wayne Hughes hit a twenty yarder for a 3-0 lead and then I began to find plenty of space, I completed my hat trick on sixty-one minutes planting a header from a Lewis cross into the net.

Fourteen minutes later I grabbed my fourth, with a simple six-yard tap-in, a few minutes later I wasted my easiest chance hitting the ball straight at their goalie from a few yards out, but my fifth came when I was put through by Gary Stevens with six minutes remaining and I dribbled round the goalie to tap home (I emulated a player named Brian Clark, who also hit five goals for Cardiff in the Welsh Cup against a team called Barmouth in 1970), but we lost disappointingly by 3-0 to Wrexham in Round Four.

I ended up as Cardiff's top goal scorer for the 1980-81 season with 19 League and Cup goals, followed by Stevens with 8 goals.

Peter with his mother and former partner Sharon in Florida.

I was very happy in Walesand Sharon, my partner, and I lived in a beautiful village by the sea called Llantwit Major, about fifteen miles outside of Cardiff. I also liked Cardiff very much, it was a nice City, with everything there, and my sons Michael and Darren would come and stay with us most School holidays.

Sharon was great with the kids (she had a son named Oliver and a daughter Lara), we would also take them all on camping holidays driving through Europe to the South of France, Venice and Tuscany in Italy. Looking back they were some of the best holidays of my life.

I had made it known to Morgan that I wanted to leave the club at the start of the 1981-82 season, as we were a struggling club both in the league and financially. I had heard that Orient had made an offer of £60,000 to get me back, but nothing materialised, and Cardiff had brought in Dave Bennett from Man City as a replacement, so I was left out of the side on a few occasions. After a few defeats early in the season the pressure was certainly starting to get to the boss. It was about this time that I had a confrontation with him, which resulted in me being suspended for two weeks and fined two weeks wages.

I had the confrontation with Morgan for allegedly refusing to travel as 13th man to an away game at Sheffield Wednesday, which incidentally wasn't true. I told him that I would prefer not to travel if I wasn't even the substitute and that he should give the experience to one of the younger players who would really appreciate the opportunity. I felt I was being made a scapegoat and so I appealed to the Football League and even threatened taking them to court.

The fine was reduced to a week's wages. Interestingly Brian Winston, the Orient chairman, was a member of the League Management Committee that heard my case, not to say it had any bearing on the result of the case?

The 1981-82 season was not successful for me or Cardiff City. We started off poorly and by November Richie Morgan had been fired and was given a job as 'Football Administrator' and replaced by the former West Bromwich Albion fullback of fourteen years, Graham Williams, who had been out of the game for many years. He had taken over a club that was going into freefall and he couldn't improve the situation and he lasted just fifteen league games of which nine were lost and he was also dismissed.

I was on the transfer list when Williams arrived, so initially I wasn't selected for any of these games and was hardly playing any football during this period. I was recalled for the Welsh Fifth Round Cup match against Wrexham on 9 February 1982, and subsequently scored a hat trick in our 4-1 victory before 2,767 fans, to the delight of everyone else except Graham as it did make his team selection prior to this game look somewhat suspect. In the South Wales Echo the following day 10 February 1982, journalist Joe Lovejoy (today one of the top sports writers for *The Sunday Times*) wrote:

Kitch rubs it in with a hat trick

Peter Kitchen is back in the job he should never have lost – spearheading Cardiff City's attack. Last night he gave the club an embarrassing reminder of the valuable talents they have wasted for most of the season. The £120,000 striker who has languished in the reserves while the first team struggled for goals, destroyed Wrexham with a memorable exhibition of finishing which had the Ninian Park faithful chanting throughout the match:

'Kitchen is back, Kitchen is back'

His superbly taken hat trick was the highlight of a 4-1 victory, which sees City through to the semi-finals of the Welsh Cup. Kitchen provided the City attack with a cutting edge, which they had always lacked in his absence.

The clubs stubbornness in refusing to play him since his dispute with Richie Morgan in October seems all the more petty and illogical in the light of his successful return to first team action, having scored 7 goals in 4 games.

Last night's hat trick made it a truly triumphant return, he waited for his chance to prove himself and scored his seventh hat trick in a 12-year professional career and as Kitchen stated: 'it was possibly my best, usually there's been a penalty or a scrambled goal in there, but this time all three were a bit useful'

I think the term 'bit useful' is a modest understatement as each of three goals were gems.

The first, after twenty-four minutes, was a thunderous shot from 15 yards after Gary Stevens knocked down a long kick from Ron Healey. The second came four minutes into the second half, Kitchen accepted a pass from Phil Dwyer and with his back towards goal, he executed a lightening turn before stroking the ball home from ten yards.

The third in the sixty-sixth minute was the best of the lot. Collecting Dwyer's headed pass on the edge of the penalty area, he went around Joey Jones and took the ball wide of goalkeeper Eddie Niedzwicki before steering in into an unguarded net.

For coolness and composure that goal will take a lot of beating by any player. It must be stated that Kitchen also provided an accurate centre for Gary Stevens to open the scoring on thirteen minutes.Cardiff Boss Graham Williams stated: 'I was delighted with our performance and I'm not at all surprised that Kitch did so well, you can see in training that he's a top class finisher. He always hits the target.'

In March 1982, Williams had gone and in came Liverpool-born Len Ashurst as boss, it was just before his forty-fifth birthday. Ashurst, was a great player with Sunderland between 1948-1952, making 404(5) League appearances and had experience as a manager with Hartlepool United, Gillingham and Sheffield

Wednesday with 304 matches in charge and a record of exactly 100 wins, quite a career for such a young man.

On 20 March, we had an exciting 5-4 home victory over Cambridge United, Gary Stevens grabbed a hat trick and I netted two, pity only 3,239 fans were at Ninian Park to witness it, not surprising really, we had only scored one goal in the previous six league games.

I only played in 25(2) League games that season, scoring 8 goals, Stevens topped scored with 13 League goals from 38 appearances.

However, I realized that Cardiff City as a club weren't going anywhere, there was just no ambition and hence we were a mediocre Second Division team. We had some good players but unfortunately not enough. I had joined them for a new start and I hoped to get into Europe through the Welsh Cup. When I first arrived they looked to me to be a big club with good support and a massive potential. But this was to prove incorrect and the club's undoubted potential has never really been realised, even to this day.

In recent years Cardiff City have at last realised some of their potential and after moving to a new stadium, they have enjoyed an FA Cup final appearance and also a short period in the Premier League. Unfortunately they have since returned to the the Championship and this season finished in mid table under former Leyton Orient manager Russell Slade.

I became very disappointed with Ashurst, because I had played in three Welsh Cup matches, scoring the hat trick against Wrexham to get the Bluebirds into the semi final against Hereford United, which we got through on aggregate 2-1. He had also selected me when he initially came to the club and I had begun to re-establish myself in the team and was committed to the fight against relegation.

Although I was leaving the club on a free transfer at the end of that season, which I had negotiated myself, I thought I would make the Welsh Cup Final squad against Swansea, Although I travelled to the match, Ashurst didn't include me in the team or even as a substitute, so I didn't get a medal and I was very disappointed. It was typical of a game that shows no sentiment.

Cardiff lost in the Final by 2-1 to a strong Swansea City side, who were in the old First Division and who had a number of well known players including Gary Stanley ex-Chelsea, Ray Kennedy and Ian Callaghan ex-Liverpool and Welsh Internationals Allan Curtis and Robbie James.

In the final match of the season, Cardiff's visitors were Luton Town, who had already been promoted as champions of the division and we had to win to stay up.

I was named as a substitute and as the game went on, our 6ft 2ins striker Gary Stevens missed quite a few 'sitters' and even though he knocked in 44 career League goals from 138(12) appearances, I found him to be a very average footballer.

Len Ashurst brought me on with just twenty minutes to go, the Bluebirds being 3-0 down. I scored one and made another but there just wasn't enough time to rescue it, we lost 3-2, and so Cardiff City was relegated.

When interviewed after the match, I made my feelings known. I told the press 'If I had played from the start, then City would not have been relegated that season'. Why not tell the truth, I was leaving the club anyway, and as we all know football is all about 'Ifs and buts'.

Ashurst left Cardiff in 1984, he had a short spell as boss of Sunderland, until May 1985, he returned to Ninian Park in August 1989 and stayed for a couple of more years.

I enjoyed the two years I had in Cardiff and everyone at Ninian Park was very friendly and we had great support from the fans, they really deserved better than they got. I think that the Cardiff fans always appreciated me and I never received any abuse or heckling when I played, even after I stated in the press that I wanted to leave. I soon realised that I was not going anywhere if I had stayed in Wales,

It was a backwater in terms of football and I really wanted to get back to London for both personal and professional reasons.

Although my record there wasn't as prolific as at Doncaster or Orient, in a struggling and very average team, it wasn't that bad. The Cardiff Chairman Bob Grogan, a businessman from the North East wasn't a real Cardiff supporter and it showed in the way that he dealt with the players. I had been spoilt at Orient by Brian Winston and Harry Zussman and never experienced the same friendliness than I had with Orient, anywhere else in my career.

I remember for one match Grogan brought in the great sprinter Alan Wells and the runner and now broadcaster Brendan Foster to watch a game and asked them to come into the dressing room before the game as he felt we needed a pep talk from them about motivation.

Whilst I respected them both for what they had achieved in their respective sports, football isn't like sprinting or long-distance running and I for one cer-tainly didn't need any motivational bullshit. I personally was disgusted because it was condescending and showed what he knew about football. In essence, we just didn't have enough good players and weren't good enough as a team, It wasn't motivation that we needed but some good new quality players.

I left on a free transfer, which I agreed by terminating the last year of my contract. My divorce was also playing on my mind. In effect, I didn't get a penny out of the divorce, Susan got all the equity from the sale of the house and I even had to pay all the costs of over £3000. I also had to send her £100 per week net from my £375 gross weekly salary for maintenance and I therefore needed to try and recover some money as I was supporting two families.

I had several offers from English clubs, these included Brian Horton the new manager at Hull City, also Hereford United, Scunthorpe United and this also included one from Billy Bremner, then manager at Doncaster Rovers. He phoned me and tried to sign me but initially only offered £220 per week and no signing-on fee. I asked for a three-year deal including a testimonial, for the previous seven years I had been at Belle Vue and in the new deal I said I would accept £300 if I got the testimonial (I had initially asked for £350 per week as I wasn't getting a signing on fee). Unfortunately Bremner wouldn't or couldn't agree to this and so I never went back to Rovers. It was interesting that in the Doncaster press just afterwards, he was quoted as saying that he couldn't match my wage demands, yet never mentioned the fact that I had offered the club an alternative option so that I could rejoin them.

I also had an offer to go Sparta Rotterdam who offered me £400 per week plus a signing-on fee of £10,000, but they wanted me first to go on a trial for a week, which I refused.

I had negotiated a free transfer as I felt that if I could get a reasonable offer from a good English club and because there would be no transfer fee involved, I would also be able to collect a reasonable signing on fee to offset the losses from my divorce. However, it was a bad time for football finances and Bristol City had just announced that they were in administration with several other clubs also in a dire financial crisis. Consequently, the bottom had dropped out of the transfer market and the English clubs just weren't in a position to offer the kind of money I was looking for.

Whilst considering what options were open to me, and always hoping that a London club might make me an offer, I received the offer to go to Hong Kong.

Chapter 6
Joins The Happy Valley Club
in Hong Kong

So in August 1982, after my free transfer from Cardiff City, I went to play in Hong Kong on a one-year deal. I didn't get any upfront lump sum but the deal included accommodation for myself, my partner and her family and return flights home and insurance. I was on a basic salary of £500 per week (with only 15% tax) plus bonuses, which were very generous and my partner Sharon moved with me. (She later also moved with me to Epping, and then to USA. We had a very good relationship for more than ten years, but in truth, eventually the pressures and problems that teenage kids bring, especially when they aren't your own and a gradual growing apart over a five to six year period brought an end to our relationship in 1996, although we have remained friends ever since. I am still in contact with her and her children Oliver and Lara).

Initially, I thought that I would enjoy the football in Hong Kong, as it was so very different to playing in England. The players were technically quite skilful but were very naïve in terms of football tactics, style of play etc, and I also hoped that I might carve out a career here, although after a few months I found it increas-ingly

Peter at Hong Kong Airport with Happy Valley officials.

difficult to maintain my motivation and also not to feel homesick as I really missed seeing my sons. The lifestyle was good, as was the money, but it didn't feel right and once I had realised this I knew I had to come back to England. I scored quite a few goals in pre-season friendlies and we went on tour to China for three weeks to Kunming and Beijing. The most interesting game I played was before a crowd of more than 60,000 against a China Select XI in Beijing and I scored both goals in a 2-0 win. We also went to Macao for a two-week tour. I enjoyed my brief stay out there, it wasn't like anything I had experience before in my career.

**Peter on tour in
Beijing, China
for Happy Valley in 1982.**

There were three other English players in the team, all of whom had signed the previous season for the club. In midfield was:

Micky Horswill, the ex-Sunderland, Manchester City, Plymouth Argyle and Hull City player, who had made over 240 career League appearances.

Nick Deacy, the former Welsh International player, who had played for Hereford United, Workington (loan), PSV in Holland, whom he had won two Dutch Championships in 1975-76 and 1977-78, Vitesse Amhem in Holland, Hull City and Bury before joining Happy Valley with 128(12) league appearances, scoring 11 goals and

Dave Wiffill, who had started his career with Frome Town before joining Bath City in February 1980, two months later after playing just 14 matches, he was snapped by Manchester City for £25,000, however he never made his mark in the Football League and was released in May 1982 to play in Hong Kong with Bulova before joining Happy Valley. After a couple of years he returned to the UK to join Bristol Rovers and in October 1987 he returned to Yeovil Town. Recently he was player-manager of Gloucester County League side Thornbury Town.

All the other players were Far Eastern nationalities but mainly of Chinese descent or from the Philippines.

We had to attend official club dinners every two to three days, which ultimately developed into brandy drinking contests between the British and Chinese players, one or more of us invariably got carried out of the restaurant. The Chinese loved brandy and at every table there were always one or two bottles of Remy Martin, which we started on after several bottles of Tsingtao beer (our shirt sponsors). I became an expert in using Chopsticks and tried almost every kind of Chinese food.

Looking back on this period it seems like it was an extended holiday. Although we trained very hard and did a lot of hill running (up to the Peak on Hong Kong Island), we didn't play enough games for me to get properly match fit.

I also came across George Best a few times again whilst in Hong Kong as he was making several appearances as a guest player for South China.

I can't recall much about the League games I played for Happy Valley, which were certainly not memorable as we spent most of our time trying to stop the opposition playing which is why I started to argue with the Head Coach. He was, I must say, very naïve and based his whole football philosophy on the Italians, who had just won the World Cup, i.e.: to get everybody behind the ball and try and counter attack on the break. Needless to say, I think of the handful of games I played, about four or five we drew most of them were either 0-0 or 1-1.

My frustrations with the coach's tactics, which came to a head in late November 1982 when we were playing Seiko, one of the strongest teams in the league. We had been offered a very good bonus of £200 per man to win the game. We had spent the first half defending and the supply of the ball forward was nonexistent except for a few aimless passes over the top. After a half time team talk when I complained to some of my team mates to pass the ball forward to feet instead of launching it over the top to chase aimlessly in 90°F temperatures, we went out for the second half.

After 20 minutes of a similar pattern of play and a score line of 0-0 the coach decided to bring me off. I was so angry that when I approached the dugout I told the coach that he didn't have a f*****g clue about the game, that he was f*****g useless and he couldn't coach a boys team.

Behind the dugout were the five Club directors who witnessed my full verbal volley which obviously didn't go down well with them or the coach, as the Chinese value their status very much and I had obviously insulted one or more of them.

As a consequence I was suspended for two weeks from training with the first team although no one officially spoke to me, only the Assistant Coach. The first details of the extent of the problem was what I heard from my Chinese team mates who said that it was in the papers that my future at the club was under discussion.

I arranged a meeting to discuss the situation with one of the Directors who spoke English and he made me aware that I was being sacked and my contract was to be terminated. I was quite prepared to leave although I needed to sort out the practical arrangements around my registration, flights back to England etc. I had rented out my house in Epping so I had to compensate for the fact that I would have to find temporary accommodation when I returned home.

After some negotiations I received a severance payment of £5000 and flights home for the family and myself, and also confirmation that I would be released from my contract and get my international clearance, which arrived about two weeks later.

When wearing a beard, Peter Kitchen was often told he looked like George Best (shown in this photo)

Chapter 7
My Return to Brisbane Road

In December 1982, I returned to England and asked Orient if I could train with them to keep fit and to await my International clearance and while I would also be seeking a new club. Whilst training with them, I was asked by Orient boss Ken Knighton to sign for the O's, who were in trouble in the Third Division.

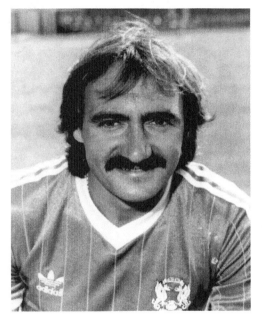

At Orient 1983

There were some good players at the club, many of whom I already knew like Bill Roffey, Kevin Godfrey and Tommy Cunningham and an out of favour Peter Taylor, a terrific player who just wasn't being played at all in the first team. However the team had no confidence at all and whilst waiting for my clearance I remember watching them get thrashed at home 5-0 by Oxford United.

Even Mervyn Day, who had been a great goalkeeper and Bill Roffey, who had always been a battler, looked deflated and disillusioned. I believe my signing had an immediate impact on morale and after the win over Preston on my debut, it started a mini-revival.

I signed an eighteen month contract on a fixed basic of £300 per week plus a £500 bonus should I score twenty first team goals over the period, I also received a £4,000 signing-on fee.

I played a reserve game against Southend United, then I returned to League action against Preston North End. David Peach scored from the penalty spot, he was good at that, and I scored the winner in our 2-1 win before a poultry crowd of 1,668 (maybe no one had told the fans I had returned), but I suppose with O's second from bottom not many more were expected on a wet Friday night

The form of the team certainly improved on my return and we won six of the next seven games, so did the crowds. We went to Millwall and won 1-0, a nice goal from Keith Houchen, who was quite a decent header of a football.

The next home game saw the crowd increase to nearly 4,000 and we turned it on beating AFC Bournemouth by 5-0, our best score in many a year. I hit the first and then goals from Kevin Godfrey (2), John Cornwell and Houchen secured a fine win.

After a defeat at Sheffield United we went on to record three straight wins, I scored at Bradford City for a great 3-2 win and we had home wins against both Chesterfield and Portsmouth, in the latter match I broke my toe and missed eight games.

On 12 April 1983, I returned to Belle Vue, Doncaster, and scored a brace in O's 3-0 win, which virtually condemned my old club to relegation back down to Division Four. I always enjoyed scoring goals, but these two gave me less pleasure than usual. It was nice to see many of the old faces, but sorry to see only just over 2,300 at the ground.

It was back to business and on the final day of the season we had to beat Sheffield United to also stay in the Third. We did it in style with an emphatic 4-1 win over the Blades before a crowd of 4,468. I scored the second with a low header and so we ended the season in 20th position, Iwas happy with my performance since returning, finishing on 9 goals from 20 League appearances. Kevin Godfrey was the leading goal scorer on 11 goals from 42(3) League appearances.

**In Action for Orient
v Sheffield United**

Ken Knighton, who was a strict disciplinarian, was sacked and his assistant Frank Clark was put in charge.

The 1983-84 season did not start off too well for me, we were knocked out of the League Cup over two legs by Aldershot, we lost the first leg away by 3-1 and drew the home leg 3-3, I came on as a sub and scored our third with eleven minutes remaining. I then missed the early part of the season, only coming back at the end of November. The team had done very well during my absence with just four defeats from sixteen games. I came back in the away fixture at Hull City on 26 November and scored in our 2-1 defeat. I then scored the opener in a 2-1 win over Preston North End.

Scoring for Orient at Sheffield United, March 1984.

We had some up and down results, some good wins against some heavy losses, like a 6-2 defeat at home to Wimbledon in February 1984 which showed why they were the Canon League's leading goalscorers. Dean Thomas opened the scoring for the visitors. I then beat three of their defenders to score one of my better goals. It seemed we might be in the hunt, but in the end they were too good for us and we were hit by the heaviest home defeat since the 7-3 reverse by Chelsea back in November 1979 and a 6-3 defeat at Sheffield United, I scored in that game as well.

During training, we didn't tend to work that much on specific coaching sessions and played a lot of 5-a-side football, which was always popular with the players. Frank Clark's style of play was to build up through midfield and to use the two front men (myself and Keith Houchen), as targets, for us to hold the ball up and allow the midfield and wide players to get beyond us. We played some good football under Clark and there was a big improvement in our play and results.

I thought that things were going well for the team and myself, and I also thought that Clark rated me quite highly as I was then playing regularly in the team.

We had a good squad of players with a good balance of experience and youth. There was myself, Bill Roffey, Tommy Cunningham, Keith Osgood and Barry Silkman, who was also used as a coach. There was also Kevin Godfrey, Kevin Hales and Keith Houchen and some promising players like Mark McNeill and Shaun Brooks. As the season progressed, I found it therefore quite strange that I was suddenly being brought off more and more and also being left out of the side altogether.

Thinking back, I remember I was standing on 18 goals and we playing away at Brentford, I was playing really well and scored a goal towards the end of half time, to take my total to 19 goals since my return to the club. I was on a bonus if I scored 20 goals since my return to the club from the Far East.

At half time Frank Clark replaced me even though I was feeling fine, I thought to myself, 'I'm sure it was because he needed to check with the chairman whether they could afford to pay me my goal bonus.'

I always suspected that there were other factors behind this and have made comment to the fact that Clark may have seen me as a threat to his own career.

In February 1984, we won 4-3 at Exeter City with defender Tommy Cunningham scoring a hat trick. For once I was not on the score sheet, but it was nice of manager Frank Clark to mention in his programme notes that he took me off in the closing minutes because I had just about run myself into the ground up front.

The following week we lost 3-2 at Brentford in the Associated Members Cup, it was our very first appearance in this competition and the home side was out to impress their new boss, the former Arsenal favourite Frank McLintock and John Docherty partnership. After just sixteen minutes, we found ourselves two goals down but eleven minutes later Shaun Brooks and Kevin Godfrey set me up for an easy goal.

Brentford scored a third on thirty-nine minutes. We came out fighting in the second half and I swept home a Godfrey cross with thirteen minutes remaining. We maintained the pressure right to the final whistle but could not find a equaliser.

Four goals against the Lions

Onto my favourite match of the season for obvious reasons, my four goals that secured us a 5-3 win over Millwall, which took me to the twenty goals that I needed for my £500 bonus.

Stephen Studd in the local *Guardian & Gazette* wrote:

Kitchen's Conquests Goals 1 and 2

Peter scores 4 goals against Millwall. At the time this happened, he was only 1 of 11 players who have scored 4 times in a Football League Match or FA Cup for Orient.

The First and Second goals are featured above, and below.

Kitchen's Conquests Goals 3 and 4

The Third and Fourth goals are featured above, and on the right.

Orient ended a run of six games without a win with a stunning Easter holiday spectacular that will earn a place in the club history books and in the memoirs of Peter Kitchen after the O's striker hit four goals and also made one for captain on the day John Cornwell, in the 5-3 win over Millwall in a match that saw O's come back from behind three times.

Kitchen's goal blitz started in the 39th minute when Mark McNeill picked up the ball on the edge of the box for an angled shot that Kitchen tapped in the first of his historic quartet.

Then Kitchen ran riot, he collected a pass from midfield, brilliantly shot passed Paul Sansome for his best goal of the day, many players would have blasted it but he kept his composure to steer the ball home. After heading wide from a McNeill cross, he completed a superb afternoon by nodding in Keith Osgood's high flick from the post and then slotted in a pass from Andy Sussex five minutes from time for his fourth.

It was the first and only time he had scored four goals in a senior match. Funnily enough in his end of match wrap-up of the game, quite a few of the players were praised by manager Frank Clark, but no mention for four-goal hero Kitchen.

I netted a penalty in the away match at AFC Bournemouth the following week, which turned out to be my last goal for the O's. In goal for O's was young ster Kevin Shoemaker, we lost 3-2 with all the goals coming in the second half, but he could not be faulted with any of their goals.

My goal came after Mark McNeil was fouled and I converted the spot-kick. My final game for Orient was a 2-1 home defeat by Oxford United before a 5,695 crowd, and the O's had finished in their highest position in quite a few seasons, in eleventh spot.

I thought I would be with Orient for at least one further season. In April Frank Clark informed me that I would be offered a new contract, but five weeks later I was told he wasn't offering their leading goal scorer in the previous season, a new contract.

Instead they brought in a young Richard Cadette from Wembley FC and Ian Juryeff joined in February 1985 for £10,000 from Southampton because by December 1984 they had suffered fourteen defeats and scored just 26 League goals. They eventually were relegated into Division Four, for the first time in their history, finishing in a poor twenty-second spot.

I'm sure if I had stayed the O's would not have been relegated. I was only thirty-two years of age, fit and could have done a good job for them, I had another 15 to 20 goals a season in me for a couple more seasons.

So, my Orient days had come to an end.

When I came back from Hong Kong, the chairman Brian Winston had told me that he would like to see me become the player-manager, and I suspect Frank

Clark always saw me as a threat to him. This wasn't the case as I hadn't really considered what I wanted to do long term and would certainly have needed more time to have even been able to fulfil that role.

I always suspected as well that my leaving the club might have also been due to some boardroom politics that were going on in the background, as there were rumours of a rift between Brian Winston and Neville Ovenden, although I was never directly aware of this.

I wanted to stay at the club and I felt that I had another two good seasons of scoring goals for them. I was still very fit, and yes, whilst I had started to lose some pace, my goal scoring ability in and around the penalty box was still as sharp as ever, having proved that during the season.

To get a proven goal scorer is always very difficult, yet Orient already had one that they decided they didn't need, a decision that defies logic and is typical of the consequences of people making poor decisions. It was ultimately to lead to the further demise of the club and one that they have only now recovered from. When I joined Orient in 1977, they were on par with a number of London clubs, like Crystal Palace, Fulham, Charlton and Millwall, yet all these clubs have been able to maintain their league standing or to progress into the Premiership whilst the O's are basically in Division 4, no matter what they call it today. I can only put this down to a lack of foresight, poor decision making and a lack of funding and investment in players.

Having been released from Orient at thirty-two and with few options left to me, I had to face up to the fact that my professional career was coming to an end. It is quite a daunting prospect to face and one I don't envy footballers today having to come to terms with even though they do earn far more than we ever did.

Chapter 8
My PFA role, and my big fan
David Speedie

During my playing career I was the PFA representative for most of the clubs I served between 1975 to 1984 and stopped only I when I left after my second spell with Orient. The role involved being the players' representative for disseminating information from the PFA, to the players and distributing circulars etc.

At one of the PFA award dinners (this was after I had retired) in around 1986 I was coming out of the Dorchester Hotel in London, oh so very slightly inebriated, when a similarly drunk David Speedie, who was at Chelsea at the time, came running over to me shouting on the top of his voice 'My Hero, My Hero' to his Chelsea team mates, one of whom was Kerry Dixon, and he shouted to him 'Come and meet my football Hero'.

He proceeded to put his arm around me, telling everyone what a brilliant player I was with Doncaster Rovers and that I had great skill and that he used to watch me as young lad from behind the goal and that I was his hero when with Donny. It certainly impressed my Turkish friend Ahmet, who I had taken as a guest. Ahmet who was a 5-a-side team mate had a clothing company and now owns a shop on the Kings Road in London and was and still is a Chelsea season ticket holder. Speedie turned out to be a fine player, born in Glenrothes in Scotland on 20 February 1960, but his family moved down to Doncaster when he was very young. He starting his football career as a junior with Barnsley in 1977, he had a long career with such clubs as Darlington, Chelsea, Coventry City, Liverpool, Blackburn Rovers, Southampton, Birmingham City on loan, West Bromwich Albion, on loan, West Ham United on loan, and Leicester City, ending his League career in 1994, before going on to play with Crawley Town. During the latter part of his career, he was often seen at Belle Vue, prompting rumours of an impending move!

Speedie also won ten caps for Scotland. Today he is the Managing Director of Lightyear Recruitment Company in Wigan and he also acts as a Players' Agent.

Well, I certainly wished they had such Agents in my playing days, to look after our financial and contractual affairs. There are some wonderful stories about him, one conveyed by a Blackburn Rovers fans. It was when Speedie came out for a pre-match warm-up, it was a cold day, he was wearing a big black curly wig and everyone was asking who was this new player we'd signed, he then took it off with a big smile, it was a priceless moment, as were all his great goals. Speedie scored 145 goals from 535 appearances, in a great career that spanned some sixteen years.

Chapter 9
Off to the States to play
indoor soccer with Las Vegas

I left for Las Vegas in Nevada on 10 September 1984, but was released on 15 December and after a bit of travelling around the States, I returned to the UK during February 1985.

I didn't receive a signing-on fee, but received a living allowance for accommodation and also flights and insurance for my partner family and me. I was to receive a basic salary of $40,000 per annum plus bonuses.

I played for Las Vegas Americans, which was a new indoor soccer franchise, who had moved from Memphis. We played in the Thomas & Mack Center, which could hold over 16,000 fans. A number of the players moved with the club. There were also a number of players who moved from the San Diego club who had been champions of the major indoor soccer league a couple of seasons previously and who formed the basis of the team.

I was recruited at a trial I attended at the JVC Centre at Highbury during the summer but primarily as one of the second line of players. Indoor soccer was played like ice hockey in that they changed players every two to four minutes to give the first line players a rest. I played in a pre-season tournament at San Diego, which we lost in the semi-final, and I scored a goal in each of those matches. So I was off to the States, having had very few offers to play in England.

Playing in the States certainly appealed to me, I thought it would allow me to play longer in the game and I was becoming disillusioned with the English League game, it was becoming so tactical that I felt it was becoming boring and had lost its excitement and I came across a lot of people in the game who I felt just didn't know what they talking about.

The Las Vegas Americans - Peter standing next to Santa!

There are so many people who talk a good game but have no insight into what really motivates players or indeed the kind of players needed in a team to win matches. The easy option is always to be organised and to be defensive, It takes a brave manager to advocate attacking football and combine this with a defensive organisation.

Head coach Alan Mayer stated in the press: 'I had watched Kitchen and I like what I saw, he has impressed me tremendously and he's better than I actually thought he'd be, he's made the transition in a week, most players takes about five weeks to get used to the indoor game.

Peter is perfectly built for the indoor game, he's very fast over short spaces and he's good in the box and a tremendous finisher.'

The lifestyle in the States was just fabulous and it was great for me and the family (my partner and her two children), but in all honesty, I could never adapt to the frantic nature of indoor soccer which was so like ice hockey in that players barged into each other and there wasn't a lot of skill needed or passes made. It was very much about dribbling and shooting and the more shots that hit the plexi glass that surrounds the pitch the better even if they missed their prime target, the goal, as this excited the crowds.

The best thing about the matches was the razzamatazz surrounding the games and the way the players were introduced to the crowd. There was always lots of pre-match family entertainment but when the match was ready to start, it was done like only the Americans know how.

We would enter the arena through the goal, which was shrouded in mist (Dry Ice) with the stadium in total darkness except for a spotlight pointed at the goal and with a slow drum beating. Players were introduced one at a time and we had to wave to the crowd and line up by the centre circle. We also had to sing the American national anthem, the Stars and Stripes, before every game.

I remember a match at Baltimore when they did it differently for the home side. We still did our thing, but they would enter from a giant football which was lowered from the ceiling to the centre circle once a large explosion or blast rang all around the indoor arena.

We had a mixture of nationalities in the squad with nine players from the States, four from the British Isles (including me and three Irishmen, namely Martin Donnelly, Martin McCoy and Gerry O'Kane from Newry Town), two players from Yugoslavia, two from Germany, and the rest from Argentina, Chile and Cyprus.

There were a few interesting characters in the squad, the first was an American, who was actually born in Hungary named Julie Veee.

I have been told that in recent years Veee has painted some very good soccer posters, many of which are held at the National Soccer Hall of Fame in New York.

There was Gert Wieczorkowski, a German who marketed himself as having the 'biggest moustache' in US football, and finally Nicky Megaloudis who was from New York and great at doing impromptu impressions of everyone in the team. Helmut Dudek had the hardest shot in the indoor game. Bobby Hadzic a former Yugoslavian player who played for Dynamo Zagreb and Val Tuksa one of the finest indoor defenders.

The way the players were introduced and the razzamatazz of the games were great but the play on the pitch certainly lacked culture. I played during my brief stay against Dallas Sidekicks, San Diego, Pittsburgh, Chicago, Kansas City, Minnesota and Phoenix.

I was still very fit and the way we trained and the medical support really showed up the amateurish way the clubs in the English League were in terms of their medical backup and training schedules at the time.

I had never played indoor soccer in my life before, I had only seen videotape and I made my intention clear when I filled in the player information sheet as a goal scorer.

I didn't foresee any problems having played fifteen years in the English league, I thought if you can score goals there you can score them anywhere, I was confident I could make the transition smoothly. I arrived two weeks before the camp opened so I could become accustomed to the boards, and the smaller field and goal area.

I was confident I could make it, even though the club also had on their books three great indoor goal scorers in Juli Veee, Yilmaz Orhan and one of the top strikers in the indoor game Fred Grgurev, who had scored 259 career indoor goals, including 23 career winning goals and **31 HAT TRICKS.** The Americans love their stats!

During my stay in the indoor league, I only played in seven league games, with no goals and one assist and as mentioned, I mostly came on as a second line player. Other English players who I came across whilst in the states were Gordon Hill and John Gorman. The head coach at the time was an Alan Meyer, who was a U.S. international goalkeeper, who played six times in the national side, he also played in the NASL between 1974 to 1981 for Baltimore Comets, San Diego Jaws, Las Vegas Quicksilver, San Diego Sockers and California Surf, with a total of 166 games.

Meyer got sacked in December and stayed on at the club as the goalie and that's the time I also got 'put on waivers', a term used to advise other clubs that a player is available for transfer. I hadn't been in America long enough to have established myself so I did not receive any offers. We therefore decided to use the time to travel in the USA so we took about three weeks off to drive down to Los Angeles and then along Highway One to San Francisco. I had managed to negotiate myself a £5000 severance payment from the Las Vegas Americans for three months of my contract as well as return flights for myself and my partner and her family to come back to the UK.

The Assistant Coach was Tony Simoes, who was a great Portuguese international player, known as Antonio Simoes who played for Benfica and in the NASL with the Boston Minuteman, San Jose Earthquakes and Dallas Tornado.

He had also appeared for Portugal in the 1966 World Cup, held in England, and played in six World Cup games in the tournament against Hungary, Bulgaria, Brazil, Korea, England and also against the Soviet Union in a 3rd/4th place game. In fact the only match they lost was against England by 2-1, with the winning goal being scored by Bobby Charlton, with a thirty-five yard scorcher. He wore the number 7 shirt and played alongside some Portuguese greats, like Eusabio, and big Jose Torres upfront.

Simoes was a really nice guy and was probably the only one with any real knowledge and intelligence about the game. My partner and I occasionally went out with him and his wife socially and a couple of times we babysat their two daughters for them.

I remember his wife who did not like the U.S.A, and wanted to go back to Portugal. It was during the time we were travelling to a match at Phoenix, that he told me that he had been an envoy for Portugal following a military coup in the late seventies and early eighties when the new Government asked him to act in that capacity.

Chapter 10
Brief spells with both Dagenham and Chester City

After my return from the States in February 1985, I joined up with my former Orient boss Ken Knighton who was at Southern League side Dagenham, and I played seven games during my month's stay. I received £120 per week and a small signing-on fee, which I used to buy a pair of soccer boots, as I didn't have any, they were still in the States.

I can't recall too much about my stay with the Daggers, the memorable aspect is that I arrived back home without any soccer boots and I used my signing on fee to quickly buy a new pair from Sedgewicks sports shop in Walthamstow (who also used to supply boots to the Orient in my time there).

It was a worrying time for me as I was coming to the end of my professional career and I didn't have much money left after my divorce in 1982 and spending money during my stay in the States.

I can't really recall much about this period of my playing days, as I really didn't enjoy the experience. The first match I played was on 28 February 1985 against Nuneaton Borough, a 2-1 home win before just 573 fans and I finished up on 28 March in a 1-0 defeat at Weymouth, which attracted 658 fans. Five days earlier I played for the reserves during March in the Capital League at home to Orient, we drew 2-2 before a wonderful crowd of 112 (one hundred and twelve people). The O's had a few first team players in the team that night, including Hales, Stride, Harvey, Cadette and Brooks and the O's scorers were Cadette and Stride.

In goal for us in a number of the games during my brief spell was Lloyd Scott, the former O's goalie and today a wonderful worker for cancer charities.

Scott himself informed the Author: 'I remember I was with Kitch at Orient, in fact I was his kit boy at Dagenham, and also played in some charity games with him.'

My move to Chester City

After this short and uninspiring spell with Dagenham, I was approached by Micky Speight, the caretaker-manager of Fourth Division Chester City to see if I was interested in joining them as player-coach. I decided to go and give it a try, I stayed in digs for a couple of weeks. Just before the next game Speight was appointed manager on a permanent basis and I signed up on non-contract terms, earning a match fee of £250 per game.

I made my debut against Halifax Town when I came on as a substitute for

Speight, in a 4-0 victory. Five days later I made my full debut, wearing my familiar number ten shirt and I scored, a rather easy goal from the boot, in a 2-0 win over Aldershot.

However, I didn't really want to move back up North. I suppose having lived in Las Vegas for a few months, I couldn't face the miserable weather and the cold and damp of Manchester.

What finally turned me against the move was a visit with Speight on a scouting mission to watch Tranmere Rovers play Blackpool, it was about two degrees below and lashing down with rain! A far cry, from the glorious sunshine of Nevada.

I played in three further League games, my last being at Wrexham in April 1985, and we lost them all to finally finish in sixteenth position in Division Four.

I recall thinking that this was no longer for me, playing in the Fourth Division and perhaps time to call it day. I decided I wasn't going to sign for Chester on a permanent basis and therefore I felt there was no point in continuing playing on and so I agreed with Speight to terminate my contractual agreement with them and left before the end of April 1985.

Peter's last League goal, scored for Chester v. Aldershot

Playing at the time with Chester was a young twenty-year old Manchester-born lad named Lee Dixon, the son of the former Manchester City goalkeeper of the fifties' Roy Dixon, and Lee went onto great things with a number of clubs, making 458 appearances for Arsenal between 1987 to 2002, before he retired at the age of thirty-eight. He also won 22 caps for England during his long career of more than 800 senior games that spanned some twenty years.

I became very disillusioned with football, the people running the clubs, the managers and coaches, that I decided not to play football again and I stuck by my word and I didn't kick a football in an 11-a-side match for about two-years.

Chapter 11
Career comes to an end,
so I thought!

Packs-up football for a sales job

It was during the period after returning from the States and whilst playing at Chester that I worked as a sales representative for a large sports outfitters and distributor, which I had to give a try as I needed to start to earn some money. The company were based in SW London, not far from Plough Lane, and were called Starcraft Sports Co. A previous employee I later found out was Tosh Chamberlain, an ex-Fulham favourite.

Starcraft was the UK distributor for Hummel sports clothing from Denmark and I was recruited because the Company were supposedly hoping to become shirt sponsors of English football clubs. They already supplied Swansea City and Wimbledon and were hoping that with my contacts I could get them into several others. Or so I was told!!

In truth Hummel apparently had terminated the contract with the company and were no longer using them as the distributor.

Despite me securing several orders for Hummel clothing with a number of sports shops, Starcraft were unable to deliver and I was finding it very difficult to keep going back to the stores unable to supply the goods. It was during this time that the warehouse burned down.

Mr. Shabbir, the proprietor, asked me if I wanted to stay on, but he expected me to take a cut in salary, which I could not afford to do, so I handed in my resignation.

Working in Harlow and winning my first Irish cap!

Without a main job and only receiving the money from Dagenham and then Chester, I needed to start earning money fairly quickly, as I was still paying £100 per week maintenance for my sons from the remnants of any money I had left from the States.

I answered an advert in the local paper for a job in the Leisure Services Department at Harlow Council and to my surprise was offered the role of Sports Development and running the Children's holiday Play Schemes as an Assistant Recreation Officer, starting on the 1st July 1985.

The person interviewing me was a guy named Chris Lightfoot who had been a teacher and a former semi-professional goalkeeper with Romford and I suspect that this may have influenced the decision. Chris unfortunately was only there

165

for a further three months before leaving to go the USA to organise soccer camps on the East Coast near Pennsylvania, however his parting gift to me was to help me get funding from the Council to take a postgraduate Diploma in Business Management studies.

In 1986, I went to Harlow College on day release for two years and achieved a CNAA Diploma in Management Studies in 1988. I completed my course at Harlow College which also coincided with the right time to progress in my now chosen career in Leisure Management, and after attending an Interview in Sevenoaks I was offered the job as Manager of a Leisure Centre in Edenbridge in Kent starting in January 1989 and which began my association with the Sevenoaks District.

Just after the move to Kent I received a number of offers from various county senior and junior football clubs, but I turned them all down. At the age of thirty-seven I had to concentrate on my new job whilst enjoying playing in the charity games for the TV Commentators XI.

It was during 1986 that I played on St Patrick's Day in an exhibition match. I played for a Republic of Ireland Select XI. We lost the match 7-3 and in the match programme my name was listed as Peter O'Kitchen. The special invitation indoor match was to launch the opening of the new soccer franchise the New York Express (formerly Cosmos), the Irish side was managed by the great Eoin Hand. The Irish team was made up of Irish League players because Eoin had just been sacked as the Manager of the Republic team and as such was no longer authorised to take the full Irish squad, yet had to fulfil the fixture commitment. (He had been replaced by Jack Charlton). Similarly, the shirts we wore were the green of the Republic of Ireland but didn't have the Irish badge as the official endorsement, only the shamrock on the breast.

(I've still got the shirt but never received the cap!!)

In the Irish side we had a young Brixton lad named Roger Wynter, whose only claim to fame was playing for England Schoolboys at Wembley against Northern Ireland, and one night at the Wembley Indoor Arena during the early Eighties, when a seventeen year-old, he stole the limelight, scoring eight goals that won Millwall the Evening Standard's London Five-A Side championship and was voted player of the Tournament. He looked like there was a bright future ahead for him, but he didn't get a chance to do much. In fact after just one sub appearance in the League, the Lions sacked him after a criminal conviction in 1984, and he ended up in the non-league with Tooting & Mitcham.

Poor old Wynter, who was a black lad and introduced to the fans as O'Winter, had to endure the Irish Americans in the crowd jeering him. They probably had had a bit too much Guinness or whisky, and shouted out in strong Irish accents 'Be Jesus, you're never Irish'.

Chapter 12
Plays for Tommy Taylor at Margate in the Southern League, aged thirty-nine

Whilst playing for the Commentators Xl, we played in a charity match against a Charlton Vets Xl and up against me was my ex-Orient team mate Tommy Taylor. I must have impressed him with my fitness because out of the blue I got a call from him a few days later. Tommy Taylor was boss at Southern League side Margate, and he asked me if I wanted to turn out for them and play a few games. I initially declined as I thought that I was far too old at 39, however he kept insisting that I could still do a job for them and so I thought I might as well give it a try.

They had a lot of youngsters as well as one 'old man' in thirty-six year former Orient defender Bill Roffey, who was still doing his thing at full-back. I was paid a signing-on fee of £1000 and a basic salary of £100 per week. I remember that on one of my first visits to training one evening, the players had put a Zimmer frame on the peg in the changing room with my training kit. (A Zimmer Frame is a walking frame that old people use to help them get about).

I decided to give it a try and after a friendly against Theo Foley's Northampton Town, I made my Southern League debut in a 2-1 defeat at Burnham on 17 August 1991, at the age of thirty-nine. Then three days later followed a 4-0 defeat at Hastings Town. I eventually got going and scored my first goal for them on 26 August, in our 2-2 draw with Ashford Town before 510 spectators. I then scored twice five days later in a 3-1 win over Newport Isle of Wight.

My next goal came in a Southern League Cup game at home to Erith & Belvedere on 8 October, a 3-2 victory, just 172 fans watched this match. I didn't score again and I finished with them on 26 December 1991 when I came on as a substitute in a 1-0 win over Canterbury City, that goal being scored by Bill (Roffey), I thought to myself, I better give it up as I was approaching my fortieth birthday. I did so, and thus my playing career came to an end.

Old Bill played a total of 71(2) appearances for Margate, having joined them from Canterbury City in 1992. He then joined Tonbridge Angels and became their Assistant Manager in 1996 before resigning a year later. Today Bill spends a lot of time coaching in the States.

The following message was received from Steve Trice, Historian of Margate Football Club by the Author during April 2005 after an initial enquiry about my career with them.

'We were in the Southern League, Southern Division at the time and despite being thirty-nine years of age, Peter Kitchen looked a class apart, he seemed to be one of the fit-

test players in the team. His touch was brilliant but he understandably lacked pace and that told against him, plus Margate was not a very good side at the time. It was obvious he must have been a fantastic player in his prime. He made a total of 11(7) appearances for us, scoring 4 goals.'

Chapter 13
My time with Wimbledon
FC's Youth Academy

It was whilst playing with the TV Commentators Xl that I became friends with Roger Smith, who organised the side and was also scouting for Arsenal at the time. Roger had been a professional at Spurs but had never made it into the first team and had gone to Exeter City on a free transfer where he made about half a dozen first team appearances. Roger was a good friend of the late Ray Harford, who was at Wimbledon and when the job of Youth Development Officer came up, Roger was appointed into the position. He subsequently asked me if I would like to do some coaching in the evenings at one of their training centres (prior to the formation of the football academies) at Slade Green near Dartford. This suited me fine as it was quite close to where I now worked in Swanley as Manager of the White Oak Leisure Centre.

I had obtained my FA Preliminary coaching badge whist with Cardiff and I converted this to a EUFA part B certificate whilst with the Dons. I considered taking a full coaching certificate but never had the time to do this, as it is a two-week residential course plus the need to attend a number of coaching seminars and sessions every few months.

Manager of Wimbledon Under 15s. Peter is the first from right on back row, and Roger Smith is first on the left.

The Goal Gourmet

I started in 1991, and I spent nine happy years with Wimbledon Football Club, as they were then known, as a coach and manager of their U-13's, 14's and 15's and was very much involved in their youth development policy. Several players who made it into the First team played in the teams I managed, although most have now been sold onto other football League clubs as part of the demise of the club and prior to its transfer to Milton Keynes.

Some of these players I coached included defender Mikele Leigertwood who played for Wimbledon, Leyton Orient on loan before joining Crystal Palace in February 2004 for £150,000. Mikele had made 104(9) career league appearances up to the end of the 2005-06 season, and in in July 2006 he moved to new Premiership side Sheffield United. Midfielder Nigel Reo-Coker, who after 57(1) league appearances for the Dons, joined West Ham United in January 2004 with 78(7) league appearances, Joel McAnuff who had made 122(20) league appearances for the Dons, West Ham United, Cardiff City before signing for Crystal Palace in May 2005. Striker Wayne Gray who had made 92(61) league appearances for the Dons, and on loan with Swindon Town, Port Vale, Leyton Orient and Brighton before helping Southend United to promotion to League One in May 2005 and finally there was defender Robert Gier who after making 67(4) League appearances for the Dons, joined Rushden & Diamonds in both in May 2005 and May 2006, in June 2006 he joined Yeovil Town. . Others who were in my teams and who have stayed at Milton Keynes Dons and played in the first team have included Alex Tapp, having made 50 appearances, but who suffered through injuries over the past couple of seasons, Ben Harding, the midfielder has played for the Dons over the past couple of seasons, Leon Crooks the defender has been a regular during the 2005-06 season and Dean Lewington (son of the former Watford manager and my former Fulham team mate Ray Lewington), who has been a regular over the past couple of seasons, with over 120 games for the Dons. They were a good bunch of lads and I enjoyed working with them all.

During this time, Roger Smith became the Wimbledon Academy Director and was instrumental in establishing the club as having one of the best youth policies in the country.

I left in 1999, because of some of the changes and requirements placed on the Academies by the FA and Roger left a couple of years later when the club had serious financial problems and went into receivership before relocating to Milton Keynes.

In April 1994, I enjoyed a brief career as a sports reporter when I started to write a few match reports on the O's in the local Guardian newspaper. I tried not to be too overcritical of manager Peter Eustace, but I found some of his team selection strange at times. The club seemed to have a policy when it came to players of quantity rather than quality. I thought the club lacked ambition and was at that time the victim of the past ten years when they sold all their good young players and brought in players from other clubs' reserves on the cheap, and I was not afraid to say so. The end result was a team of very ordinary footballers, and it was not unexpected to see them relegated when John Sitton and Chris Turner took over.

I thought to myself 'Unless they start showing some ambition they will always remain in the lower divisions'.

It was around this time that I was beginning to become fed up with the bureaucracy of local government and increasingly felt that if I had been given the chance, I couldn't have done worse that a lot of managers I was seeing in the game at that time. I think I had learned how NOT to manage from some of them.

I was so desperate to see the O's improve that during April 1994 I declared my interest, through an article I wrote, in the manager's job at the club, although I never formally applied. I would love to have achieved what Kevin Keegan did at that time for Newcastle United. I understand that because of my press criticism of the club I was not in Chairman Tony Wood's favourite books.

I did hear from one of the directors that Tony Wood had taken offence to one of my articles after I had criticised the club's policy under him and Frank Clark of not spending any money on some good experienced players and always trying to buy everyone else's reserves or cast-offs. To be fair to Clark, he did watch a lot of youth and reserve football around the country in an effort to bring in new blood during his spell with Orient and he did bring in some decent players, but every good team needs a balance of both youth and experience and to get such players you need to spend some money.

I also applied for the manager's job at Doncaster Rovers in January 1994, and I was interviewed for the job, but was unsuccessful, and I thought to myself if I couldn't get the manager's job at the two clubs I was most successful with then it wasn't worth applying anywhere else.

Chapter 14
Playing for Charity with Rod Stewart's Vagabonds and the TV Commentators XI

At a chance meeting with highly acclaimed Yorkshire TV and later Sky football commentator Martin Tyler at the PFA dinner in 1987, he asked me if I wanted to play a charity game for the Commentators XI team. This was the start of my many years playing for various charity teams. I scored a hat trick in my first game, which was played at Collier Row and the former O's player and West Ham United manager Glenn Roeder also played in that game for the team. In later matches Pat Rice of Arsenal fame also turned out for us, as well as a number of ex-professionals and backroom staff of the BBC and ITV sports coverage teams.

The TV Commentators Xl team was something I really enjoyed being involved with and I played for them right up to 2000. We played it fairly seriously as they were very competitive and obviously the players involved understood the game and were always totally committed to trying and win, although it's fair to say that the after-match drinking and socializing was always just as important to us.

In the Commentators side were people like John Motson, Jim Rosenthal, Alan Parry, Richard Keys and as previously mentioned Martin Tyler. Robin Russell of

TV Commentators XI, 1992. Peter second from right on back row. Other famous faces include John Motson, Trevor Brooking, Jim Rosenthal, Pat Holland, Alan Parry and Martin Tyler.

the FA and Gordon Riddick a stalwart of Brentford, Luton and Watford (he even turned out for Orient) were regulars as was Roger Smith previously mentioned from Wimbledon and Colin Booth, a good friend who later died of bowel cancer.

There were also occasional guest appearances from the likes of Trevor Brooking, Frank Lampard Snr, Andy Gray, John Gorman, Gary Lewin the Arsenal and England Physio and Dave Galley the Liverpool Physio, when he was at Luton.

I was once a studio guest of Sky's Richard Keys when Orient beat West Bromwich Albion in the FA Cup some years ago, so I suppose that does technically make me a TV commentator!

We haven't played for a few years together but I suppose if a match was arranged, we would mostly all turn out again (except for Motty). It's a question of finding enough over 50's to fit into a pair of shorts and run around without a respirator. I have kept in touch with most of the players and only recently some of us met up for John Motson's 60th birthday celebrations in July 2005.

I had been keeping myself fit for many years by playing 5-a-side since I finished playing professionally in 1985. This was in the local sports centre's 5-a-side League in Epping, Essex on Thursday nights with some friends. We were known as Granville because several of the players lived in Granville Road and we were sponsored by Granville Insurance owned by one of the players. One of our players, Mike House, a good friend who had played for Epping Town, was still playing recently at sixty-two years of age. I continued playing regularly until I left Epping in 2003. I also played in the Harlow Sports Centre lunchtime 5-a-side League once I started working in Harlow with the Council's Leisure Department.

Playing with Rod Stewart's team

I also played for Rod Stewart's Vagabonds team for about four years between 1995 and1998.

Highgate-born Roderick David Stewart loves his football. He had dreams of becoming a player and was an apprentice with Brentford, but soon switched to singing. He built a beautiful football pitch in the grounds of his Epping mansion so that he could play as often as he liked when he was in England.

Rod was very serious about the game and he kept himself extremely fit and still plays today at the age of sixty. His older brother Don who was already in his 70's is also very fit and was the referee for all the games we played. Rod is only allowed to spend up to 90 days in the country for tax reasons but when he is in the UK he was always looking for the team to play matches.

He was always very hospitable and after matches during the summer the team were always invited to swim in the open-air pool at the side of the house. Afterwards we would all retire to the Theydon Oak pub in Epping for several

**Rod Stewart's Vagabonds XI Peter standing next to Rod.
Rod's brother Don is acting as referee.**

pints. It was interesting to see that a number of 'Rod Stewart look-alikes' would appear at the pub as well as if they knew when he was in the country.

The team was mainly made up of players from the team his father used to manage, Highgate Redwing, plus several guest players like myself, and some of the local Epping Constabulary. There were also a number of famous faces who would regularly turn up for a game including Bradley Walsh, now of Coronation Street fame and other well known footballers like Dean Holdsworth, Ian Wright, Mark Bright, and David Hurst of Sheffield Wednesday and Southampton. Terry Gibson, ex-Wimbledon and Manchester United, was also a regular in midfield.

In one match we were playing, the front three was Kitchen, Holdsworth and Bright and when I limped off with a pulled hamstring I was replaced by Ian Wright. Gordon Strachan, who is a close friend of Rod's, was also a regular visitor and occasionally turned out for the side.

It was during this time that Rod split from his then wife Rachel Hunter who had regularly watched the matches. It was interesting that I received several phone calls at the time from magazine reporters asking for comments about the break up. Fortunately my experiences in football had taught me how the press operates so I was able to politely respond that I "was unable to comment".

Chapter 15
15-years playing with the Corinthian Casuals Vets until 52 years of age scoring 280 goals from 228 appearances

Playing for the Corinthian Casuals School Vets, part of the club that was founded in 1882, has been a wonderful part of my life, having had the opportunity of playing all around the world. The Club Secretary and Vets Team Manager is Brian Wakefield who was a goalkeeper who once captained Oxford University and played for Kingstonian, he was nicknamed 'The Cat '. He was a fringe player with Leyton Orient, after joining them from Corinthian Casuals FC, he was offered a professional contract by manager Les Gore but turned it down, and so in 1960, Leyton Orient signed instead veteran goalkeeper Bill Robertson from Chelsea for £1,000.

I first started with the Casual Vets in 1991 when Colin Booth, who also played for the Commentators Xl asked me if I fancied a game for them, and after only a few games I was invited on the forthcoming tour to the USSR.

During my professional career I experienced the slow but inevitable transition from being the 'up and coming' youngster to becoming the old pro in later years. With the Corinthian-Casuals I repeated the process often being the callow

**Corinthian Casual Veterans. Peter first from right on front row.
Brian Wakefield is first in top row.**

youth with my team mates whose combined ages sometime approached 500 years!

There were still things I hadn't got used to like the 'pay for play' concept (i.e. the match fee, the absence of a match programme or the anxious study of the league position at 4.45pm). The most obvious differences were the environment in which the matches were played – the green and historic buildings of Eton, Winchester and Charterhouse were vastly different from the concrete and steel of League grounds like Burnley, Bolton and Sheffield.

The pre-match talks were very different – with the Vets we didn't focus on our opponents or their pattern of play, but rather on covering our deficiencies e.g. avoiding the back-pass to the goalkeeper, also the lack of the 'industrial language' use by the football league manager to emphasize his 'over the top' and 'win at all costs' philosophy.

The 'three cheers' for the opposition was the norm by the Vets team and its management with the expletives and obscenities that were often exchanged with one's fellow professionals at the end of a bruising battle was never evident.

The pace of the game was of course much slower and there were many opportunities to take get some breathe during a game. I remember one game we played against Bembridge on the Isle of Wight, I was able to take a breather and admire the yachts passing the island at the beginning of the Round Britain Race. I wouldn't had got away with that as a pro – there would have been volleys of abuse from several quarters!

At the end of a Vets game there was still a frantic rush – as a pro it was usually to speak to the press, watching if any scouts from other clubs were around or to sign autographs, but with the Vets it was to get to the shower first before all the hot water ran out, to be first to the bar for 'refreshments' before retiring to the local hostelry.

Yet, in the end nothing much had really changed – the game is dissected, tactics are criticized, excuses are made and no likes to leave in case they are talked about, but, I loved every minute!

I played regularly up to early in 2005, until the old legs have started to go and I must have averaged around nineteen goals each season that I played for the Vets.

We played every week mainly against the public schools around the London area such as Eton, Charterhouse and many more and our philosophy is to set a good example in terms of passing the ball and to teach the boys good sportsmanship and standards of behaviour.

In 1991, the Moscow trip was memorable, we played two games, one of which was against a USSR Vets XI, we lost 4-3, but I netted a hat trick in that one, and when they toured England later in the year I scored in the return match, a 1-1 draw. It was the only time that the Clubhouse was drunk dry of vodka!!

In 1993 we played three games in Florida, one was against a team managed by the former Fulham goalkeeper Peter Mellor in a place called Clearwater. We won all our games and I was top scorer on that tour.

Tour of South Africa

In August 1996, we went to South Africa and played six games in twelve days against opposition with an average age of only thirty-five. Our average age was fifty-one, we won two and drew four games. I was captain and top scorer on that tour. The tour opened in the province of KwaZulu-Natal with matches against three well-known amateur clubs. It was then down by plane to Cape Town and all the clubs, with the exception of the Cape District XI, were teams that played regularly in veterans' leagues.

Amongst the highlights of the trip, was a visit to Robben Island where Nelson Mandela was imprisoned and a visit to the State Parliament in Cape Town.

We beat Stella FC 2-1, Wanderers FC 1-0, Cape District XI by 1-0, Blue Bells FC 1-0 and drew with Savages FC 3-3 and Avendale FC 1-1. The touring party was:

Carl Adair, Dave Alexander, Barry Cooper, Peter Crees, Les Eason, John Harding, David Harrison, Peter Kitchen, Dave Laurie, Ian Longworth, Gordon Mousinho, Mick Preston, Mark Rose, Tony Slade, Dave Smith and Brian Wakefield with R.H. Glasgow and G.G. Howlett, the vice-presidents of the club also accompanying the players.

We returned home from Johannesburg Airport, and all dressed in a club blazers and tie when a gentleman came up to a group of us and asked who we were. He was told we were a football team from England and he replied 'You must have an awful lot of Administrators with you'.

In 2001 and 2002, at the ripe old age of forty-nine, I also played for C.C. Vets on tour to both Brazil and then in 2002 in Shanghai in China.

The tour of Brazil in 2001

In Brazil, we opened the tour against a strong SPAC Veterans team on Saturday 25th May 2001, in their side was Vladimir, who made 803 appearances for Corinthians Paulista, and he also gained 3 full Brazilian caps. They opened the scoring on just 7 minutes when Vladimir turned the ball home past our goalie Peter Crees, but we equalised immediately when Trevor Waller headed home a Martin Spong cross, it was short lived when Mauro scored from close range.

On 29 minutes we equalised when Spong broke away to give their goalie Cassio no chance, but just two minutes later Nego ran through to score. In the second half Vladimir scored another on 55 minutes to make it 4-2.

We tried to get back into the match: I had a point blank shot saved by Cassio's legs, a few minutes later Mark Fabian volleyed just over and in the final minutes after a superb cross from Paul Roberts I headed wide, and so we lost our first tour match by 4-2.

The second match three days later was against The Corinthians Paulista Masters, and the name Masters said it all. In their squad, every player had won a Sao Paulo State Championship medal and six were full Brazilian internationals and so there was little surprise at the overwhelming 9-0 scoreline. The match was shown live on Brazilian TV to an estimated 10 million viewership.

In the stadium there were around 3000 fans and as we were sitting in the dressing room in walked a host of former great Brazilian international players to shake our hands and then stand beside us in the tunnel. As we walked out into the sunlight we were greeted with singing, cheering and a barrage of firecrackers, the TV Cameraman was walking up and down the line and zooming on each one of us.

We spent the whole game chasing shadows with their Samba style of play,

They were five goals up by half time through Joao Paulo – a hat-trick, Zenon, Biro Biro. The second half continued in the same fashion with four goals from Pitta, Luiz Fernando, then on 52 minutes Geraldao turned poor Tony Blunt five times before shooting home. Five minutes later Pitta scored his second and the scoring was complete in the final seconds when Luiz Fernando volleyed sweetly home. I left the field with a few minutes remaining being replaced by both Paul Roberts and John Harding, the latter nearly scored in the final second the ball being deflected for a corner, but he fell and tore his hamstring. John was around sixty-four, although he was a top-class amateur player in his day, having captained Great Britain, the Combined Universities, the Army and he played for Pegasus.

The teams were:

Corinthian-Casuals Vets: Peter Crees, Ronnie McNamara (Tony Blunt), Mark Rose, John Russell-Smith, Mark Pope, Trevor Waller (Brian Adamson), Graham Pearce, Steve Smith, Mark Fabian, Peter Kitchen (Paul Roberts // John Harding) and Robert McNamara.

The Masters: Soliti, Ronaldo, Wilson Mano, Nelsinho, Vladimir, Paulinho, Biro Biro, Zenon, Carlinhos, Ataliba, Joao Paulo. Playing Subs: Solitinho, Geraldao, Agaldo, Alves, Luiz Fernando, Altinete, Marcio, Edson, Adaozinho, Moretti, Pitta and Mirandinho.

Mirandinho was with Newcastle United thirteen years previously, having made 54 Division One appearances and scoring 20 goals. (Francisco Ernami Lima de Silva – better known as Mirandinho joined United from Palmeiras of

Brazil in August 1987 for £575,000, to become the first Brazilian to play in the English League. He stayed for two seasons. United had been relegated, Mira had returned back home and manager Willie McFaul was sacked).

After the match a huge firework display took place and the local media rushed onto the pitch for interview, it was an amazing atmosphere as the fans sang and danced to the beat of the drum, moving side to side. The reception, which followed took place in a huge banqueting hall, which overlooked the ground. It was a just a wonderful day.

We were also guests of Corinthians Paulista at their stadium when they clinched the Brazilian championship against Botofogo. Unfortunately, I was left back in the hotel suffering with extreme diarrhoea. You could say I had been booked for dissent(ry)!!

The next match on Thursday 31 May against the Paulistano Veterans and we managed to turn around the seventy-minute match and we won at a canter. I scored four of goals in a 6-1 win.

We scored on 12 minutes when Steve Smith headed home a Trevor Waller cross, I extended the score when we were awarded a penalty and I rolled the ball in to the bottom right-hand corner. Our third came on 41 minutes after Mark Rose smashed home from 25 yards.

The second half opened and after eight minutes I scored with a deft touch from a corner. Our hosts to their credit came back and Richard Zats slotted the ball past Peter Crees.

On the hour I nodded home from a Rose centre and five minutes later we turned on the English magic. A long ball by Graham Pearce found Rob McNamara in the corner. He chested the ball down in one move and knocked the ball to Martin Spong, who in turn laid on the ball to me and I scored my fourth and our sixth

In June 2001 we played in the John Mills SPAC Vets invitation cup in Sao Paulo, Mills is the man who made the tour possible. We started with a 0-0 draw against the SPAC Pre-Vets before beating the SPAC Strollers 2-0 with goals from Mark Fabian and Tony Blunt, our last game also ended 0-0 against SPAC Vets and so we secured a place in the final on goal difference. The final table finishing:

	P	W	D	L	F	A	Pts
SPAC Pre-Vets	3	1	2	0	3	0	5
Corinthian-Casuals	3	1	2	0	2	0	5
Vets	3	0	0	3	0	6	0
SPAC Vets	3	0	0	3	0	6	0
SPAC Strollers	3	0	0	3	0	6	0

So we were up against the SPAC Pre-Vets in the Final. The match ended goalless, although Leonardo had a good chance saved by our guest goalkeeper Renato. The match went to penalties and Trevor Waller and Wilson for SPAC converted to make the shoot-out 1-1.

Then Graham Pearce's spot kick was saved and Piero made no mistake with his kick. Mark Fabian and I converted our kicks, as did, Tata and Edoardo for SPAC leaving the score going into the round of kicks as 4-3 to SPAC, up trod Martin Spong, who missed his kick to give SPAC Pre-Vets the cup.

After the match we had a lovely sit-down meal and later we were taken to an exclusive Sao Paulo nightclub, and we were well looked after at the VIP bar and it was a big thank you to both Timmy Banks and John Mills for making this such a great tour.

Tour to China in 2002

The tour of China was enjoyable, we left Heathrow on the evening of Saturday 1 June 2002 and arrived at Shanghai Airport at 11.30 a.m. the following day. After a short trip in a crowded minibus we arrived at Xindongfang Hotel, it was very elegant with a fountain in reception and marble floors. Shanghai itself looked a very modern city and not what a communist city would be like. The people themselves seemed very happy and friendly, which surprised many of our touring party. The squad received an early wake-up call from Brian Wakefield and John Harding for our tour to the Bund which ran along the banks of the river with large structures and modern shops and takeaways, so the lads were glad for some western food, although it seemed more for the tourists as the locals seemed fit, not many obese people in China.

We opened the tour against the British Consulate and beat them 1-0, our average age was around forty-five in contrast to our younger hosts, the game which I did not play in was delayed because the referee was late in turning up and we took an early lead with a header from Andy Jennings and that was enough to secure victory.

During the following morning we all went on a tour to visit the Olympic Stadium and in the afternoon it was off to the Yeyaun Gardens. The following day before our next game against Shanghai 2000, we visited the Jade Buddha, which was set in a monastery.

Then it was off again to the Jingan Workers Stadium to play a young Shanghai side, which was on the verge of entering the Chinese National Amateur League. They were aged between eighteen and twenty-one, they were more than a match for their more aged visitors and the early indications of the match was that they were a very useful outfit.

Shanghai took the lead on twenty minutes, Ca Oyue ran half the length of the field to smash the ball past goalie Paul Harrison, soon after the same player scored a second. They made it three five minutes later when Huang Le hit a beauty from twenty-five yards. We pulled one back through Mick Tomlinson (not the former Orient player) just before the break.

In the second half we reduced the arrears after a Nigel Stops cross was put through his own goal by Jiang Rong Bin. I should have put away the equaliser but I shot over the bar from five yards, but I made amends on seventy-four minutes after the referee, who must have felt sorry for the Vets, awarded us a dubious penalty, I strolled up and rolled into the bottom right hand corner, but in the end the young home side got the last laugh and scored two goals against a tiring Vets side to win 5-3.

Over the years, we have had a few ex-professional sportsmen playing for us, although I have probably played the most over the fourteen years I have been with them. Some of those to have appeared include:

Graham Pearce, the former Brighton left back, who appeared with Paddy Grealish for them in the 1982 FA Cup Final. Steve Gritt, the former Charlton and Gillingham player Steve Coppell of Manchester United and England fame Alan Pardew , the present Manager of Crystal palace, and Gavin Peacock, the former QPR and Chelsea player.

Graham Pearce also went on tour overseas with us. He was a printer by trade who played part-time football for Barnet in the old Alliance Premier League. He impressed the Brighton & Hove Albion manager Mike Bailey, when they played against Brighton in the FA Cup in January 1982, so much that he bought him for £20,000. Pearce went onto have a long career both as a player and later as a manager in the Conference.

And from cricket, we have had with us Bill Athey, Mark Ramprakash, Alex Tudor and more regularly Alex Stewart the former England captain. We have even had Jess Conrad, the 60's singer, play in goal, although when he leaned that he had to pay subs of £3 on a weekly basis he never played again.

Others in our team are guys who have played Semi-Pro or at a good Southern League standard, although in recent years it has become increasingly harder to get quality players who want to play on a regular basis.

Funnily, one of the best players I have played with in the team was a Roddy Haider, who won a record number of 65 England Amateur caps (10 caps whilst with Kingstonian and 55 with Hendon) and played for Woking, Kingstonian and Hendon, in fact he was voted as the latter's best ever player and he was in Hendon's side that beat Enfield 2-0 in the 1972 FA Amateur Cup Final at Wembley in front of 38,000 fans. He really understood the game and was excellent at linking up the play. He was a real team player, very creative and very unselfish and was certainly good enough to have played professionally. He did have close links with Charlton Athletic and had a few games in their Combination but stayed an amateur and decided to continue to work in his insurance job.

Another real character in the team was John Harding, a Liverpudlian with a great sense of humour, a person who was always positive and he was almost always laughing. He enjoyed a distinguished amateur football career at University with Pegasus, the Corinthian Casuals and Old Hertfordians and also for the British Army team and the Great Britain team. He played for England Amateurs between 1959 to 1965. He was also an academic who became a Professor of Arabic. He gave up playing football on his sixtieth birthday in 1997. I remember our tour to Moscow: he was a voracious drinker, yet he was always ready for training or to play matches. He was a good footballer and a very likeable and well respected character, who made everyone laugh around him.

We were always asked why do we keep on playing long after our sell-by date when logic and body screams after each game 'retire!' The answer was our collective love for the beautiful game, our deep respect for each other, the convivial sociability in which our weekly meetings are held, the hospitality, generosity and friendship extended to us by all the schools we played at, and last, but not least, the dread of the ultimate condemnation: 'No passion'.

Brian Wakefield the manager of the CC Vets, wrote:

Yes, Peter Kitchen was introduced to the club by Colin Booth, who played for us and also played with Peter for the Commentators XI. He thought Peter would be ideal for the team as he enjoyed playing in a relaxed atmosphere with players that he could relate to and was not averse to socialising in the bar after the game. Moreover he was a proven goalscorer.

Peter made his debut for the Vets against Christ's Hospital, a school in Horsham on 20th February 1991. He played only a handful of games that and the following season but from the 1992-93 season he played on a more regular basis. During the course of fifteen seasons, he played in 228 games, scoring a remarkable 280 goals. His most successful season was in 1995-96 when he scored 40 goals from 25 appearances.

Peter fitted easily in the Veterans scenario – he was a quality player who could score goals and relate to the style of play, which was free-flowing football aimed to show the schoolboys how the game should be played.

If Peter was comfortable on the pitch, he was just as comfortable in the post-match inquests. It was customary for the team to retire to a local hostelry, chosen for its ambience, which had become a regular haunt whenever we played in that locality. He was equally comfortable when on tour and was keenly interested in such tourist locations as the Kremlin and the Cape. One got the impression that he found the environment more fulfilling than he experienced when he played professionally.

To conclude, Peter was a great asset to Corinthian Casuals and since his retirement in 2005, at the ripe old age of fifty-three, he will be greatly missed.

Peter' remarkable seasonal records with the CC Vets were as follows:

Season	Appearances	Goals
1990-91	4	7
1991-92	5	13
1992-93	19	25
1993-94	15	24
1994-95	11	12
1995-96	17	24
1996-97	25	40
1997-98	10	17
1998-99	10	13
1999-2000	20	26
2000-2001	16	17
2001-2002	18	18
2002-2003	22	20
2003-2004	20	15
2004-2005	16	9
Totals	**228**	**280**

Playing many New Year's for the Jim Rosenthal XI

I have played these past few years for the Jim Rosenthal XI in Cookham Dean in Bucks against local sides and in the last game I played, the former Watford, Liverpool and England star John Barnes played up front alongside me. Richard Keys, Alan Parry, Gordon Riddick (ex-Orient) and the former Oxford United man Malcolm Shotton also played for us.

Jim arranged a charity match between his select XI and the Cookham Dean Vets XI. We won the first match but lost the last two games.

Chapter 16
After Epping, moves to Kent

In 1996, as previously mentioned, I moved out of the house in Epping I had bought with Sharon back in 1984 and initially I bought a flat in an old Georgian complex in the town. A neighbour of mine who occasionally shared a BBQ and a bottle or two of wine was Justine Greening. Born in Rotherham in 1969, she was then a Financial Manager with Centrica Plc, and was also involved in politics as a local councillor in Epping.

Justine Greening became a Cabinet Minister in the previous Tory government as well as in the last coalition government, firstly as the Transport secretary and later as the Minister for Overseas Aid and Development. She has again, been reelected as the Tory MP for Putney in the General Election on May 7th of this year and has retained her job in Prime Minister, David Cameron's new cabinet.

She was elected as the Tory MP for Putney in May 2005 with 15,497 votes, unseating the Labour MP Tony Colman. It would not surprise me if she became a future Prime Minister in the mould of Margaret Thatcher, she has determination with much tenacity to get things done.

I lived there for three years but I realised I couldn't keep commuting to Sevenoaks in Kent on a daily basis, so I bought a house in Farningham, near Dartford in Kent.

I'm now happily ensconced in Kent and living and working in the Sevenoaks District, as the Operations Director of the Sencio Community Leisure Company, which operates the four leisure centres and a golf course in partnership with Sevenoaks District Council. I live in the village of Farningham, near Dartford after moving there in 2000. I have now worked in the Leisure industry for over twenty years since hanging up my boots.

We currently operate four Leisure centres, three of which are large complexes with a variety of leisure facilities as well as a Public Golf course with both 9 and 18 holes, a Pitch and Putt course and a driving range, so this keeps me very busy and focused.

We are a small management team, led by the Managing Director, Mark Whyman, and we recognised that if we continued to work for the District Council we would just continue to face cuts in expenditure and Services. We established an Independent Company in January 2004 and so far the venture has proved successful and we made a healthy surplus in our first full year of trading. Although very demanding, it is nice to be working with more autonomy and with more business focus and less 'Political restraint'.

As you can see, today I enjoy living in Kent...

Peter And Katherine at Peter's 60th Birthday Party, Feb 2012.

In September 2006, I moved from Farningham in Kent and with my partner Katherine, who also sold her house, we bought a house together, a lovely 200 year old cottage with lots of character, in the pretty village of Ightham, near Sevenoaks in Kent. Ightham is in an area of outstanding natural beauty and because of it's location close to London, is ideal for making regular trips to the capital or via the channel tunnel to Europe as well as all the major road and rail networks and even close to Gatwick for our regular holidays abroad.

In November 2009, at the age of 57 years old, I was offered the chance to take early retirement, which was an opportunity too good to pass up, especially as I hadn't been enjoying work for the previous 2 years. The Company agreed to enhance my final salary pension, which meant that I would be financially sound and would not need to work again. In the latter part of my working career, my mantra had become ' Work to Live ' and not ' Live for work ' because I believe that life is so very short and that it should be about experiences, activities and doing things and certainly not about material things . I would describe myself as someone who always tries to look forward, so I couldn't wait to start the next chapter in my life.

In February 2012, I celebrated my 60th Birthday at the George and Dragon, the local pub in my village and was very pleased to celebrate with my family, close friends and many old friends from football, my TV Commentators team mates, John Motson, who had just been awarded an OBE came along with his wife Anne, as well as Jim Rosenthal, with his wife Chrissy.

"I love retirement and now have much more time for myself, so Katherine and I are able to keep very fit and active and we either go walking, jogging or cycling near our home virtually every day and I realise now that our health is the most cherished thing we all have as we get older.

Katherine and I also go skiing every year to either France or Austria and I have become quite a good intermediate skier, especially after buying my own customised fitted boots ! She prefers to do mountain walking rather than skiing, but in 2012 we both managed a skiing trip to the resort of Rusutsu in Hokkaido Japan, with my son Michael and his family when we visited them in Japan the month after my 60th Birthday. We wanted to go to Japan to celebrate Yoko's 40th Birthday in April and to see my grandchildren, Alfie and Tommy and to meet my new Granddaughter, Atalie Sumire, who is now 4 years old and a very beautiful little girl.

**Peter's granddaughter
Atalie, 18 months old, 2012**

Coincidentally, in the last 2 years, I have been able to see much more of my grandson Alfie, who is now 14 years old and at boarding school in the UK. He has stayed with me on many occasions, either at weekends or when on school holidays from Gordon's School, which is near Woking in Surrey.

Well the last few years have been very eventful and Katherine and I have been enjoying some really nice holidays. We spend some time with Katherine's daughters, Louisa and Samantha

**Peter with his grandchildren, Tommy,
Atalie, and Alfie.**

and their respective husbands, Richmond and Alex and Katherine's grandchildren and in August 2013, we all went for a long weekend to Honfleur and Deauville in Normandy, France and a day at Deauville racecourse.

(Left) Peter with a Bottle of
Chateau Margeaux,
a 60th Birthday Present from
Michael & Yoko.

Peter with his son Michael

(Left) Peter with Michael,
Katherine, and Yoko March 2012

In 2014, I bought a BMW Convertible and Katherine and I ' christened ' this by doing a wonderful 3 week driving holiday to the South of France, via the wine regions of the Loire and Bordeaux, following the *canal du midi* to the medieval city of Carcassonne, the Roman town of Arles where Vincent Van Gough lived and where he painted some of his finest work, finally staying in Villefranche Sur Mer, close to Nice on the French Riviera, before coming back via Monaco, Italy and Germany.

Peter With Katherine 's grandchildren at Deauville Racecourse, in Normandy, July 2013. (From L- R) Louie, Zac, Yasmin, and Bailey.

In February of this year (2015), we had a fantastic 3 week trip to the USA, initially staying a week in my timeshare

Peter 'posing' in his new BMW Convertible, 2014.

**Peter with Jose Antonio,
Malaga, April 2015**

in Cocoa Beach, Florida, before flying to Los Angeles and then driving down the Pacific coast highway from Santa Monica via Long beach and Newport beach to San Diego, before then driving to Las Vegas for a week. It was amazing to see how much Las Vegas had changed and grown since I played Indoor soccer there 30 years before and I was able to make a nostalgic visit to the Thomas & Mack stadium where we used to play our home matches.

Over the past few years, we have also had the time to make at least 3 visits each year to Katherine's apartment near Malaga and have met and made some very good Spanish friends. Jose Antonio and his wife Loli have welcomed us into

Peter with Jose Antonio's family, Malaga, April 2015. (Left to Right: Carlos, Juanfri, Peter, Katherine, Loli, Jose Antonio, Jorge, Lorena, Antonio (behind Loli and Jose Antonio), Mario (right of Lorena), Mamen and Paqui.

their wonderful family and we always look forward to a lunch at their beach-front house where such specialities as freshly caught and cooked Giant squid and Galician octopus are regularly served along with some wonderful tapas and of course lots of wine .

Jose Antonio coaches football for the local boys team who his grandsons play forand he is also a season ticket holder at Spanish La Liga team Malaga, so football is always a universal language between us. Jose Antonio's son Carlos and his friend Juanfri have also been a great help to Katherine and I with language translation and communications and a great source of information on Spanish food and on new musical inspiration.

I recently bought myself a new Apple iphone 6 and joined Facebook, so I guess I have finally landed in the 21st Century!!

Chapter 17
On a Personal Note

The first thing I must just point out is that I am not at all related to the cricketing umpire by the surname of Kitchen or the actor Michael Kitchen who has appeared in several of the recent James Bond movies and also in the lead role in the TV series 'Foyles War.'

For my hobbies they would include music, I love the group REM, whom my son Michael turned me onto back in 1987. REM are a very innovative rock band that try to produce a new style with each album whilst not losing their very distinctive sound as well as being politically and environmentally aware. I also think Michael Stipe, theirlead singer has a great voice and writes the best ever love songs and he is probably the person I would now most like to meet (because I think he would be very interesting and definitely NOT because he is bi-sexual). I also like Morrissey, the Cranberries, Natalie Merchant, Tracy Chapman and previously Fleetwood Mac and Pink Floyd.

I do, however, have a very diverse taste in music and I have a very large collection of CDs and vinyl records. I also collect commemorative cups and mugs. I have a great interest in the First and Second World Wars and collect books on these and I go on an annual pilgrimage to the battlefields.

Peter with friends Duncan Sturrock and Bill Yates at the grave of Richard McFadden, (Clapton Orient player killed in WW1, 1916) in the British Cemetary in Couin, France.

This first started around 1980, when I was at Fulham, when I was invited by my great friend Duncan Sturrock and a group of his friends during the close season. Duncan and his wife Jean and their two sons were the first family friends I made when moving to Epping and we have remained close friends ever since. He is a Reading FC supporter and I am pleased that they are doing so well and hopefully May 2006 will see them reach the Premiership for the first time in their history. They are doing so well and May 2006 saw them reach the Premiership for the first in their history.

At the time of this first Somme visit I had no specific motive, other than it was somewhere different to go. I found the whole area and experience so moving that it had a profound effect on me. It was then that I became fascinated and wanted to learn more about the Great War and in particular the Battle of the Somme.

Over the years we made quite a few friends with some of the locals, none more so than with Thierry Gaudefroy, the owner of the 3 Pigeons Bar, situated next to the Basilique Cathedral, in the centre of Albert.

Whenever I visit the Somme area, I just feel I owe the soldiers who gave their lives a great debt of gratitude and it always makes me feel very fortunate to have enjoyed a successful playing career as a professional footballer, without having to face anything worse than just a few heavy knocks from the odd late tackles.

Bill Yates, and Thierry Gaudefroy (owner of the Three Pigeons Bar) with Peter June 2006-in Albert, France.

So this is the reason for me to happily write the Foreword to a book written by Leyton Orient's Supporters Club Deputy Chairman, Stephen Jenkins, on the O's players involvement in the First World War entitled '*They Took the Lead*', published in December 2005, and a fine book it is too. I have also written another foreword for the revised edition of this book, which was updated and reprinted in July 2014

I am also an avid reader when I get the chance and always like to have a good book when I am on holiday. I also occasionally buy second-hand books. My favourite TV series is Rising Damp, starring the late Leonard Rossiter who I think was a comedy genius. I never get tired of seeing Rigsby try to seduce Miss Jones and my son Michael bought me the complete series on video for my 50th Birthday. To move on, I also really enjoy cooking and I cook a lot at home and one of my inspirations is Keith Floyd. He always has to have a 'slurp' from the drink in his hand and he never measures the quantities in the pan and always makes cooking look like fun.

Finally, I just love travelling, which I have done a lot of in my life and in the overseas tours all around the world, with the Corinthian Casuals Veterans team. I always watch the Michael Palin travel documentaries and have several of his books from the series. Although I am very committed in my job, I would say that I work to live as opposed to living for work. I have completely changed my priorities and I have to know that my next trip is already booked so that I can count down the weeks in between. As often as possible I try to go to France either for a daytrip or a long weekend, and I really enjoy the laidback way of life there and the café culture as well as the wine and food.

Life is definitely too short and it seems only like yesterday when I made my League debut for Rovers in 1970. What has become so apparent is that our health is the most important thing to have, as we get older. I have always taken my fitness for granted and have been quite a heavy drinker over the years, however in March 2000 I was diagnosed with Ulcerative Colitis which is a degenerative disease of the colon and very uncomfortable when it is active. With the help of my doctor, John Fraser (who incidentally is the club doctor for Charlton Athletic FC) and my Consultant Dr. Walter Melia (a rugby rather than football man based in Blackheath) I have been able to keep it under control, although I have had to cut down substantially on my alcohol intake.

It has made me very aware of the food I eat and I now have a very healthy diet. I just wish I had known how important this was whilst I was playing professionally as I am sure it would have helped improve my fitness and performance.

I have some close friends in Duncan Sturrock and Roger Smith, who I mentioned earlier, but I probably spend more time with Bill Yates who I became friends with in 1996 when at 44 I found myself living alone for the first time in my life since I was 18. Bill had a career in the City with the NatWest Bank and avoiding giving his money to any ex-wives he was available to go on holidays with and at that time to occasionally drink to excess, although never as much as I did. We have lots of similar interests and have been good mates for over 10 years now.

I also spend a lot of time with my current girlfriend, Katherine Corbett, who I would describe as the kindest and most considerate person I have known, someone who is most supportive in everything I do.

We have been together for about five years and although we don't live together at this time, we are considering that as a possible future option. In 2006, Katherine and I were planning to buy a new home, and O's legend Peter Allen, who is a solicitor, is helping us with the legal aspects of our future investment. We make quite a few trips to Southern Spain where Katherine has an apartment and we may consider living there in the winter months when we have retired. Katherine is a Beauty Therapist, who has also trained in nutrition and weight management and she is also a fitness coach.

There have been some recent lows in my life. 2003 was not a happy one for me with the death of my son Darren at the age of only twenty-eight from a brain haemorrhage.

And March 2005 was a very sad time with the death of my mum, more recently the news that my former wife Susan has breast cancer, although I understand that the treatment she has been undergoing has been effective.

On a happier note, during September and October 2005, I visited my son Michael and his family in Osaka, Japan, consequently I missed out on another football tour with the Corinthian Casual Vets in August 2005 to Cape Town, South Africa. Although I have just announced my retirement from playing with the Vets, It is with some regret that I will not be playing every week, but I have told Brian Wakefield that if he is desperate for players then on the odd occasion I will squeeze the shorts on again and so I would have loved to have visited South Africa again and a meeting up with Neil Kaufman in Johannesburg.

Honoured by both Orient and Doncaster in August 2003

It was a privilege to be at the Matchroom Stadium on 9 August 2003 to be honoured by both my former clubs during the interval of the opening League match of the season and to held in high esteem by both clubs and their fans. It was nice to see both sets of supporters on the day very 'positive' towards each other and not the usual Home and Away fan mentality!!

**Peter receives the acclaim of both sets of supporters
at the Orient v Rovers match, August 2003.**

The Goal Gourmet

My girlfriend and I were guests of the club and we were right royally entertained by the O's Vice Presidents club. At half time I was presented with two inscribed cut glass decanters, one from both clubs, one from the Rovers chairman John Ryan And I was honoured during a lap of honour with a standing ovation from both sets of supporters.

This was a very emotional occasion as it is not a common occurrence for a player to receive this acclaim from both the home and away sets of supporters. It was Rovers first match back in the Football League, which they won 3-1.

The Peter Kitchen Bar

In front of the Peter Kitchen Bar at Leyton Orient, 2003.

A few years ago when I was told that a bar at Brisbane road had been named after me. I felt very honored and was very proud of this since I was quite a heavy drinker at the time - and having a bar named for you is quite an accolade. However on my annual trip to the ground my euphoria was cooled when I discovered that "The Peter Kitchen Bar" was, in fact, a burger and snack bar... seriously though, I am still very honored by both this and the naming of a block of flats after me.

Block of Flats named for Kitchen near Matchroom Stadium

When one considers more than 950 players have appeared for the club, I feel very honoured that one of the block of flats near The Leyton Orient FC ground has been named after me. The four blocks are called Kitchen Court, Johnston Court, Bloomfield Court, and Cunningham Court.

The names were chosen by Bellway Homes, the company that owns the flats, after consultation with the club and the fans - they selected what they felt were

Kitchen Court at the Matchroom Stadium, completed in 2006.

the four of the greatest names in the club's history. These are myself, Tommy Johnston, Jimmy Bloomfield and Laurie Cunningham. I am very happy that my name was reckoned among them.

Chapter 18
What Of The Future for
Both Doncaster And The O's

It was a tense and nerve wracking match at Oxford United in May 2006, when O's had to win to gain promotion to League One after almost sixteen years in the basement division and they did it in the last minute with a goal from Lee Steele, who took his chance professionally, for a 3-2 win, which condemned them to relegation into the Nationwide Conference and Grimsby Town for another season of League Two football, after losing in the play-off 's.

It was great to see them do it with an attacking style of play and I was very happy for all those involved with the club, Barry Hearn, Stephen Jenkins, David Dodd, manager Martin Ling and his assistant Dean Smith and of course all the loyal fans who have turned up year-after year to support their team.

So the match culminated what was a wonderful season for the O's, a great FA Cup run and a promotion.

I have admired what Barry Hearn has achieved at the club, they have a wonderful new stadium and all is set for some great times.

Forrmer O's players at Leyton Orient's 125th anniversary dinner in 2006. Peter, bottom row, 3rd from left.

And what of Rovers?

I am also a great admirer of John Ryan, the Chairman, who has transformed the club over the last few years and it would not surprise me if they were promoted to the championship this season. Their crowds are the best they have been for years and this really shows what a difference a supporter can make who is prepared to put his money into the club and by also making the right decision in terms of the manager he appoints.

I was invited down to Rovers on 29 November 2005 for their televised League Carling Cup clash with Premiership side Aston Villa, and I most impressed with their 3-0 victory, covered live by Sky Sport, I met Alan Parry, who was commentating with Chris Kamara and so the cameras panned on me a couple of times during the match, I met the Villa chairman Doug Ellis, and a Rovers shirt was presented by chairman John Ryan before the match and when I did a lap of honour I was greeted with a tremendous reception from the Rovers fans.

Peter in the Rovers shirt presented to him by John Ryan.

The Villa players kicked the ball to me and then I did a Johan Cruyff turn and kicked the ball back to them to the delight of the crowd. It was a suburb evening.In the quarter final Rovers narrowly went out of the Carling Cup to 'lucky' Arsenal, after a penalty shootout.

Well, isn't that that just great with both O's and Donny facing each other in 2006-2007! Who knows, maybe we shall see both teams promoted in May 2007.

I am really looking forward to seeing the Rovers new ground which is due to open in December 2006. Seeing the Rovers play in a New Community Stadium will be a fitting tribute to the contributions by John Ryan and his fellow Directors, and for the loyal fans who have supported them through the lean spells.

The fans and I wait in great anticipation!

The new Community Stadium opened in December 2006.

Donny and the O's become 'Yo Yo' Club

Well a lot of things have happened at Doncaster and the Orient since the first book was written in 2006 and I have been able to watch my old clubs on many occasions since, in addition, I have become involved in some of their community initiatives personally .

In December, 2006, I attended an 'End of an Era' dinner at the Dome in Doncaster, where I met up with some of my old team mates including big Brendan O'Callaghan and also with my former manager Stan Anderson. I have since been a guest of the club at the new Keepmote stadium on several occasions, which is very impressive and to see how John Ryan and the Board of Directors have developed the club is fantastic. Doncaster Rovers have enjoyed a period of huge success over the past 8 years and hopefully they can continue to build upon this.

I was a guest of the Club at the Johnstone's Paint Trophy final at the Millennium stadium in Cardiff, which Rovers won in 2007 against Bristol Rovers and in 2008 Katherine and I were guests in the Royal box at Wembley, when Rovers beat Leeds United 1-0 in the Play Off final to gain promotion to the Championship for the first time in over 50 years ?

It was a fantastic day and Rovers thoroughly deserved their victory, much to the annoyance of several of the old Leeds United ' Greats ', Peter Lorimer and Norman Hunter, who I bumped into during an after match toilet break !!

Although Rovers were relegated just 3 years later ; in 2013 it was fantastic to witness the most amazing finish to a game I have ever seen in my time watching football. I was a guest of the club at their last league match of the season away at Brentford, who needed a draw to gain the second automatic promotion spot, whilst Rovers had to win and other results go their way for them to gain automatic promotion.

Before the match, John Ryan, the Rovers Chairman asked me to come onto the pitch with him and another Director of the club, Dick Watson, to applaud the fans for their support and for making the journey to the game. It was an amazing experience to have my name chanted and to be cheered by the Rovers fans behind the goal so long after I last played for the club.

The game was a fairly tense affair and 0-0 at the end of normal time. The game went into added time and with 4 minutes of this already played, Brentford were awarded a penalty, meaning the outcome now seemed a forgone conclusion, however, the Brentford No 9; Trotta, on loan from Fulham, took the ball from their normal penalty taker and prepared to take the penalty kick himself. Amazingly, the ball rebounded off the bar and was hooked clear by a Rovers defender to another Rovers players who raced the full length of the pitch before crossing to the far post for James Coppinger, who had also sprinted forward, to control the ball and fire into an empty net. The fans went delirious and with the news that Bournemouth had failed to win their game, it meant that Rovers had won the Division One Championship.

**Peter before the Brentford game with
Doncaster Rovers fans behind the goal - April 2013**

Last month, James Coppinger had a testimonial match at the Keepmote stadium for his 11 years service for the club and I was asked to write a contribution for the match day commemorative programme."

Unfortunately Rovers have since been relegated to Division 1 and finished this season in a mid table position, with Paul Dickov as the manager . Earlier in 2015, after a failed attempt at gain outright control of the club in a partnership with Louis Tomlinson, a member of the Boyband, One Direction, John Ryan has relinquished the Chairmanship and has severed his ties with the club that he has supported since he was a boy.

On a positive note for myself, I was immensely proud to be told that Rovers have named one of the Bars at the Keepmote stadium after me, similar to the one at Leyton Orient and I feel very honoured to now have a ' Peter's Kitchen' bar so named at their ground and now at two stadiums

The 'Peter's Kitchen' bar at the Keepmote Stadium, Doncaster, 2015

At Orient, there have also been a number of changes at the club and early in the 2014/15 season, the owner, Barry Hearn sold the club to an Italian businessman, however the fortunes of the club on the pitch have gone downhill since and after the departure of manager Russell Slade to Cardiff City and 3 further management changes during the season, the club were relegated to Division 2 on the last day of the season away at Swindon Town.

This was such a contrast to 12 months ago when in May 2014, the club reached the Division One Play Off final at Wembley. I was in the Royal box as a guest of David Dodd, Chairman of the Orient Supporters club and a Director of the club at the time, for the final against Rotherham United. At Half time, Orient were winning 2-0 and playing so well that it seemed that all they had to do was to see out the second half and they would be in the Championship, however they were stunned by 2 Rotherham goals in the second half, one by Alex Revill, a former Orient player and the match went to extra time. Neither team managed to score and the game then went to penalties, with Rotherham winning the penalty shoot out and condemning Orient to another season in Division One.

It was such an anticlimax to a great season of euphoria and only a week before, at the Player of the Year dinner at the Dorchester hotel in Park Lane, watched by Orient supporters, Lord Andrew Lloyd Webber and his brother Julian, I presented an award to David Mooney, the first Orient player to score 20 goals in a season since I achieved this feat in 1978.

Following the clubs relegation this season, the Manager has again been sacked and there are already rumours circulating that the new Italian owner wants to sell the club, so what the future holds for this wonderful little club is anyone's guess.

In the last few years, I have been actively involved with the Supporters club and I have been asked on several occasions, to attend Birthday Parties and Wedding receptions of Orient supporters and also to make after dinner speeches, which I find very flattering so long after I played for the club and I am immensely proud to be held in such high esteem by Orient fans. I also wrote a foreword for Neil Kaufman's book, The Official Leyton Orient Quiz book, published in September 2012 .

It has also just been confirmed that I will be appearing as a substitute in an ' Orient Legends' game against a ' Harry Redknapp's X1 ' at the end of May, who will have in his team, the comedian, TV & Film actor Russell Brand amongst many others. This is for the Prostate cancer charity and will be held at the Matchroom stadium and despite not having kicked a ball in 9 years, it will be a wonderful experience to again run out onto the Orient pitch at 63 years old, wearing the No 26 shirt and I just hope that I can bag a goal or two !!

I am still friends with Dennis Barefield, the ' Sparky ', who was the Orient fan who welcomed me to the club on my first day of pre season training in 1977 as told earlier. I have also become a close friend of Steve Jenkins and David Dodd and attend quite a few social functions with David, who in 2011 was presented with the ' Freedom of the City of London ' for his services to Leyton Orient Football club at a ceremony at the Guildhall, conducted by the Clerk to the Chamberlain, Murray Craig, incidentally a Luton Town supporter "

David Dodd: Chairman of the Leyton Orient Supporters Club wrote:

"It is a pleasure to be asked to place on record some thoughts about Peter for this revised edition of his book.

Without doubt he is one of the most prolific goalscorers to ever wear the O's shirt, Peter Kitchen thrilled so many of the club's fans during his two all too brief spells with the club. Peter's two fantastic goals at Stamford Bridge in the O's victory over Chelsea in the fifth round FA Cup replay in 1978 are the most prominent among my favourite never to be forgotten personal memories of Peter the footballer

- more so as the game was played on my birthday, the 27th February, and so gave me one of the best birthday presents I have ever had !

At that time I really only knew Peter as an O's player and it wasn't until his second term with the club when he began to come into the Supporters Club and the old players bar with some of his team mates for a post match drink that I started to get to know more about him.

David Dodd is made a 'Freedom of the City of London' at the Guildhall, for his services to Leyton Orient FC, pictured with Murray Craig, Clerk to the Chamberlain, 2011.

Over the years Peter has shown a great interest in the activities and progress of the Supporters Club to which he is a frequent and much welcomed visitor. Aside from his invaluable help and guidance with the O's Somme Memorial project, outlined elsewhere by my friend and O's colleague Steve Jenkins, Peter has made guest speaker appearances, attended book launches, helped with fund raising projects and provided useful input and guidance on a number of issues relating to the Supporters Club.

Peter in the Orient Supporters club in 2014 with Dennis Barefield - 'The Sparky.' Dennis was the O's fan who he met on the first day of training in 1977.

On a more personal level Peter has become a very good friend with whom I have shared many enjoyable times at lunches and events of all kinds. I was particularly honoured to have had Peter along as a special guest when I was presented with the Freedom of the City of London at a ceremony in 2011.

Peter is an interesting conversationalist and raconteur on a broad range of life's topics aside from his obvious interest in football related matters, and very convivial company to be in. It is a pleasure to enjoy his friendship.

Peter will always be regarded as a true O's legend and I feel sure that readers of The Goal Gourmet will enjoy learning more about Peter the footballer and Peter the man. I wish him all success with the book and for the future."

David Dodd
May 2015

Being remembered and Honoured even Today

My affinity with both Doncaster Rovers and Leyton Orient and my popularity with their fans still amazes me even after all these years and I feel very honoured to have such a special place in the history of both clubs.

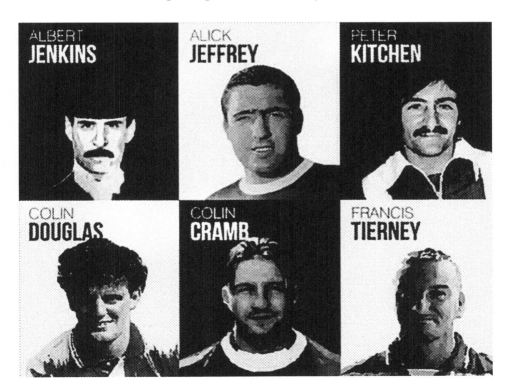

205

The Goal Gourmet

I have just learned that a flag featuring '6 Legendary Players' who have played for the club over several decades since the 2nd World war, is being erected on the 'Black bank', behind the goal at the Keepmote stadium in Doncaster. The players were voted for by Rovers fans and include the late, great Alec Jefferies amongst others and I am very proud that I have been included amongst them and my name and face will be on the flag.

As an occasional visitor to see Orient home games, I am often invited to walk on the pitch and it is always an amazing feeling to be greeted so warmly by fans. I have also been asked by Leyton Orient , to be an Ambassador for the clubs new 'Walking Football fitness initiative' aimed at getting older men and women from the local community, involved in regular exercise and I will be helping the club launch this new initiative on September 17th, 2015 taking part in a game and culminating in a 'Question and Answer' session afterwards.

Chapter 19
The Managers I played for

During my long professional League career some fifteen years I had played for a number of managers, well, these are my opinions of each one of them, with a profile from published sources at the end and their managerial career records.

Lawrie McMenamy—Doncaster Rovers 1970-71
Maurice Setters—Doncaster Rovers 1971-74
John Quigley—Doncaster Rovers 1974-75
Stan Anderson—Doncaster Rovers 1974-77
George Petchey—Orient 1977
Jimmy Bloomfield—Orient 1977-79
Bobby Campbell—Fulham 1979-80
Richie Morgan—Cardiff City – 1980-81
Ken Knighton—Orient 1982-83
Frank Clark—Orient 1983-84
Mickey Speight—Chester City 1985

Lawrie McMenemy 1970-71

He was a very imposing figure, standing at about 6ft 4ins, with a very strong Geordie accent, coming from Gateshead. I only played under him for one season, but he had charisma and I could tell he had insight into the psychology of the players. His real strength was in motivating players rather than in coaching.

He would talk to players on an individual basis and changed his style to suit their different temperaments rather than bellowing at everyone indiscriminately. He was a great advocate of being very fit and made sure we trained very hard. He used to often have us running around the Doncaster racecourse, although fortunately never over the hurdles!!

I always remember some of the things he would shout about during training session, i.e. when we were doing the hard running sessions, he would say 'If you cheat at this you are only cheating yourselves' and 'The good habits you get now in training will stay with you all through your careers'.

These McMenemy principles stayed with me throughout my playing career and no matter what I had done the night before, I never missed training and always trained as hard as I could. I was very disappointed when he was sacked and it certainly put the brakes on my career taking off for a few more seasons.

When he took over at Grimsby Town, it was reported that he had taken the Grimsby players to the docks at 4am to watch the fisherman bringing in their daily catch and made the point to the players of just how lucky they were to be footballers and this was 'real' work. Needless to say, Grimsby won promotion under his management. I really liked Lawrie and I am very glad that he went onto have an illustrious career in management, which he thoroughly deserved.

Lawrie McMenemy was born in Saltwell Park, Gateshead on 26 July 1936, an injury ended his own playing career with Newcastle United in 1961 and he was appointed coach with Gateshead, he moved to Bishop Auckland as manager and coach in 1964 and guided them to the League championship of the Northern League and County Cup winners. In 1966, he was appointed coach of Sheffield Wednesday, after two years came his big chance when being appointed manager of Doncaster Rovers, taking them to the Fourth Division championship in the 1968-69 season. When Rovers chairman Fred Wilson was ousted for local builder Ben Bailey it spelled the end of McMenemy. In 1971, he was appointed manager of Grimsby Town in 1971 and they won promotion as Fourth Division in 1971-72.

He was appointed as manager of Southampton in 1973, and oversaw them during one of the most successful periods in their history with an FA Cup Final victory over Manchester United in 1976 and First Division runners-up in 1983.

He has held numerous positions in football, including MD of Sunderland FC between 1985 and 1987, Assistant Manager of the England National Team to Graham Taylor between 1990 to 1994, VP of the League Managers Association between 1992 to the present, Director of Football at Southampton between 1994 to 1998, manager of the Republic of Ireland between 1998 to 2000. McMenemy is today rated in the Guinness Book of Records as one of the top twenty most successful managers in post-war football. In 2002, he was appointed an Ambassador to the Football Association.

He has appeared on numerous TV shows, a football analyst, and is an after dinner speaker of note and also speaks on motivation and management.

McMenemy's Managerial Career Record (League and Cup)

	From	To	P	W	D	L
Doncaster Rovers	Nov-68	May 197	118	40	35	43
Grimsby Town	May-71	Jul-73	93	49	15	29
Southampton	Nov-73	Jun-85	539	225	144	170
Sunderland	Jun-85	Apr-87	85	26	22	37
TOTAL			**835**	**40**	**216**	**79**

Maurice Setters 1971—1974

Setters had been a 'big name' player in his career having played for Manchester United amongst other clubs and had a reputation as a 'hard man' and one he really enjoyed and played up to. He was a bit 'flash' for Doncaster in those days and he drove a new leather seated racing green Jaguar car.

He appeared to me as an arrogant, aggressive character, who expected every player to adopt the 'Kick, Bollock and Bite' mentality that he had. He had been a player of limited ability but he had made the most of his opportunities and there was no doubting his commitment and 'win at all costs' approach.

He was an intelligent manager in football terms and he did have some good ideas. I always listened to him and tried to do the things that he asked of me to do and so I learned quite a lot from him. He often talked about how a good player Denis Law was and how sharp he was in and around the penalty area, especially in anticipating chances. He taught me about deception on the field, i.e. shouting to team mates and opponents 'my ball' when he was going to attack the ball before suddenly dropping off and collecting the ball comfortably because the opposing forward had ducked out of the challenge that never came.

I recall one game, we were playing Aldershot away, I was on the subs bench and at half time we were 3-0 down. As the half time whistle blew he stood up, began shouting obscenities in the direction of the players and referee coming off the field of the pitch and then he turned and kicked the trainers bucket and sponge into the crowd, completely soaking some of the spectators at the side of dugout.

After giving all the players a roasting and demanding an improvement in the second half, he turned to me and said that we were so bad he wouldn't embarrass me by bringing me on, then there was a knock on the dressing room door. He opened the door, and was faced with a policeman and a middle-aged lady, who looked somewhat bedraggled and dripping wet from the water that the boss had thrown over her.

The policeman proceeded to inform him that the lady had made an official complaint as she had been to the hairdressers that morning and her hair was now ruined thanks to him.

In true Setters style, he immediately got out a five pound note and his words to the policeman was for the woman to take the money and next time to have her f***ing hair done properly!

One of the downsides to his management style was that I always felt that he had his favourites and this was quite evident to most of the players as he often only singled out certain players for criticism.

I must admit I wasn't disappointed to see him go and I felt like a weight had been lifted off my shoulders and I think a relief to most of the other players. His dour play and physical game saw Rovers having to apply for re-election in 1973-74 and were on the way to doing so again the following season, when he was fired.

On the plus side, he did bring though a number of good youngsters in the Doncaster side like Mike Elwiss, Terry Curran, Brendan O'Callaghan, Steve Uzelec and Steve Wignall

Maurice Edgar Setters was born in Honiton, Devon on 16 December 1936, he started playing football with Honiton & Cullompton Schoolboys, he signed as an amateur with Exeter City before turning pro' two years later. In January 1955, he signed for West Bromwich Albion for £3000 and after playing 120 games, scoring 12 goals, he moved to Manchester United in 1959 for a fee of £30,000 and won an FA Cup winners' medal in 1962, after playing in 159 games, with 12 goals, he then played for Stoke City, Coventry City and Charlton Athletic, with a total of 434 appearances and 31 goals, he joined Doncaster Rovers as Manager as manager in August 1971.

He joined Rovers at a bad time with a lack of transfer funds and with the economy in recession and crowds falling even with the scoring of Kitchen and O'Callaghan, the defence was a problem, leaking 80 goals. In the 1974-75 season, the team was in poor shape with crowds down to just over one 1200 people and in November Setters was suspended by the club and John Quigley place in charge andthen he was formally sacked, he took the club to the Industrial Court and won

£1340 for unfair dismissal. It should be remembered that he had no cash to spend and he did bring in a fair number of decent youngsters.

He did not manage another club himself but became well known in his partnership with Jack Charlton together at Sheffield Wednesday and Newcastle United and then with Eire in 1986. They were both in charge at two World Cups in Italy (1990) and USA (1994) and to the Finals of the European Champions in 1998.

However, he also had his critics, Eoin Hand stated in January 2004, that a generation was lost while Setters was running the underage football in Ireland and player Roy Keane called Setters in his book Jack Charlton's sidekick and a 'yes man and a bluffer'. It was no surprise that they didn't like each other, as they had a bust-up in the States in 1994, when Keane was made to publicly apologise to Setters.

Setters' Managerial Career Record (League and Cup)

Team	From	To	P	W	D	L
Doncaster Rovers	Aug-1971	Nov-1974	157	47	42	68

John Quigley November Nov 1974 to Feb 1975

On the other hand john Quigley, or 'Quigs', as he was known, was a much more approachable man than Setters ever was, and certainly gave me more belief in myself.

He took over as caretaker-manager at Doncaster Rovers for a short time prior to the appointment of Stan Anderson as manager, he didn't really think he ever expressed a desire to have the job himself on a permanent basis.

He was a really nice guy and I remember one day he lent me his car to drive to Mexborough because I needed to go home to do something urgently.

He was always very encouraging of the players and he always played down his own career and used to say that he was merely a midfield ball winner and then he would give the ball to those players who could 'play' or create opportunities. He was actually a very intelligent player and a good passer of a ball.

He was a very competitive person and whenever we played in practice match-es he would tackle as it if was a league match. I specifically remember him coach-ing me on how to use my body to shield the ball from opponents.

He tended to be the counterbalance to Maurice Setters in that he would offer encouragement to try and motivate the players when Maurice had given them, collectively or individually, a rollicking. When Anderson came in I for one was very glad he kept 'Quigs' as his assistant. Quigley's last game in charge was the 7-4 defeat at Shrewsbury Town on 1 February 1975

I was very sad to hear of 'Quigs' death in November 2004.

John Quigley was born in Glasgow, Scotland on 28 June 1935, he started off with the amateur side Ashfield club before joining Nottingham Forest in 1957, making 236 appearances with 51 goals, he was a key figure in Forest's FA Cup success. He joined Huddersfield Town in 1964. He later played for both Bristol City and Mansfield Town. He was appointed manage of Doncaster Rovers in November 1974 and he made a total of 474 League appearances, scoring 64 goals.

He later spent time coaching in both Kuwait and Saudi Arabia. He returned to Nottingham and spent time coaching children, however after recovering from a stroke, he died suddenly at the Queen's Medical Centre on 30 November 2004, aged sixty-nine.

Quigley's Managerial Career Record (League and Cup)

Team	From	To	P	W	D	L
Doncaster Rovers	13/11/74	1/3/1975	14	2	4	8

Stan Anderson February 1975 to November 1979

Anderson was also a very different personality to Setters and appeared to be a very calm, composed and self-assured man. He had jet-black hair and having just come back from managing in Greece, he looked very suntanned and fit.

He called me into office and said that he had seen me play before and how much he rated me and that he wanted to build the team and the way we played around me, which was music to my ears.

He was a great advocate of passing the ball and playing attacking football and always told the players to get the ball into the penalty box as soon as they could when they were in the last third of the pitch. The great thing about this was he used to differentiate between just hoofing the ball in and playing it in, so he wanted me to attack the near the post and Brendan (O'Callaghan) the far post, and we worked at this a lot in training.

He would also tell the players to give the ball into my feet, even if I was closely marked, instead of me having to chase long hopeful balls over the top. This certainly played to my strengths and also to Brendan's game and when Ian Miller was brought into the side, it only got better for the two of us.

Anderson was a very thoughtful, intelligent manager and our style of play reflected this. We became a really good attacking side and very entertaining and we scored lots of goals as a team. I liked and respected Stan immensely, both as a person and as a manager, and he certainly knew how to motivate and to get the best out of me and the other players. When he won the Bells Manager of the Month Award, which he did on several occasions, he would always fill me up a bottle of whisky from the huge bottle he received from Bells.

Unfortunately, despite my improved playing and goal scoring performances, there was no sign of a move to a bigger club and I realised that the only way to get away from Belle Vue was to refuse to sign a new contract.

I had always hoped that Stan Anderson would get a top job in English football and come back to sign me, but this never happened.

Stan Anderson was born in Hordern on 27 February 1934, he started his playing career a junior with Sunderland. He had a long and distinguished career of fourteen years with Sunderland, Newcastle United and Middlesbrough, the right half made a total of 504 League appearances, scoring 45 goals. He moved in football management in April 1966 with Middlesbrough and stayed for seven years, after a brief spell in charge with Queens Park Rangers in 1974, he was appointed manager with Doncaster Rovers in February 1975 and after nearly three-years in charge, he was the manager of Bolton Wanderers in the 1980-81 season. Today Anderson lives in retirement in Doncaster.

Anderson's Managerial Career Record (League and Cups)

Team	From	To	P	W	D	L
Middlesbrough	1/5/1966	25/1/1973	305	130	81	94
QPR	7/10/1974	16/10/1974	6	1	2	3
Doncaster Rovers	3/3/1975	20/11/1978	174	67	47	60
Bolton Wanderers	28/1/1980	31/5/1981	62	17		27
TOTAL			547	216	147	184

George Petchey August 1977

I never really got to know George Petchey because he was sacked within the first week of the season, so he never enjoyed any of my or his team's success and which went onto enjoy a famous FA Cup run in 1978.

I say *his* team, because several of the players had come through the youth team policy he had put in place, like Paddy Grealish, Glenn Roeder, Bobby Fisher, Nigel Gray, whilst others he had brought from Crystal Palace, like Phil Hoadley, John Jackson, David Payne and Bill Roffey. He had also signed Joe Mayo and Allan Glover from West Bromwich Albion as part of the Laurie Cunningham deal and myself from Doncaster. Peter Allen had been a part of the furniture for more than ten-years, now that's what I call loyalty!

I had gone through the pre-season training and found George Petchey to be a very self-effacing individual, a really nice man and a good coach and I felt that with the players at the club we had the makings of a very good team. After losing the first League game at Luton Town by 1-0, we had a disastrous result at home to Blackpool by 4-1, he was then sacked by Chairman Brian Winston immediately after the game.

George William Petchey spent his entire playing and most of his managerial career with London teams. Born in Whitechapel, London on Wednesday 24 June 1931. He joined West Ham United in August 1948 making just two appearances before moving to QPR during July 1953.

It was with Rangers that Petchey made his name as a tough tackling wing-half, making 255 senior appearances in the six years with them, scoring 22 goals. In May 1960 he joined Crystal Palace and was ever present in their side that won promotion to Division Three.

A serious eye injury forced him to retire after 153 senior appearances, netting 12 goals. He was appointed youth team manager and then assistant manager.

He took over as O's boss on 12 July 1977 and during his first season at Brisbane Road, the club reached the sixth round of the FA Cup. In February 1972 he won the Bells whisky manager of the month award.

Petchey adopted the 'one-touch' style of football, made famous by Arthur Rowe, at the time an O's consultant, O's looked to be heading to the 'old' First Division in 1973-74, but they eventually stumbled in the second half of the season missing out by a single point, needing victory and two points versus Aston Villa in April, the match ended 1-1, so it was Carlisle United who were promoted instead.

Petchey guided O's to the Final of the Anglo Scottish Cup before losing to Nottingham Forest in the two-legged Final by 4-1, but gained some excellent victories along the way against Norwich City, Fulham, Chelsea, Aberdeen and Partick Thistle.

Like most O's managers, his biggest problem was to find a forward who could hit the net on a regular basis in fact out of a total of 254 matches under his charge, 89 were drawn, quite a number goalless, so it was a great pity that he never saw the fruits of Peter Kitchen's goal scoring feats with the club.

After his departure from Brisbane Road, he did not stay away from the game too long, being appointed Manager of Millwall in January 1978. He remained as boss until November 1980, however he was appointed their general manager.

In November 1982, Petchey became involved with Brighton & Hove Albion looking after their youth and reserve development. A year later he was promoted to chief coach and when their boss Chris Cattlin was fired in April 1986, taking charge for the final League match of the 1985-86 season, a 2-0 defeat at Hull City on 2nd May. He was asked to take over as Manager but decided to leave them soon afterwards. He scouted for both Sunderland and Watford, before retiring from the game. He was tempted to return to the Goldstone at the age of sixty-three in January 1994, as youth development officer under manager Liam Brady. Following Brady's departure in November 1995 he was appointed assistant to new boss Jimmy Case and took temporary charge following Case's dismissal in December 1996, although no first-team matches were played.

When Steve Gritt was appointed on 12 December 1996, Petchey left, but reaching retirement age, he continued to assist Brighton by helping look after the under-14 year old lads for nothing. Today, Petchey lives in retirement in Brighton, Sussex.

Petchey's Managerial Record (League and Cups)

Team	From	To	P	W	D	L
Leyton Orient	12/8/1971	26/8/1977	265	76	93	96
Millwall	5/2/1978	30/11/1980	129	42	32	55
Brighton & Hove A		May-86	1	0	0	1
TOTAL			**395**	**118**	**125**	**152**

Jimmy Bloomfield 1977 – 1979

When Jimmy Bloomfield first arrived at Brisbane Road, my initial thoughts were, 'Oh No', not another big-headed and arrogant football manager. Having been in charge of big money spenders in First Division, Leicester City, he breezed into the dressing room in his first meeting with the players looking very dapper in a three-piece pin stripped suit and told everyone that 'He was a First Division manager and he intended remaining that way'

The general gist of this meeting was that he was doing us all a favour by coming to Orient…

The Chairman Brian Winston had told the players the week before that the person he was after as the new manager, knew how much he wanted him to take the job and so he was 'pushing him very hard' This meaning that he was obviously demanding a lot of money and / or a huge salary to come to the club.

It was a very unsettling time for me as I had just come to the club and was in the process of buying a house and now I would have to impress a new manager all over again, who I didn't know and I wondered whether he had ever heard of or seen me play.

The first few games I played under Bloomfield, he wanted me to spend the whole time trying to stop the opponents full-back from breaking forward, so although I was working very hard at tracking back, I wasn't playing my natural game and not getting into the box enough, so being conscientious, very professional and keen to impress the new boss, I was listening to him and not to my instincts.

I recall an early game at the Baseball Ground against Derby County, which we lost 3-1. I had run my bollocks off but got nowhere, after the match several of my former Rovers team mates who had been watching, came to see me after the game and I remember Ian Miller specifically saying that I wasn't playing to my strengths, which really struck a cord with me.

I resolved after that match that I was going to play how I had always done with Doncaster and if the boss didn't like it, he would have to lump it or get rid of me. I was as good as my word and after making this commitment to myself, I started to play and score goals as I had done previously with Doncaster, and nothing was ever mentioned afterwards by Jimmy.

Jimmy wasn't a bad guy at all, in fact he was a very nice man really and quite a comical character.

I remember one of his team talks, it was away at Sheffield United, for the opener of the 1978-79 season, which he started by saying to the players 'Paddy (Tony Grealish), you will be Team Captain, Jacko (John Jackson) will you will Club Captain, Roff (Bill Roffey), you will be Vice-Captain, Peter (Bennett), you will be vice Club Captain, Bobby (Fisher) you will be Vice, Vice Team Captain!!!!

The Goal Gourmet

I think he must have realised how ridiculous he was sounding, so he suddenly said "In fact, you are all captains when you are out on the pitch." Anyway we won 2-1 and both big Joe Mayo and myself scored before a big crowd of over 19,000.

I have already made reference to other team talks in an earlier chapter about stopping the opposition players rather than playing to our strengths, about his lack of ambition and why I felt I needed to try and get away from Brisbane Road, I loved the people at the club and the fans but were they ever going to win anything under Jimmy Bloomfield and his defensive tactics, the answer was no.

James Henry 'Jimmy ' Bloomfield was born in North Kensington, London on Thursday 15 February 1934, the 5ft 9ins midfield player started his career with Hayes before joining Brentford in October 1952, making 42 League appearances, scoring 5 goals.

He moved to Arsenal in July 1954 for £ 8000 and stayed at Highbury for six-years, maturing into a brilliant midfield player, he made 210 League appearances, with 54 goals. He moved to Birmingham City in November 1960 for £30,000 he later had spells with Brentford and Plymouth Argyle before being appointed as O's player-manager on 8 March 1968, he made a total of 47 (2) senior appearances with 4 goals before retiring to concentrate with his managerial duties in May 1969.

His playing career spanned some seventeen years and he made a career total of 494 League appearances and scoring 93 goals. He joined Orient as player-manager from Plymouth Argyle on 8 March 1968.

Within two years of being in charge at Orient, he remarkably took the club to a Third Division Championship. It was no surprise that he would eventually end up in the 'old' First Division. He has some nice offers over the years, but the best would have been an offer from the Ethnikos club in Greece, who offered thirty-six year old Bloomfield a £20,000 a year deal to get the best young manager in the country, he decided to stay in England.

On O's Third Division championship winning season of 1969-70, he once remarked: "The rewarding thing about the way we won the title was the standard of football we achieved. There was no brute force, just skilful football."

He joined Leicester City on 23 June 1971 but not before they had to pay £5000 in compensation. At Filbert Street, Bloomfield was reported to be the highest paid manager in the League and led them to some successful seasons before he resigned on 23rd May 1977.He became a marketing consultant to Admiral, the Leicester based sportswear firm.

Bloomfield was not in the soccer wilderness for long, there was talk of him taking over the England manager's job but it was O's chairman Brian Winston who brought him back to Brisbane Road on 12 September 1977. Winston phoned Bloomfield to ask if he wanted his old job back, having discussed the offer with his family, they were in total agreement that she should take it.

216

Bloomfield told the press "I enjoy working with Brian Winston because he genuinely loves the club, he stood on the terracing as a boy and is consumed with ambition for Orient."

His biggest achievement was to take O's to the semi-final of the FA Cup, although for long periods he was in and out of hospital and it was Peter Angell who took charge of the team. When the team were celebrating and doing a knees-up in the dressing room after the 2-1 win at Chelsea, Brian Winston slipped away to phone the news to Bloomfield, who was in a London hospital having test, and what a tonic it was for him.

After the transfer of John Chiedozie to Notts County for an O's record fee of £600,000, Bloomfield had a conflict of opinion over the deal with Chairman Winston and resigned as manager in May 1981. He was appointed a part-time scout with Luton Town in October 1981.

After a long battle against cancer, Jimmy Bloomfield died at his North Chingford home on 3 April 1983, aged forty-nine.

Bloomfield's Managerial Record (League and Cups)

Team	From	To	P	W	D	L
Orient	1/7/1968	31/5/1971	134	48	42	44
Leicester City	23/6/1971	23/5/1977	264	75	99	90
Orient	12/10/1977	27/8/1981	167	50	58	59
Totals			**565**	**173**	**199**	**193**

Bobby Campbell 1979-1980

Bobby Campbell was the most persuasive man I have ever met in football. More than that I'm not prepared to say, as I don't have the time to spend in court!

I knew within three weeks of signing that I had made the biggest mistake of my football career and one that would ultimately put paid to any thoughts of my dream of playing at the highest level of the game.

We were playing at Luton Town and after a very poor first half display, being 3-0 down, we trudged off the field at Kenilworth Road with heads down expecting to receive an ear bashing and some criticism for an inept display.

What followed was the worst example of a 'pep talk' I have ever witnessed in football. As the last player came through the door, a red-faced Bobby with eyes bulging and froth coming from his lips, violently slammed the door closed so hard that the frame split and the door collapsed off one of the hinges. After all the players had sat down, he jumped up in the air and brought his fists down so hard on the trainers couch, which was in the middle of the room that the table legs buckled.

He was absolutely out of control and shouting and swearing indiscriminately at all the players. He then went for each player individually and whilst putting his face within a few inches of each one and a finger almost in their eyes, he was literally frothing saliva out of his mouth. He then started abusing each player in turn, by insulting them.

To the first player he came to, he shouted:

*"You are a f****** cheat, the next one, "You are a f******coward, the next one: "You are a f****** moral coward, etc etc, when he got to me he said, "And you, you c***, you think you have f****** arrived, well you f****** well haven't, and if you don't buck your f****** ideas up, you'll be out"*

The poor players went out for the second half with heads down and were totally demoralised, it was no wonder that the second half was not better and we ended up losing the game by 4-0.

The episode certainly made me realise that this approach doesn't work and that managers have to really understand why a team is not performing. It is rarely a lack of commitment but more about confidence and motivation and sometimes so-called 'bad luck'.

Today, no manager would get away with this behaviour and players would probably take legal action.

Another example of his management style was whilst we were on a pre-season tour in Sweden during 1980 and we staying in a small town called Solvesborg. One night three of us had been out on the town and the other two lads, who were married (no names mentioned) had pulled a couple of girls and arranged for them to come back to the hotel the following night. However Campbell and his assistant Mike Kelly (who was not dissimilar to Campbell in his temperament and approach, so they made a good team) wanted everyone in bed by 11pm that night, so they both came around to everyone's room to check we were all in bed and as they said 'to tuck us in'.

They said that we all needed some rest and sleep because of the hard training we were doing because of the schedule of matches. Apparently, the two girls had been hiding in a wardrobe when they came around the first time. But the two must have gone back to check a bit later because just after I had fallen asleep, which was approximately one hour later, I was woken up by banging on doors down the corridor and then eventually on my door by Mike Kelly. (*Kelly was born in Northampton on 18 October 1942, the goalie made 116 career League appearances with QPR and Birmingham City, before going to play in the States during 1974 with Minnesota Kicks. Today, he is the goalkeeping coach with Crystal Palace.*)

I was told that all the players had to go to a certain room where Campbell wanted to speak to everyone.

When everyone was in the room, he exploded again in a torrent of abuse aimed specifically at the two married players and he was clearly trying to make an example of their misdemeanour in front of everyone. He told them they were going to be fined and he even threatened to tell their wives.

What was ridiculous about the whole incident was that we were there for a further forty-five minutes or so and by the time we all got back to our rooms and back to sleep we had lost half the night. The manner in which they both handled this was totally unnecessary, as they could have dealt with the two players concerned in a way that wouldn't have disturbed everyone else.

I was so pleased when I left Craven Cottage and to get away from Campbell.

Robert 'Bobby' Campbell was born in the Scotland Road area of Liverpool on 23 April 1937 and his debut for Pool in September 1959, after turning professional with them five years earlier. After a total of 14 first team appearances, he moved to Portsmouth in November 1961 for £1000 and during his four-year stay he made 60(1) League appearances, scoring 2 goals. He moved to Aldershot in July 1966, but after only 2(3) games, he was forced to retire at the age of thirty through injury and soon built up a reputation as a coach with Portsmouth, Queens Park Rangers and Arsenal.

Campbell moved into management with Fulham, at Craven Cottage he inherited a side pushing for promotion to the 'old' Division One, but within four years he took them down to the Third Division, and changed players like they were going out of fashion, only one remained during his four-year spell: Les Strong. Towards the end of his time at the Cottage, he did not have a good relationship with the fans and refused to sit in the dugout and also to write any notes in the programme so it was no surprise that in October 1980, he was booted out. He joined Aldershot as their Assistant Manager then onto Portsmouth, taking them to the Third Division championship in 1983, but was surprisingly sacked (the reason being unknown) in May 1984, Arsenal, QPR and Chelsea, where he enjoyed a successful spell at Stamford Bridge from March 1988, taking them to the Second Division title in 1989, but in the higher grade their fortunes declined and he was sacked as manager in May 1991, but he remained at the club working as their chairman Ken Bates' personal assistant. Today he lives in retirement.

Campbell's Managerial Record (League and Cups)

Team	From	To	P	W	D	L
Fulham	18/12/1976	31/10/1980	170	49	45	76
Bristol Rovers	22/11/1978	12/13/1979	46	11	12	23
Portsmouth	21/5/1982	11/6/1984	88	40	17	31
Chelsea	6/4/1988	7/6/1991	153	68	45	40
Totals			**565**	**173**	**199**	**193**

Richie Morgan 1980-81

The Cardiff city boss Richie Morgan was a nice guy and he appeared to be very laid-back. He had played for Cardiff City, although his appearances had been limited and had worked for the club over a number of years in their commercial department.

The half back, who was born in Cardiff on 3 October 1946, started his career with Cardiff Corries, who joined City in 1967 and in the ten years he was a player, he made just 69 League appearances, although he did represent Welsh Schools and gained one cap for the Welsh U-23 side.

Don't ask me how he became manager, as he appeared to have no background for the job, although he was a Cardiff man through and through and he would do what their General Manager Ron Jones (the famous Olympic athlete) or Bob Grogan, the Chairman asked of him and Richie was a man, who certainly wouldn't 'rock the boat'.

Richie was the manager in name only, as it was Brian Harris, who had the real football brain and I always got on well with both of them and initially I had no problems. I always gave 100% and was totally committed to the club, I finished as their top goalscorer in my first season which helped them avoid relegation, although it was a close thing.

Brian Harris left the club at the end of May 1981 and I suspect this really affected Morgan because he was now on his own and it appeared to me that he had limited tactical awareness or football knowledge. He tried a number of different coaches with the first team, men like Colin Prophet, the former Sheffield Wednesday player, Fred Davies, who had been with Swansea City and Bobby Woodruff, who was a former Cardiff player, but none were given the job on a permanent basis.

Tony Book, the famous old Manchester City player was also brought in for a few weeks, but maybe he saw what was happening, as he decided to leave after a few weeks, the story goes that he wanted to stay in Manchester.

After the departure of Morgan in came Graham Williams and Len Ashurst, but I was with them both only a short while, so cannot really say much about them both.

Morgan's Managerial Record (League and Cups)

Team	From	To	P	W	D	L
Cardiff City	1/12/1978	3/4/1981	105	38	24	43

Ken Knighton 1982-1983

There isn't much I can say about Ken Knighton. He really didn't make much of an impression in terms of personality, his coaching methods or management style. In reality most of the team decisions when I arrived in December 1982 were taken by his Assistant Manager Frank Clark. This was highlighted in one match when we were playing away towards the end of the season and in the team talk both Knighton and Clark identified different Captains which was a bit embarrassing for the two players concerned, being Bill Roffey and Tommy Cunningham, of course Clark was correct. At the end of the season Knighton was sacked and Clark promoted to manager in 1985. After I returned from Las Vegas, I teamed up with Knighton again for month or so when I played a few games for Dagenham in the Alliance Premier League.

Kenneth Knighton was appointed O's boss on 13 October 1981, Frank Clark was appointed his assistant a month later, in the end O's were relegated back into the 'old' Third Division during May 1982. He was born in Mappleworth, close to Barnsley on 20 February 1944 and he attended Mexborough Secondary School and was a former apprentice colliery worker down the local mine. After representing Barnsley schoolboys the 5ft 9ins and 11st. 5lbs full back started his playing career with Mexborough Rovers in the Barnsley Amateur League and he then joined Wath Wanderers. He became an apprentice with Wolverhampton Wanderers in July 1960, turning professional a year later.

He enjoyed a long-playing career with Wolverhampton Wanderers, Hull City, Oldham Athletic, Blackburn Rovers, Preston North End and Sheffield Wednesday (he was in fact sent-off for the Owls in a Division Two match versus O's at Brisbane Road on 28 September 1974, O's won 1-0).

He retired from playing in January 1976 after a career that spanned 16-years and 340 (9) League appearances with 30 goals. In January 1976, he was appointed Coach of the youth team at Hillsborough before being appointed as Manager with Sunderland. Frank Clark was his assistant.

The pair took Sunderland into the 'old' Division One in 1979-80 when the Wearsiders finished runners-up to Leicester City, yet, both men left in April 1981.

After a brief time as scout with Manchester United between April 1981 and October 1981, he was appointed as O's boss. Knighton was a strict disciplinarian and would not tolerate a lax attitude from the players, several of whom were fined. He once had a bust-up with Tommy Taylor at half time during an FA Cup tie against Crystal Palace, Taylor left for Belgium at the end of that season and O's were relegated.

Several times players found themselves the target of his criticism. After one performance at Reading, Knighton declared, "If there was a way I could stop their wages, I would." During May 1983 he was sacked and replaced by Frank Clark. He was appointed manager of Dagenham Town in May 1984 and in October 1985 was Manager with

Beazer League, Midlands Division side, Trowbridge Town, until he left them in January 1988, he then spent two years as manager of Pottishead FC.

Knighton's Managerial Record (League and Cups)

Team	From	To	P	W	D	L
Sunderland	7/7/1979	1/5/1981	82	33	22	27
Orient	13/10/1981	1/6/1982	29	8	7	14
Totals			**111**	**41**	**29**	**41**

Frank Clark 1983-1984

When Frank Clark took over at Orient he adopted a very cautious approach probably because he was in a fairly precarious position and he wasn't a person who sought confrontation or controversy.

The club was feeling the pinch financially and he didn't have a lot of resources at his disposal, although he did inherit a reasonable squad of players.

He was very committed to the club and he spent a lot of his time watching reserve and youth team football in the hope of spotting players he might be able to recruit for little outlay.

In those days the Manager was the jack-of-all-trades and he used to take most of the training sessions, drive the mini-bus to the training ground and quite a few other jobs as well, it certainly wasn't the glamorous image we have of today's football manager.

I liked Frank, although I never really trusted him but he did initially improve the team and the way we played, and was the last O's manager to have any real success with Orient, with promotion back in the 1988-89 season.

Frank Albert Clark was born in Rowland's Gill, Highfield, near Gateshead in Co Durham on Thursday 9 September 1943, he started his long, distinguished footballing career with Crook Town winning a FA Amateur Cup winners' medal in 1961. He was playing for Crook Town whilst serving his apprenticeship as a laboratory technician.

The left full back joined Newcastle United in November 1962, making his League debut at Scunthorpe United on 18 April 1964, a 2-0 defeat and in nearly 13 years with them, he went onto make 388 League and 69 Cup appearances for the Magpies. He won a Second Division Championship medal in 1965 and a UEFA Cup winners' medal in 1969.

In July 1975 at the age of thirty-two, he joined Brian Clough at Second Division Nottingham Forest on a free transfer, making a total of 116 League and 50 Cup appearances. He won a League championship medal and a League Cup winners' medal in 1978, European Cup and League Cups winners' medals in 1979.

He joined Sunderland as assistant manager to Ken Knighton and helped them to promotion to the 'old' First Division in 1980. In April 1981, he rejoined Forest as coach before resuming his partnership with Knighton as assistant manager with O's during November 1981.

During May 1983, Clark became O's 15th manager since the WW2. After relegation to Division Four in 1985, O's went close to the promotional play-offs for the following two seasons.

It was during 1988-89, the club managed a play-off place with excellent performances against both Scarborough and Wrexham in the Final that saw Clark become only the fourth Manager in its history to lead an O's team to promotion (Stock, Carey and Bloomfield being the other three men). In November 1986, Clark was appointed Managing Director of the Club with a seat on the Board after Brian Winston resigned.

During July 1991, Clark decided to concentrate on the administrative side of the Club, handing over the managerial reigns to Peter Eustace, having been appointed Assistant to Clark, a year earlier.

After eleven years with the O's, Clark left to take over from Brian Clough as manager of Nottingham Forest. Tributes came pouring in and chairman Tony Wood stated, "I'm sad to see Frank leave because we had such a fine working relationship. Frank was superb at his job."

Eustace admitted that although Clark was always fully committed to Orient, he always had a soft spot for Forest.

"Frank had a wonderful relationship with all at the Club, not having him around will be noticed for quite a while". Eustace added "I hope everyone realises all the hard work Frank put into the Club and what a wonderful manager and administrator he was."

There was more than a tear shed as the departing Clark packed his bags, he officially took over at Forest on May 12 1993, winning promotion to the Premier League in 1994 at the first attempt, under Clark, Forest reached the quarter Finals of the UEFA Cup in 1995-96. He resigned as manager of cash stripped Forest on 19th December 1996.

On 30 December 1996, he accepted the managerial job at Manchester City. His stay lasted just over a year when he was fired on 18 February 1998. He only heard of his sacking, while listening to the radio, on his way to the training ground. It was City's fifth manager that year.

In recent times, Clark has become a commentator with Radio Five Live and as a studio guest summariser for Sky Sports, in fact he was in the studio with Barry Fry for O's Promotion Final play off match against Scunthorpe United at Wembley Stadium in May 1999.

Clark also works for the League Managers' Association and completed a book a few years ago, entitled 'Kicking with both feet' mentioning his stay with O's, he also runs a football consultancy and does some media work.

In a recent interview, Clark looked back on his career and listed the Orient promotion season of 1989 as one of his top accomplishments. "I always look back at my time with Orient as being rather special it was just a wonderful moment in time,"

"Winning promotion is something I will never forget, we had a good set of players and they deserved their success."

Clark's Managerial Record (League and Cups)

Team	From	To	P	W	D	L
Orient	1/6/1982	1/8/1991	476	83	114	179
Nottingham Forest	12/51993	19/12/1991	178	73	58	73
Portsmouth	21/5/1982	11/6/1984	88	40	17	31
Manchester City	29/12/1996	17/02/1998	60	20	18	22
Totals			**714**	**276**	**190**	**274**

Michael Speight 1985

Mickey Speight was a very hard working and honest professional footballer who played with Sheffield United, Blackburn Rovers, Grimsby Town, and Chester City, which was also his first experience in English football management and only as caretaker, so I didn't have much time with him to make any judgment on his expertise.

He was replaced as the Chester manager by Harry McNally at the end of the 1984-85 season and went on to work in Norway and stayed for sixteen years as coach to such clubs as Drobak/Frogn, Vidar, Moss, Sogndal and Mjondalen, before the fifty-two year old was running his own business in 2004 and living in a place called Moss in the south east of Norway on the Oslo fjord.

Michael Speight was born in the village of Upton in Yorkshire on 1 November 1951, the midfielder started his career as an apprentice with Sheffield United in May 1969 and made 184(15) appearances with 14 goals, he moved to Blackburn Rovers in July 1980, making 51 appearances and scoring 4 goals, and later played for Grimsby Town and Chester. He made 328 career League appearances and scored 21 goals. H e also won 4 England 'B' Caps.

Chapter 20
My trip to Japan to visit
My Family in 2005

I am very proud of my son Michael, he is very intelligent and teaches English in Japan to company executives and students. He has a lovely Japanese wife, Yoko who is a wonderful mother to my two beautiful grandsons, Alfie (who at only 4 is already bilingual) and Tommy who was 2 in July. I usually see them once or twice a year but I hope to spend more time with them once I have retired, although that is still a few years away.

**Peter (right) with son Michael Kitchen (far left),
his wife Yoko and their sons Alfie and Tommy**

Peter and his partner Katherine wearing
traditional kimonos and enjoying a typical Japanese meal.

Peter and his partner Katherine (right)
with Yoko's parents (left), Katsuko and Misaaki.

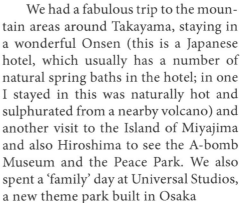

We had a fabulous trip to the mountain areas around Takayama, staying in a wonderful Onsen (this is a Japanese hotel, which usually has a number of natural spring baths in the hotel; in one I stayed in this was naturally hot and sulphurated from a nearby volcano) and another visit to the Island of Miyajima and also Hiroshima to see the A-bomb Museum and the Peace Park. We also spent a 'family' day at Universal Studios, a new theme park built in Osaka

Michael has a great interest in music and is very knowledgeable about up and coming and obscure bands and regularly played me demos of groups such as Smog, Lone Pigeon, King Creosote and the Beta band to mention just a few.

Peter at the famous Itsukushima Shrine on the island of Miyajima, off the coast of Japan, near Hiroshima.

Peter with grandsons, Alfie (left) and Tommy (right) .

Chapter 21
The O's Somme Memorial

The announcement of my retirement could not have come at a more opportune moment, as it gave me the time to become completely immersed in a project very dear to my heart. I have mentioned earlier in the book, my interest over a long time in the Great war and in particular the Battle of the Somme, since my first visit in 1980 with my good friend Duncan Sturrock. Duncan unfortunately passed away from cancer at the time of writing this update and being one of my best friends for 38 years, he will be very sadly missed.

In 2009, I was asked by Steve Jenkins, the Vice Chairman of the Leyton Orient supporters club, to become the patron of the O's Somme Memorial Committee in 2009, which I was very pleased to accept, with the aim of raising sufficient funds to build a permanent memorial on the Somme Battlefields to the Orient heroes . In 2005, I had written the foreword for Steve's book, 'They Took the Lead ', the story of Clapton (Leyton) Orient FC's involvement in the Great war, as the first English football league club to enlist en masse, when 41 players and staff, were the first professional footballers to enlist into the army in 1914. The O's

**The O's Somme Memorial Committee,
Theresa Burns, Peter and Steve Jenkins: 2010**

Somme committee, consisted of Steve Jenkins, Theresa Burns, an Orient supporter who was the Secretary and treasurer of the fund and myself, as well as support from David Dodd, in his role as Chairman of the Supporters Club. In August 2009, we launched the fund in a packed Gallery bar in the west stand at the Matchroom stadium after a Carling Cup match against Premier League Stoke City and I was very pleased to accept a first cash donation of £10 from Paul Sturrock, then the Manager of Plymouth Argyle. Due to the fantastic work and fund raising initiatives of Steve, we have raised more than £20,000, culminating in us achieving our aim in July 2011 of unveiling a memorial on the Somme battlefields in Northern France.

Once we were satisfied that we were likely to achieve sufficient funding, I contacted some friends of mine who live in Flers, a small village in the battlefield area to see if they could help identify a possible site in or near their village. Flers was where the first Tanks were used in September 1916 during the Battle of the

David Dodd & Peter unveiling The O's Somme Memorial, July 2011

Somme and an ideal location as it is close to many of the 'Infamous 'names associated with the Battle.

Mike Byott, an English resident of the village and a West Ham supporter and his French wife Sylvie, a retired GP and former Mayor of the village were a tremendous help in identifying a suitable site and gaining agreement from the Mayor and local Councillors for the memorial to be built in their village.

After a visit to Longueval in October 2010, for the unveiling of the Football League memorial to the Professional Footballers who served in the Great War, we were able to find a Company who specialised in the design and installation of these kind of memorials and Keith Rackham of H.L.Perfitt, based in Diss in Norfolk, incidentally a Box Holder at Norwich City FC, helped us to design a very unique and fitting memorial incorporating a contemporary ball and football boots from the period. Keith will be so happy that he will be going to Wembley in a couple of weeks, to see Norwich playing Middlesborough in the Play Off finals for a place in the Premier League.

It was a very special and wonderful day for us all, when in July 2011, Steve made the inaugural speech telling this most poignant of WW1 stories and former Orient player, Alan Comfort, now the Club Chaplain conducted the memorial service. It was then a great honour for myself and David Dodd, to unveil the memorial, in front of over 200 Orient fans, local residents of Flers, TV cameras, local dignitaries and members of both the English and French Football Associations.

**Peter & Steve Jenkins at
The O's Memorial, July 2013**

The O's story has continued to gain momentum and a play has been written about this called *The Greater Game* by Michael Head, an actor and producer, keeping very much to the original story. A read through of the play was held in the gallery bar, in front of 150 invited guests and the cast included former Eastenders actor and football pundit Tom Watt.

A second reading of the play was held at the Pleasance theatre in Islington for the Theatre Industry, with a view to generating interest in the play becoming a possible west end production. There were some notable actors amongst the cast including Danny Mays, who has appeared in the films Atonement and Made in Dagenham, as well as the TV series Ashes to Ashes, Danny is a passionate O's fan so he was very pleased to take part. Another cast member was Neil Dudgeon, who took over from John Nettles as DCI John Barnaby in the ITV series Midsomme Murders.

After the play, I was asked to do an interview for my thoughts about the play and went to the interview room; whilst waiting I could see and hear Neil, who was being interviewed at the time. He didn't know I was there and as he was finishing his interview, he was asked if he watched or supported a football club, to which he replied, " I live in West London and I am a season ticket holder at Fulham, however I originally come from Doncaster and my football hero as a lad in the 70's, was a striker for Doncaster Rovers called "Peter Kitchen."

Peter & Neil Dudgeon at The Pleasance Theatre in Islington In 2013. Neil watched Peter at Doncaster as a young lad.

Well I was totally unaware of this and after we were introduced, we retired to the bar to share a couple of drinks and reminisce about our days in Doncaster and I was very flattered when Neil said to me, "I don't normally do this, but do you mind if we have a selfie together."

In fact, Neil subsequently accompanied me to the Brentford v Doncaster game mentioned earlier when Rovers won the Division One Championship in 2013.

Neil Dudgeon was born in Doncaster in January 1961. He studied drama at the University of Bristol between 1979 - 1982 and made his first screen appearance in 1987.

Neil as appeared in numerous TV drama's and series including: 'A Touch of Frost', 'Inspector Morse', 'Between the Lines', 'The Bill', 'Casualty', and 'Silent Witness'. He played the part of Football League secretary , Alan Hardaker in the film, 'United', and he also made an appearance in the romantic film 'Bridget Jones, the Edge of Reason'.

Neil had a leading role as George the chauffeur in the 'Mrs Bradley Mysteries' series , starring Dame Diana Rigg , who was also born in Doncaster. Neil now plays the lead role in 'The Midsommer Murders' series , as DCI John Barnaby, which he took on in 2011 after John Nettles retired

Steve Jenkins and his book, *They Took The League*

The O's Somme story is one that continues to achieve a wider acclaim and In 2014, I wrote a second foreword for Steve's updated book, *They Took the Lead*, which he did to incorporate all the developments of the 'O's Somme story 'since the original publication. On the 15th December, Steve and myself were involved in a Commemorative service in Fulham Town hall to mark 100 years to the day, since the actual enlistment by those first professional footballers into what became known as the 'Footballers battalion 'the 17th Middlesex Regiment, with the event televised by Sky sports news. Also In December, Steve and myself were invited to the National Football museum in Manchester for a exhibition preview of the Footballers contribution in the Great war and it was really good to meet up again with the PFA chairman Gordon Taylor, who I played against many time in the 70's, when he was playing for Blackburn Rovers and Bolton Wanderers.

Steve and myself, in conjunction with Keith Rackham, have also had preliminary discussions about the possibility of having an O's memorial erected at the National Memorial Arboretum in Staffordshire and we hope that this might come to fruition in 2016, to mark the 100th Anniversary of the Battle of the Somme.

At Orient's last home game of this season v Sheffield United on 25th April, the club acknowledged Orient's contribution to the Great war, by naming it 'Clapton Orient day ', to mark the 100th anniversary of Orient's last game before 41 players and staff departed to serve in the First World War and to enable the Leyton Orient trust to further develop and deliver the Orient story to the local community. I was honoured to be part pf the commemoration and went on the pitch with two Chelsea Pensioners to present Football shirts to some of the family descendants of Richard Mcfadden, William Jonas and George Scott, the Orient players who were killed on the Somme in 1916.

Steve Jenkins, Deputy Chairman, Leyton Orient Supporters Club and Author of the book, They Took The Lead, wrote: "Proudly standing legs astride with arms folded and wearing the iconic white kit with the red 'braces', he looked full of confidence as he stood on the Brisbane Road pitch. He had told the reporter of the Waltham Forest Guardian that he had scored lots of goals whilst at Doncaster Rovers and it was his intention to score plenty for the Orient ; Peter was as good as his word and he finished the season with 29 League and Cup goals for the O's and was the second Divisions top goalscorer. This was Peter Kitchen, 'Kitch 'to all those who came to know him.

I have been an O's supporter since 1969 and success was not something I had come to expect having had so many disappointments over the years, but season 1977/78 will remain in my heart for the rest of my life, as this was when Orient almost reached the twin towers of Wembley by getting to the semi-finals of the FA

Further to its original publication in 2005, *They Took The Lead* has now been revised and updated to 260 pages, nine additional chapters and an extra 80 images, many of which are in colour. This special centenary edition will bring to you the remarkable story of Clapton Orient's major contribution to the Footballers' Battalion, as well as how the O's service in the Great War is now being remembered 100 years later - locally, around the country and abroad.

They Took The Lead sells for £14.99 plus £2.50 p&p – to order a copy of this excellent publication, please complete your details below and send with a cheque made payable to S Jenkins to 73 Havering Gardens, Romford, Essex, RM6 5BH.

The flyer for Steve's Book,
They Took The Lead, updated In 2014

Cup for the first, and currently only time in the Club's history. I can still remember spending hours lying on the floor in the lounge of my parents home making

**Steve Jenkins & Peter with Gordon Taylor, Chief Executive Of The PFA,
His Asst Simon Barker & Colin Moore, Director of
The National Football Museum In Manchester, Dec 2014.**

a huge banner for the semi-final against Arsenal with the words 'KITCHEN FRIES RICE' proudly emblazoned upon it, referring to Pat Rice the Arsenal full back and captain. I felt so proud when I heard the late Brian Moore mention my banner and those words during his commentary on the Big Match, unfortunately we lost the match 3 - 0 and the dream was over, but such a wonderful cup run for the O's.

Earlier, in the fifth round replay when the O's played Chelsea at Stamford Bridge, I witnessed one of, if not the finest goal I have ever seen scored, and it was Kitch who came up with the goods - jigging his way into the box and on a quagmire of a pitch, he beat three players including Ron 'Chopper'Harris – leaving him on his backside, and also Mickey Droy, before firing a low hard shot past the despairing dive of Peter Bonnetti and into the back of the net!

I wouldn't mind but I couldn't cheer the goal as I was in the 'Shed End' surrounded by Chelsea fans having been let into the ground by a policeman for a fiver.

Peter on The Clapton Orient Day with Chelsea Pensioners - April 2015

Peter presenting shirts on The Clapton Orient Day - April 2015

Kitch and his strike partner Joe Mayo were my favourite players at that time and I really appreciated the difference they made to the Orient – we now had the makings of a fine team.

I got to meet Kitch on several occasions during his time at the O's, particularly following my appointment on the committee of the O's Supporters Club, but it was just as a 'supporter meets a footballer'acquaintance. However, many years later and whilst reading the original edition of his book, 'The Goal Gourmet 'I discovered that I shared his interest in the Great War. It was around this time that I was in the process of trying to raise funds for a memorial to be erected on the Somme in France to commemorate the service and sacrifice made by the players, staff and supporters of Clapton Orient FC (as the O's were known at the time) during the Great War. I needed to raise a committee and I approached Peter (as I now knew him), to ask if he would be prepared to be patron and work with me and my friend and fellow O's fan Theresa Burns on behalf of the O's Somme Memorial Fund. I am so glad he agreed and within eighteen months we had raised the money enabling the memorial to be erected in the village of Flers in July 2011.

Peter has been a great support to me with the O's Somme project and we have now become good friends and indeed Peter again wrote the forward for my book which I updated last year. We have been and still are working together with various projects connected with the O's and the Great War including the ongoing developments of the play written by Michael Head 'The Greater Game ', the plans for a memorial at the National Memorial Arboretum along with numerous WW1 commemorations and exhibitions.

Peter's passion for the O's and its supporters is as strong as ever and I look forward to continue working with him to further the story of those brave Clapton Orient lads of 1916.

Up The O's!
Steve Jenkins, May 2015

A Tribute from Tom Davis

As a post-script to this, I would like to add this memory of me that came in just as we were finishing up the first edition of the book in 2006. Tom Davis had written to enquire about the release date of the book, and provided a photo and this recollection:

As a kid Peter Kitchen was my favorite O's player for obvious reasons. Generations of my family on my Father's side originated from East London, so naturally there was a only a choice of two teams - West Ham or Orient, and being nearer the Hackney end, Clapton/Leyton was the nearest. Both my Father and my Grandfather would take me regularly to the O's during the Jimmy Bloomfield/Peter Angell red braces era and as a very young kid no one epitomised that time more than Peter Kitchen. With Peter along side Joe Mayo it felt almost like our own second division Keegan and Toshack with the exciting John Cheidozie on the wing. I always remembered the programmes with the 'Man of the Orient' player profiles and looking out to see if Kitch would be featured.

When Peter Kitchen left I remember there seemed a definite hole in the team and even though he only played with us for a short time it was like a vital part had been removed. A memory that has been the most enduring to me was the come back match. In a story straight out of Roy of the Rovers the hero returns and scores.

Thankfully Peter's finest hour for the O's against Chelsea at Stamford Bridge is available for all to see. Everyone no matter who they support has their own era - mine was Orient, the Peter Kitchen era. I wasn't at the actual game but watching those 2 goals against Chelsea in the cup have got to be his legacy - Magic!!

6-year old Tom Davis pictured with Peter Kitchen, his favourite O's player in 1978

Thanks Tom, for remembering me – now more than 37 years after the fact!

Plays with 'Orient Legends XI' for Prostate Cancer Charity

As a postscript to the revised edition of this book in 2015, I had the chance to dig out my old football boots and once again, grace the Brisbane Road pitch. An opportunity arose for me to get involved in the Prostate cancer charity football match at Leyton Orient on 31st May. A good friend of mine, Martyn Webster was recently diagnosed with Prostate cancer and I felt compelled to become personally involved in some way. I contacted the match Organiser, Errol McKellar, a coach at the club, who had himself been diagnosed with and successfully treated for Prostate cancer recently

Poster for 'Orient Legends XI' held 31st May, 2015

and Martyn Ling, the 'Legends' Team Manager to offer my services and I was delighted that they both agreed I could participate in the day.

The match was between an 'Orient Legends XI', made up mainly of players from the promotion winning side of 2005/06 team, but with myself from the 70's and 80's, Alan Comfort from the 80's, Martyn Ling, who Managed the 05 / 06 team and played in the 90's and with Kevin Lisbie, who left the club to sign for Barnett only this summer, we had Orient players spanning 5 decades, which was pretty amazing.

The opposition, Men United, was managed by Harry Redknapp, the former West Ham player and manager, who has also managed Bournemouth, Portsmouth, Southampton, Spurs and more recently QPR, with TV and Film star Russell Brand as his Assistant and their team featured a number of well known TV actors, Rock Star Maxi Priest, and former players including Luther Blissett ex Watford & England, Chris Whyte of Arsenal, Trevor Sinclair QPR and England and Jamie Cureton to name just a few.

I thoroughly enjoyed the day and it was fantastic to run out on the Orient pitch again at 63 years old. I was very 'rusty' and wasn't nearly fit enough, having not kicked a ball in almost 10 years, so I only managed about 20 minutes and my knee is still sore 2 weeks on, however the pain was worth it and the well wishes from Orient and even Doncaster fans was amazing, with my Facebook page still receiving numerous posts and messages of support.

I didn't manage to score a goal myself, though we did win the game 4-3, but the most important thing was that with a crowd of almost 3000, we helped raise in excess of £20,000 for Prostate charity and if the opportunity arises for me to play again in the future, then I will certainly be involved and will start my training programme a lot earlier !!

Peter still dropping his shoulder and using his body swerve while dribbling with the ball.

Peter watching play develop, with former Watford and England striker, Luther Blissett in the background.

Peter sharing a joke with the Orient Legends goalkeeper.

Peter shaking hands with Harry Redknapp when coming off, with Martin Ling, the Legends manager in the background."

Chapter 22
The Last word - by Peter Kitchen

In writing this biography with Neil Kaufman, we have made few references to any personal incidents in my life and have tried mainly to focus on my playing career

When I look back on my career as a Professional Footballer, I do feel a sense of achievement, pride and satisfaction. I am grateful to have achieved so much and to have been such a favourite of the fans at the clubs I played for. On reflection, it was wonderful to have been so popular and to have been held in such high esteem at Orient and Doncaster especially. I still get goose bumps recalling how the fans used to chant my name after I had scored or showed some individual skill on the ball, something that many people will never experience in their lifetime. I was always totally committed to scoring goals for all my clubs and never gave less than 100% and the hard work that I put into training and playing then helped me to maintain my fitness and continue to play up to the present time. I was also very blessed not to have suffered many serious injuries and therefore able to maintain a regular training regime.

I have wonderful memories of my time at all my clubs and of the goals I scored especially at Doncaster and Orient and it is unfortunate that TV cameras weren't always around in those days as they are now at virtually every league game. I never saw any of the 100 + goals I scored for the Rovers on the TV and only a very few of the ones for Orient and Cardiff. Winning the 'Player of the Year' awards in 1976 at Rovers and 1978 at Orient are constant reminders of the wonderful times I had at these clubs and will In some ways give me some kind of immortality long after I am gone.

The experiences that I have taken from those years have helped me deal with so many situations in my life and in my subsequent career that at times it can almost be like having the benefit of hindsight. I have experienced first-hand how some people with their own 'agenda' are a barrier in preventing others from fulfilling their potential and in my case since professional football, I actively try to encourage young people, who I feel have the ability and a positive attitude to progress in their own careers.

A couple of things that my biography shows is the frustration I felt in my career, I felt that I was good enough to play at the highest level and I certainly became frustrated that at both Doncaster Rovers and Orient, I played consistent-ly well season after season and no matter how many goals I scored, I just couldn't get a move to a bigger club. I always naively believed that it was about how good you were and that if you had the ability then the opportunity would come, I never sought anything other than to fulfil my full potential doing something that I loved, however I realised that as players we were just pawns in other people's games

All I ever heard on the radio and read in the press and from other informed sources was this or that club were interested in me or had made an enquiry or an offer, but it appeared to me that I was always priced out of the market, at least that's what I always heard.

I always scored against higher divisional clubs when I played against them, like with Doncaster, against Liverpool, Stoke City, Derby County, Manchester United, Sheffield United, Hull City, Tottenham Hotspur and Crystal Palace and with Orient against Norwich City, Chelsea and Middlesbrough and for Fulham against Arsenal in Ted Drake's Testimonial, the Gunners playing their first team, for Cardiff City against Nottingham Forest, who had just won the European Cup.

I believe that composure on the ball, intelligence and the psychological aspects of football are just as important as all the tactical and physical factors, which the majority of managers find very difficult to comprehend. After all, players wouldn't get to this level if they didn't already have the physical skills and it is the intelligence, understanding, awareness and anticipation that sets players apart, not brute strength and speed.

My experience also showed me that it is actually easier to play at a higher level if you have better players around you because good players give you the ball when you want it and not when they want to get rid of it. It is a subtlety that isn't always apparent to coaches and fans unless they have more insight and don't just take note of the obvious in front of them.

As a player I knew my failings, in that I wasn't very tall or very quick over longer distances, but I was very quick over short distances, and many complemented me, saying I had exceptional ball control and that I was a very intelligent player. I also suppose I was too sensitive and thought too much about situations which did make me appear to have an attitude problem at times.

The things that I think set me apart from a lot of other strikers was having a very cool and composed nature, which you can't coach or give people. Players like Gary Lineker and Jimmy Greaves had it and players like Teddy Sheringham and Thierry Henry have it in today's game. I always seemed to make time on the ball when I was in the box and to take another touch to steady myself. I was then able to place the ball in the corners rather than snatching at the ball or smashing it at the keeper.

I can remember coming back to defend at corners and free kicks and it always felt to me like I was outside the window looking in on a circus. In these situations, most players would be screaming, shouting and pointing at their team mates to pick up with eyes bulging and totally out of control of the situation, instead of staying calm and knowing immediately who they had to pick up in the box.

The difficulty was being able to articulate this at the time and being able to quantify an intangible situation to an arrogant, opinionated football manager who can't even control themselves, let alone the players. That's why I admire Intelligent and thoughtful managers like Arsène Wenger and Jose Mourinho, because they always remain in control and cool under pressure and thereby take the pressure off their players.

I have often wondered what it would have been like to play at a big club or in a very successful team, who won leagues, promotions or cups regularly, because success breeds success and gives players so much more self confidence to express themselves. Playing every week in a struggling team that is often fighting against relegation, has a very negative effect on the players, so that it becomes harder to improve and develop or reach their potential.

Team Managers are often just trying to save their jobs, surviving on a day to day basis and most are learning on the job themselves, so they mostly employ negative, defensive tactics, trying to avoid defeat at all costs, rather than going out expecting to win. Ultimately, they are too quick to criticise and castigate their players rather than encouraging them.

I have said earlier that it is much easier to play with good players around you and I still wonder how many goals I might have scored, had I played alongside players like Trevor Brooking, Glen Hoddle or Tony Currie, who were all brilliant creative midfield players during my playing era or in the modern game with the likes of Eden Hazard, Cesc Fabregas, David Silva, Wayne Rooney or Steven Gerrard. Having said this, I am not bemoaning anything about my football career and whilst I believe I could and should have achieved more, I still feel very fortunate and proud to have lived the dream of being a professional football.

I would like to finish by thanking all my former team mates over the years, because Football is a team game and every player no matter how talented they might be, need to work within and for the team and I certainly appreciate those players I played alongside, some of whom were unsung heroes. A big thank you as well, to the supporters of all the clubs I played for, because I still believe, that despite all the money in football today, the game is still about the fans who come week in week out to support their favourite team and to cheer on their own particular football hero.

I am so glad to have this opportunity to update and finally complete my story and I hope to be around for many more years to come and whilst I always watch out for the results of all my old teams, I will always follow the fortunes more closely of my two favourite clubs, Doncaster Rovers and Leyton Orient.

Best Wishes

Peter Kitchen

Kent England
August 2015

APPENDIX

Peter Kitchen's full career— Appearances and goal scoring record November 1970 to December 1992

Peter Kitchen's professional career record 1970 to 1992

Season	Club	League		FA Cup		FL Cup		Other		Total	
		Apps	Gls	Apps	Gls	Apps	Gls	Apps	Gls	Apps	Gls
1970--71	Doncaster Rovers	13(1)	6							13(1)	6
1971- 72	Doncaster Rovers	6(3)	1							6 (3)	1
1972- 73	Doncaster Rovers	37(1)	6	3	2	2	1			42(1)	9
1973- 74	Doncaster Rovers	37(1)	10	4	2	2	3			43(1)	15
1974- 75	Doncaster Rovers	42(1)	21	2	2	2	1			46(1)	24
1975-76	Doncaster Rovers	43	22	1	0	6	2	2	2	52	26
1976 -77	Doncaster Rovers	43	23	2	3	4	2			49	28
1977-78	Orient	42	21	8	7	3	1	3	0	56	29
1978-79	Orient	22(1)	7	3	2	1	1	3	0	29(1)	10
1978-79	Fulham	17	5							17	5
1979-80	Fulham	8(5)	1					2	0	10(5)	1
1980-81	Cardiff City	39(1)	13	1	0	3	1	2	5	45(1)	19
1981-82	Cardiff City	38	8			1	0	3	3	42	11
1982-83	Orient	20	9							20	9
1983-84	Orient	26(3)	12	1	0	2	1	1	2	30(3)	15
1984-85	Chester City	3(2)	1							3(2)	1
1984-85	Dagenham Town							7	0	7	0
1990-91	Margate									11(7)	4
Total		436(19)	166	25	18	25	12	34(7)	16	520(26)	213

Notes: Other Games
Doncaster Rovers—appearances in 1975-76 was in Sheffield County Cup
Orient—appearances in 1977-78 and 1978-79 in Anglo Scottish Cup
Fulham—appearances in 1979-80 in Anglo Scottish Cup
Cardiff City—appearances in 1980-81 AND 1981-82 in Welsh Cup
Orient—appearance in 1983-84 in Associate Members Cup
Dagenham Town—appearances in 1984-84 in Alliance Premier League
Margate—appearances in 1991-92 in Southern League and Southern League Cup

Doncaster Rovers 1970-71—Division 3

Peter Kitchen made his League debut in November 1970 at Shrewsbury Town, scoring within a minute. He made 13 +(1) League appearances, and scored 6 goals.

Opposition	Date	Venue	Score	Goals Scored	Att
Shrewsbury Town	27/11	a	3-0	1	5184
Swansea Town	05/12	h	1-2	1	4174
Halifax Town	12/12	a	0-4	-	3175
Rotherham United	19/12	h	0-2	-	6471
Gillingham	13/02	h	2-2	-	2735
Chesterfield	20/02	a	0-4	-	8042
Aston Villa	26/03	h	2-1	1	7879
Tranmere Rovers	02/04	a	0-1	-	3015
Bradford City (sub)	10/04	h	3-1	-	4361
Bury	13/04	h	2-0	2	4974
Reading	17/04	a	0-1	-	5570
Fulham	24/04	h	0-1	-	4399
Rochdale	2704	h	1-2	1	2884
Torquay United	01/05	a	1-2	-	3196

Doncaster Rovers 1971-72—Division 4

Peter Kitchen made 6 + (3) League appearances, scoring 1 goal

Opposition	Date	Venue	Score	Goals Scored	Att
Barrow (a sub)	28/08	h	0-1	-	3696
Exeter City	11/09	h	2-1	-	3616
Stockport County (a sub)	01/01	h	2-2	-	3241
Workington (a sub)	18/03	h	0-0	-	4214
Brentford	21/03	h	0-3	-	5256
Exeter City	25/03	a	0-1	-	3370
Southend United	31/03	a	1-2	1	16073
Reading	01/04	h	1-1	-	2875
Gillingham	04/04	h	1-1	-	2769

Doncaster Rovers 1972-73—Division 4

Peter Kitchen made 37 + (1) League appearances, scoring 6 goals, 3 FA Cup appearances with 2 goals and 1 League Cup appearances with 0 goals = 41 total appearances, scoring 8 goals.

Opposition	Date	Venue	Score	Goals Scored	Att
Workington	12/08	a	0-2	-	2032
Hartlepool (L. Cup)	16/08	a	0-1	-	6752
Mansfield Town	19/08	h	0-1	-	3540
Cambridge United	26/08	a	1-3	-	2941
Barnsley	29/08	a	2-4	1	3377
Stockport County	01/09	h	2-2	1	2222
Gillingham	08/09	a	0-3	-	1575
Southport	15/09	h	2-0	-	2055
Crewe Alexandra	20/09	a	1-0	1	1820
Lincoln City	23/09	a	1-2	-	6455
Hereford United	26/09	h	0-0	-	3111
Bradford City	29/09	h	1-0	-	2511
Northampton Town	06/10	h	3-0	1	2489
Torquay United	11/10	a	0-1	-	1952
Peterborough United	14/10	a	1-3	-	4237
Aldershot	21/10	h	1-0	1	1997
Chester	24/10	h	0-0	-	2240
Darlington	28/10	a	1-0	-	1544
Hereford United	04/11	a	2-3	-	8332
Crewe Alexandra	11/11	h	0-2	-	1687
Bury (FA Cup)	18/11	h	3-1	1	2630
Bury	25/11	h	4-1	1	1793
Hartlepool United	02/12	a	0-0	-	2964
Scarborough (FA Cup)	09/12	a	2-1	1	7109
Colchester United	16/12	h	1-0	-	1880
Reading	23/12	a	0-1	-	4762
Lincoln City	26/12	h	1-1	-	3325
Mansfield Town	30/12	a	0-0	-	5187

Doncaster Rovers 1972-73—Division 4
(Continued)

Opposition	Date	Venus	Score	Goals Scored	Att
Cambridge United	06/01	h	0-0	-	1735
Reading (FA Cup)	17/01	a	0-2	-	361
Stockport County	19/01	a	1-2	-	2586
Gillingham	26/01	h	0-1	-	3059
Torquay United	03/02	h	1-0	-	1594
Southport	09/02	a	2-2	-	3566
Workington	16/02	h	1-1	-	2026
Aldershot	17/03	a	0-1	-	3435
Exeter City	20/03	h	5-1	-	1823
Bury	31/03	a	0-5	-	2039
Hartlepool	07/04	h	2-1	-	1488
Exeter City	14/04	a	1-0	-	3609
Barnsley (a sub)	27/04	h	0-0	-	2721

Doncaster Rovers 1973-74—Division 4

Peter Kitchen made 37 + (1) League appearances with 10 goals, plus 4 FA Cup appearances with 2 goals and 2 League Cup appearances with 3 goals = 43 +(1) total appearances, scoring 15 goals.

Opposition	Date	Venue	Score	Goals Scored	Att
Stockport County	25/08	h	1-1	-	2851
Notts. County (League Cup)	28/08	a	4-3	3	7735
Bradford City	01/09	a	1-1	-	4123
Torquay United	07/09	h	0-1	-	3313
Barnsley	11/09	h	1-0	-	3070
Brentford	15/09	a	0-2	-	4957
Peterborough United	17/09	a	1-5	-	6648
Workington	22/09	h	5-2	2	1517
Gillingham	29/09	a	1-5	1	3864
Peterborough United	02/10	h	3-1	1	2383
Reading	06/10	h	0-0	-	2516
Newcastle United (FLC)	08/10	a	0-6	-	16065
Chester	0	a	0-3	-	2150
Hartlepool	20/10	h	2-2	1	1676
Barnsley	23/10	a	0-2	-	3301
Darlington	27/10	a	0-1	-	2057
Swansea City	03/11	h	3-1	1	1523
Newport County	09/11	a	1-3	-	2852
Exeter City	14/11	a	2-1	-	5259
Bury	17/11	h	1-1	-	2088
Lincoln City (FA Cup)	24/11	h	1-0	-	3628
Crewe Alexandra	08/12	a	0-4	-	1360
Tranmere Rovers (FA Cup)	15/12	h	3-0	1	2444
Gillingham	22/12	h	1-2	1	1878
Scunthorpe United	26/12	a	1-2	1	5775
Torquay United	29/12	a	0-3	-	3487

Doncaster Rovers 1973-74—Division 4
(Continued)

Opposition	Date	Venue	Score	Goals Scored	Att
Bradford City	01/01	h	2-2	-	3480
Liverpool (FA Cup)	05/01	a	2-2	1	31483
Liverpool (FA Cup R)	08/01	h	0-2	-	22499
Brentford	12/01	h	1-2	-	3009
Stockport County	20/01	a	0-0	-	4050
Colchester United	27/01	h	2-0	1	4285
Rotherham United	03/02	h	1-2	-	5955
Workington	10/02	a	1-3	-	1667
Chester	17/02	h	1-2	-	2472
Reading	24/02	a	0-5	-	9187
Darlington	10/03	h	0-0	-	1467
Mansfield Town (a sub)	26/03	h	0-0	-	1894

Doncaster Rovers 1973-74—Division 4

Peter Kitchen made 42 +(1) league appearances with 21 goals and 2 FA Cup appearances with 2 goals and 2 League Cup appearances with 1 goal = 46 +(1) total appearances, scoring 24 goals.

Opposition	Date	Venue	Score	Goals Scored	Att
Stockport County	17/08	h	2-1	-	2383
Mansfield Town (L. Cup)	20/08	h	2-1	1	3078
Exeter City	24/08	a	1-2	-	3819
Newport County	31/08	h	0-2	-	2157
Swansea City	07/09	a	3-3	2	1554
Bury (League Cup)	10/09	a	0-2	-	4587
Rochdale	13/09	h	4-1	1	1928
Scunthorpe United	17/09	h	1-1	-	3116
Crewe Alexandra	21/09	a	1-2	-	4102
Northampton Town	24/09	a	0-2	-	4269
Rotherham United	28/09	h	0-0	-	4710
Chester	02/10	a	0-3	-	2922
Brentford	05/10	h	2-1	-	1692
Bradford City	12/10	a	0-2	-	3128
Lincoln City	15/10	h	2-2	1	2034
Workington	26/10	a	3-0	1	1256
Torquay United	02/11	a	0-2	-	2492
Chester	05/11	h	1-1	-	1286
Shrewsbury Town	08/11	h	1-3	-	1673
Lincoln City	13/11	a	0-4	-	5300
Mansfield Town	16/11	a	2-5	-	5634
Oswestry Town (FA Cup)	23/11	a	3-1	2	2000
Reading	30/11	a	0-2	-	4243
Hartlepool	07/12	h	3-0	1	1357
Chesterfield (FA Cup)	14/12	a	0-1	-	5267
Cambridge United	21/12	h	0-1	-	1677
Scunthorpe United	04/01	a	0-0	-	2472
Hartlepool	11/01	a	1-2	-	2950
Reading	18/01	h	1-1	-	1505

Doncaster Rovers 1973-74—Division 4
(Continued)

Opposition	Date	Venue	Score	Goals Scored	Att
Barnsley (a sub)	24/01	h	1-1	1	4153
Shrewsbury Town	01/02	a	4-7	2	3632
Torquay United	08/02	h	3-0	-	2166
Barnsley	15/02	a	1-0	-	6451
Mansfield Town	22/02	h	4-3	2	7278
Newport County	28/02	a	2-0	1	2252
Northampton Town	08/03	h	2-0	2	5319
Rotherham United	15/03	a	0-1	-	8049
Stockport County	17/03	a	2-0	-	1995
Swansea City	21/03	h	3-2	1	5011
Cambridge United	28/03	a	1-4	1	4159
Southport	31/03	a	1-2	1	1515
Crewe Alexandra	01/04	h	2-1	-	4845
Workington	05/04	h	0-0	-	3232
Brentford	12/04	a	1-1	1	5147
Bradford City	19/04	h	4-1	2	3640
Exeter City	22/04	h	3-3	1	4251
Darlington	26/04	a	1-4	-	2647

Doncaster Rovers 1975-76 — Division 4

Peter Kitchen made 43 League appearances, scoring 22 goals, he also made 1 FA Cup appearances, no goals and 7 League Cup appearances with 2 goals and 2 appearances with 2 goals in the Sheffield County Cup = 53 total appearances, scoring 26 goals.

Opposition	Date	Venue	Score	Goals Scored	Att
Cambridge United	16/08	h	0-2	-	2999
Grimsby Town (L. Cup)	20/08	h	3-1	-	3218
Tranmere Rovers	22/08	a	2-2	-	2013
Grimsby Town (L. Cup)	25/08	a	0-0	-	5552
Crewe Alexandra	30/08	h	3-1	-	2467
Bournemouth	06/09	a	1-0	1	3511
Crystal Palace (L. Cup)	09/09	h	2-1	-	6268
Brentford	15/09	h	1-1	-	6353
Watford	20/09	a	1-2	-	4228
Barnsley	24/09	a	1-0	-	6681
Southport	27/09	h	5-2	3(1pen)	5219
Northampton Town	03/10	a	1-2	-	6155
Torquay United (L. Cup)	08/10	a	1-1	-	2785
Stockport County	10/10	a	2-1	1	3159
Torquay United (L. Cup)	13/10	h	3-0	-	9784
Swansea City	18/10	h	2-1	1	6640
Bradford City	22/10	a	4-3	-	3687
Darlington	25/12	a	2-2	-	3725
Reading	01/11	h	1-1	-	7293
Huddersfield Town	04/11	h	4-1	1	10650
Hartlepool	08/11	a	1-2	-	3592
Hull City (L. Cup)	11/11	h	2-1	1	20476
Newport County	15/11	h	5-1	-	7793
Bury (FA Cup)	22/11	a	2-4	-	7094
Exeter City	28/11	a	0-1	-	2848
Tottenham Hotpsur (L. Cup)	03/12	a	2-7	1	25702
Tranmere Rovers	13/12	h	3-0	1	5684
Workington	20/12	a	1-3	1	1642

Doncaster Rovers 1975-76—Division 4
(Continued)

Opposition	Date	Venue	Score	Goals Scored	Att
Lincoln City	26/12	h	2-4	1	14353
Scunthorpe United	27/12	a	1-2	1	5969
Crewe Alexandra	10/01	a	2-1	1	2501
Watford	17/01	h	1-2	1	5845
Rochdale	20/01	h	1-2	1	3586
Brentford	24/01	a	1-0	-	4885
Hartlepool	14/02	h	3-0	2	5035
Newport County	21/02	a	3-2	1	1543
Barnsley	24/02	h	2-2	-	8250
Darlington	27/02	h	3-2	2(1 pen)	5587
Reading	06/03	a	1-0	-	6637
Northampton Town	09/03	h	0-4	-	8737
Stockport County	13/03	h	3-1	1	4231
Swansea City	16/03	a	1-2	-	3128
Exeter City	20/03	h	0-0	-	4149
Torquay United	27/03	a	2-2	1	2121
Workington	30/03	h	1-0	-	4081
Cambridge United	03/04	a	3-3	1	1633
Southport	06/04	a	1-1	-	1599
Bournemouth	10/04	h	1-1	-	4097
Barnsley (S C C)	12/4	a	3-2	-	1618
Rochdale	16/04	a	0-1	-	1462
Lincoln City	17/04	a	0-5	-	4096
Scunthorpe United	19/04	H	0-1	-	4097
Sheffield United (SCC)	07/05	a	2-1	2	4602

Doncaster Rovers 1976-77—Division 4

Peter Kitchen made 43 League appearances, scoring 23 goals and 2 appearances in the FA Cup with 3 goals and 4 appearances in the League Cup with 2 goals = 49 total appearances, scoring 28 goals.

Opposition	Date	Venue	Score	Goals Scored	Att
Lincoln City (L. Cup)	15/08	h	1-1	-	5594
Lincoln City (L. Cup R)	18/08	a	1-1	-	7098
Southport	21/08	a	2-2	-	1964
Lincoln City (L. Cup 2nd R)	24/08	N	2-2	(1 pen)	3726 (won on penalties)
Torquay United	28/08	h	0-4	-	4382
Derby County (L. Cup)	31/08	h	1-2	1	14888
Brentford	04/09	a	2-2	-	3804
Newport County	10/09	h	1-0	-	3739
Aldershot	14/09	h	1-2	1	5017
Swansea City	18/09	a	1-1	1	3504
Darlington	25/09	h	4-0	2	3618
Stockport County	01/10	a	1-2	1	7132
Barnsley	09/10	h	2-1	1	6707
Huddersfield Town	16/10	a	1-2	1	7494
Bradford City	22/10	h	2-3	-	6816
Colchester United	25/10	h	3-2	1	3856
Rochdale	30/10	a	0-1	-	2436
Halifax Town	02/11	a	0-6	-	2350
Hartlepool	05/11	h	2-0	2	2631
Shrewsbury Town (FA Cup)	20/11	h	2-2	2	5232
Shrewsbury Town (FA Cup R)	23/11	a	3-4	1	6134
Crewe Alexandra	27/11	h	3-0	2	3465
Exeter City	04/12	a	2-0	-	2891
Bournemouth	18/12	h	0-0	-	3485

Doncaster Rovers 1976-77—Division 4
(Continued)

Opposition	Date	Venue	Score	Goals Scored	Att
Scunthorpe United	27/12	a	1-1	-	7128
Southend United	28/12	h	0-3	-	5605
Hartlepool	01/01	a	0-0	-	2206
Cambridge United	08/01	h	1-1	-	3682
Rochdale	11/11	h	2-0	1	3008
Aldershot	15/01	a	0-1	-	3462
Southport	22/01	h	3-1	-	3441
Workington	29/01	a	1-1	-	1350
Torquay United	05/02	a	1-0	-	2642
Brentford	12/02	h	5-0	1	4095
Swansea City	26/02	h	2-1	-	4359
Newport County	01/03	a	2-1	1	1724
Darlington	05/03	a	3-1	-	3407
Stockport County	11/03	h	1-0	-	6340
Barnsley	19/03	a	1-1	-	10180
Huddersfield Town	25/03	h	2-0	-	11042
Watford	29/03	a	1-5	-	5476
Bradford City	02/04	a	1-3	-	6882
Southend United	09/04	a	1-2	(pen)	4691
Scunthorpe United	11/04	h	3-0	2	4676
Halifax Town	12/04	h	3-0	1	4840
Colchester United	15/04	a	0-1	-	4668
Workington	19/04	h	6-3	3	3782
Watford	23/04	h	1-0	-	4476
Crewe Alexandra	30/04	a	2-1	1	2359

Orient 1977-78—Division 2

Peter Kitchen made 42 League appearances, scoring 21 goals, also 8 FA Cup appearances with 7 goals and 3 League Cup appearances with 1 goal and 3 Anglo Scottish Cup appear- ances with no goals = 56 total appearances, scoring 29 goals.

Opposition	Date	Venue	Score	Goals Scored	Att
Fulham (A S C)	02/08	a	0-1	-	3700
Norwich City (A S C)	06/08	a	1-1	-	3124
Chelsea (A S C)	09/08	a	0-2	-	5702
Fulham (L. Cup)	13/08	a (N)	2-0	1	4704
Fulham (L. Cup)	16/08	a	1-2	-	4372
Luton Town	20/08	a	0-1	-	8061
Blackpool	23/08	h	1-4	-	5328
Sunderland	27/08	a	1-1	1	28261
Derby County (L. Cup)	31/08	a	1-3	-	16948
Oldham Athletic	03/09	h	5-3	2	4704
Charlton Athletic	10/09	a	1-2	-	8751
Bristol Rovers	17/09	h	2-1	1(pen)	5104
Blackburn Rovers	24/09	a	0-1	-	6326
Tottenham Hotspur	01/10	h	1-1	-	24131
Southampton	04/10	a	0-1	-	15789
Notts. County	08/10	a	1-1	1	7482
Cardiff City	15/10	h	2-1	2	5444
Fulham	22/10	a	2-1	1	9126
Millwall	29/10	h	0-0	-	8791
Bolton Wanderers	05/11	h	1-1	-	7547
Brighton & Hove Albion	12/11	a	0-1	-	20830
Crystal Palace	19/11	h	0-0	-	10027
Burnley	26/11	a	0-0	-	8506
Mansfield Town	03/12	h	4-2	3	4426
Hull City	10/12	a	2-2	1	4279
Brighton & Hove Albion	17/12	h	0-1	-	9374
Sheffield United	26/12	a	0-2	-	18370
Stoke City	27/12	h	2-0	2	6911
Blackpool	31/12	a	0-0	-	6991

Orient 1978-79 — Division 2
(Continued)

Opposition	Date	Venue	Score	Goals Scored	Att
Luton Town	02/01	h	0-0	-	9270
Norwich City (FA Cup)	06/01	h	1-1	1	14538
Sunderland	14/01	h	2-2	1	6737
Norwich City (FA Cup R)	16/01	a	1-0	1	20421
Oldham Athletic	21/01	a	1-2	-	8206
Blackburn Rovers (FA Cup)	28/01	h	3-1	2	9547
Bristol Rovers	11/02	a	1-2	-	9416
Chelsea (FA Cup)	18/02	h	0-0	-	25123
Tottenham Hotspur	25/02	a	1-1	-	32869
Chelsea (FA Cup R)	27/02	a	2-1	2	36379
Notts. County	04/03	h	0-0	-	5828
Middlesbrough (FA Cup)	11/03	a	0-0	-	33426
Middlesbrough (FA Cup)	14/03	h	2-1	1	18051
Fulham	17/03	h	1-1	1	7928
Millwall	21/03	a	0-2	-	6833
Stoke City	25/03	a	1-5	-	14595
Sheffield United	27/03	h	3-1	3(1 pen)	6725
Bolton Wanderers	01/04	a	0-2	-	17957
Blackburn Rovers	04/04	h	0-0	-	7072
Arsenal (FA Cup SF)	08/04	N	0-3	-	49698 *(Semi-Final at Stamford Bridge)*
Crystal Palace	15/04	a	0-1	-	15414
Burnley	18/04	h	3-0	-	5795
Hull City	22/04	h	2-1	1	5776
Southampton	25/04	h	1-1	-	19248
Mansfield Town	29/05	a	1-1	-	6336
Charlton Athletic	03/05	h	0-0	-	217
Cardiff City	09/05	a	1-0	1	8270

Orient 1978-79—Division 2

Peter Kitchen made 22 +(1) League appearances, scoring 7 goals, he made 3 FA Cup appearances with 2 goals and 1 League Cup appearance with 1 goal and 3 Anglo Scottish Cup appearances with no goals = 29 + (1) total appearances, scoring 10 goals.

Opposition	Date	Venue	Score	Goals Scored	Att
Mansfield Town (A S C)	05/08	h	0-1	-	3385
Notts. County (A S C)	08/08	h	2-3	-	2511
Norwich City (A S C)	12/08	a	0-0	-	2870
Sheffield United	19/08	a	2-1	1	19012
Sunderland	22/08	h	3-0	-	7373
Wrexham	26/08	h	0-1	-	6416
Chesterfield (L. Cup)	30/08	h	1-2	1	4667
Blackburn Rovers	02/09	a	0-3	-	6781
Stoke City	09/02	h	0-1	-	6587
Notts. County	16/02	a	0-1	-	8094
Newcastle United	23/09	a	0-0	-	26356
Leicester City	30/09	h	0-1	-	5430
Charlton Athletic	06/10	a	2-0	-	11024
Cardiff City	14/10	h	2-2	-	6064
Luton Town	28/10	h	3-2	2	7035
Cambridge United	04/11	a	1-3	-	6655
Sheffield United	11/11	h	1-1	1(pen)	5540
Wrexham	18/11	a	1-3	-	9122
Blackburn Rovers	21/11	h	2-0	-	4415
Burnley (a sub)	09/12	h	2-1	1	4764
Oldham Athletic	16/12	a	0-0	-	5169
Millwall	23/12	h	2-1	-	6185
West Ham United	26/12	a	2-0	-	29220
Crystal Palace	30/12	a	1-1	-	20100
Bury (FA Cup)	09/01	H	3-2	2	6192
Notts. County	20/01	h	3-0	-	4803
Ipswich Town (FA Cup)	27/01	a	0-0	-	23 337
Ipswich Town (FA Cup R) 1	30/0	h	0-2	-	18672
Newcastle United	03/02	h	2-0	1(pen)	7251
Leicester City	10/02	a	3-5	1	12050

Fulham 1978-79 — Division Two

Peter Kitchen joined Fulham for £150 000 + striker Mark Gray in February 1979, he made 17 League appearances, scoring 5 goals.

Opposition	Date	Venue	Score	Goals Scored	Att
Brighton & Hove Albion	24/02	h	0-1	-	18464
Preston North End	03/03	a	2-2	1	10890
Crystal Palace	10/03	h	0-0	-	10564
Leicester City	21/03	a	0-1	-	10396
Wrexham	24/03	a	1-1	1	9046
Orient	27/03	a	0-1	-	6610
Charlton Athletic	31/03	h	3-1	1	6955
Stoke City	04/04	a	0-2	-	15243
Notts. County	07/04	a	1-1	-	9485
Cardiff City	11/04	h	2-2	1	6067
Cambridge United	14/04	a	0-1	-	6523
Orient	16/04	h	2-2	-	8052
Newcastle United	21/04	a	0-0	-	11916
Millwall	24/04	a	0-0	-	7397
Leicester City	28/04	h	3-0	-	7002
Luton Town	05/05	a	0-2	-	9112
Blackburn Rovers	09/05	a	1-2	1	4684

Fulham 1979-80 — Division 2

Peter Kitchen made 4 + (3) league appearances with 1 goal and 2 Anglo Scottish Cup appearances with no goals.

Opposition	Date	Venue	Score	Goals Scored	Att
Plymouth Argyle (A S C)	04/08	h	1-0	-	2067
Birmingham City (A S C)	08/08	h	0-5	-	2889
Leicester City	22/09	a	3-3	-	14875
Luton Town (a sub)	29/09	h	1-3	-	9944
Orient (a sub)	09/10	a	0-1	-	5090
Birmingham City (a sub)	03/11	h	2-4	-	8243
Leicester City	09/02	h	0-0	-	8691
Luton Town	16/02	a	0-4	-	9169
Shrewsbury Town	03/05	a	2-5	1	6328

Cardiff City 1980-81 — Division 2

Peter Kitchen made 39 +(1) league appearances with 13 goals, 1 FA Cup appeaance, 0 goals and 3 FL Cup appearances with 1 goal and 2 Welsh Cup appearances with 5 goals = 45 +(1) total appearances, scoring 19 goals.

Opposition	Date	Venue	Score	Goals Scored	Att
Oldham (a sub)	23/08	a	0-2	-	5690
Chelsea (L. Cup)	27/08	h	1-0	-	6549
Orient	30/08	h	4-2	-	5671
Chelsea (L. Cup)	03/09	a	1-1	1	12959
Newcastle United	06/09	a	1-2	1	5787
Bolton W anderers	13/09	h	1-1	-	6532
Bristol Rovers	20/09	h	2-1	-	6117
Barnsley (L. Cup)	23/09	a	2-3	-	13135
Notts. County	27/09	a	2-4	1	7229
Watford	04/10	h	1-0	-	6388
West Ham United	07/10	a	0-1	-	20402
Sheffield Wednesday	11/10	a	0-2	-	15606
Cambridge United	17/10	h	1-2	-	4140
Queens Park Rangers	22/10	h	1-0	-	4453
Shrewsbury Town	25/10	a	0-2	-	4466
Chelsea	31/10	h	0-1	-	8445
Preston North End	08/11	a	1-3	1	5494
Wrexham	12/11	h	1-0	1(pen)	4780
Blackburn Rovers	15/11	a	3-2	2	7855
Luton Town	22/11	h	1-0	-	6041
Derby County	29/11	a	1-1	-	15581
Cardiff Corinthians (WC)	03/12	h	6-0	5	1080
Grimsby Town	06/12	h	1-1	I (pen)	5936
Bristol City	26/12	a	0-0	-	15039
Swansea City	27/12	h	3-3	1	21198
Leicester City (FA Cup)	03/01	a	0-3	-	17527
Luton Town	10/01	a	2-2	1	9013

Cardiff City 1980-81—Division 2
(Continued)

Opposition	Date	Venue	Score	Goals Scored	Att
Orient	17/01	a	2-2	-	3838
Wrexham (W C)	27/01	a	0-3	-	4880
Oldham Athletic	31/01	h	0-2	-	5563
Queens Park Rangers	03/02	a	0-2	-	9834
Bolton Wanderers	07/02	a	2-4	-	8115
Notts. County	20/02	h	0-1	-	4958
Newcastle United	25/02	h	1-0	1	4226
Bristol Rovers	28/02	a	1-0	-	7525
Sheffield Wednesday	04/03	h	0-0	-	6971
Watford	07/03	a	2-4	1	10114
Cambridge United	21/03	a	0-2	-	3719
Shrewsbury Town	28/03	h	2-2	-	5195
Chelsea	04/04	a	1-0	-	11569
Preston North End	11/04	h	1-3	-	4987
Swansea City	18/04	a	1-1	1	19038
Bristol City	20/04	h	2-3	1	5575
Grimsby Town	25/04	a	1-0	-	7377
Derby County	02/05	h	0-0	-	7577
West Ham United	06/05	h	0-0	-	10535

Cardiff City 1981-82 — Division 2

Peter Kitchen made 25 + (2) League appearances with 8 goals, 1 League Cup Appearances with 0 goals and 3 Welsh Cup appearances with 3 goals = 29 +(2) total appearances, scor- ing 11 goals.

Opposition	Date	Venue	Score	Goals Scored	Att
Oldham Athletic	29/08	a	2-2	-	4374
Exeter City (L. Cup)	02/09	h	2-1	-	2688
Chelsea	05/09	h	1-2	1	8884
Rotherham United	12/09	a	0-1	-	7002
Blackburn Rovers	19/09	h	1-3	-	4248
Luton Town	22/09	a	3-2	1(pen)	9015
Newcastle United (a sub)	03/10	h	0-4	-	5758
Blackburn Rovers	30/01	a	0-1	-	7001
Rotherham United	06/02	h	1-2	1	3818
Wrexham (W C)	09/02	h	4-1	3	2767
Newcastle United	13/02	a	1-2	-	15129
Chelsea	17/02	a	0-1	-	9710
Barnsley	20/02	h	0-0	-	4500
Sheffield Wednesday	27/02	h	0-2	-	5767
Bolton Wanderers	06/03	a	0-1	-	6269
Crystal Palace	09/03	a	0-1	-	7202
Shrewsbury Town	13/03	a	1-1	-	4089
Cambridge United	20/03	h	5-4	2	3239
Norwich City	27/03	a	1-2	-	11923
Grimsby Town	30/03	h	2-1	-	3920
Watford	03/04	h	2-0	-	6729
Hereford United (W C)	08/04	a	0-0	-	4832
Orient	10/04	h	2-1	1	5685
Charlton Athletic	13/04	a	2-2	-	4186
Leicester City	17/04	a	1-3	1	13650
Hereford United (W C)	19/04	h	2-1	-	3635
Queens Park Rangers	24/04	h	1-2	-	5974
Orient	28/04	a	1-1	-	2527
Derby County	01/05	a	0-0	-	111
Crystal Palace	08/05	h	0-1	-	5558
Luton Town (a sub)	17/05	h	2-3	1	10277

Orient 1982-83—Division 3

Peter Kitchen returned from Hong Kong in December 1982, he made 20 League appearances, scoring 9 goals.

Opposition	Date	Venue	Score	Goals Scored	Att
Preston North End	17/12	h	2-1	1	1668
Millwall	26/12	a	1-0	-	4740
Bournemouth	28/12	h	5-0	1	3718
Sheffield United	01/01	a	0-3	-	10973
Bradford City	12/01	a	3-2	1	3315
Chesterfield	15/01	h	2-0	1	2642
Portsmouth	18/01	h	2-1	-	3961
Southend United	13/03	h	1-1	-	3073
Wigan Athletic	19/03	a	1-0	_	2954
Wrexham	25/03	h	0-0	-	1969
Bournemouth	02/04	a	0-2	-	7039
Millwall	04/04	h	2-3	-	4345
Oxford United	09/04	a	2-2	1	4033
Doncaster Rovers	12/04	a	3-0	2	2355
Huddersfield Town	16/04	h	1-3	-	3498
Preston North End	23/04	a	1-2	-	5628
Exeter City	30/04	h	5-1	-	2407
Portsmouth	02/05	a	2-2	1	16232
Cardiff City	07/05	a	0-2	-	11480
Sheffield United	14/05	h	4-1	1	4468

Orient 1983-84—Division 3

Peter Kitchen made 26 + (3) League appearances with 12 goals, 1 FA Cup appearance, 0 goals, 1+(1) League Cup appearances with 1 goal and 1 Associate Members Cup appearances with 2 goals = 29 + (4) total appearances, scoring15 goals.

Opposition	Date	Venue	Score	Goals Scored	Att
Bradford City	27/08	h	2-0	-	2675
Aldershot (L. Cup)	30/08	a	1-3	-	1978
Lincoln City (a sub)	07/09	a	0-2	-	2899
Aldershot (L. Cup)	13/09	h	3-3	1	2236
Bristol Rovers	23/09	h	0-1	-	4206
Wimbledon (FA Cup)	19/11	a	1-2	-	4330
Hull City	26/11	a	1-2	1	6857
Preston North End (a	03/12	h	2-1	1	2679
Plymouth Argyle	17/12	h	3-2	-	2684
Millwall	26/12	a	3-4	1	5161
Bournemouth	27/12	h	2-0	-	4077
Burnley	02/01	h	1-2	-	4470
Walsall	07/01	h	0-1	-	3106
Rotherham United	22/01	h	2-1	-	2204
Wigan Athletic	27/01	h	0-0	-	2123
Wimbledon	04/02	h	2-6	1	3377
Bristol Rovers	11/02	a	0-0	-	4741
Exeter City	18/02	a	4-3	-	2347
Brentford (A M C)	21/02	a	2-3	2	2301
Southend United	26/02	h	1-0	-	3001
Sheffield United	03/03	a	3-6	1	21
Bolton Wanderers	06/03	h	2-1	1	2449
Brentford	10/03	a	1-1	1	4358
Newport County	17/03	h	2-2	-	2355
Gillingham	31/03	a	1-3	-	3090
Lincoln City	07/04	h	1-1	-	2174
Port Vale (a sub)	09/04	a	0-2	-	3169
Preston North End	14/04	a	1-3	-	3144
Millwall	21/04	h	5-3	4	3874
Bournemouth	24/04	a	2-3	1(pen)	3736
Hull City	28/04	h	3-1	-	3020
Scunthorpe United	01/05	a	1-3	-	2284
Oxford United	07/05	h	1-2	-	5695

Dagenham 1984-85—Alliance Premier League

Peter Kitchen, at the age of thirty-four, joined in February 1985 and made 7 League and Cup appearances with no goals.

Opposition	Date	Venue	Score	Goals Scored	Att
Nuneaton Borough	22/02	h	2-1	-	573
Altrincham	02/03	h	1-1	-	559
Enfield	04/03	h	0-3	-	771
Orient (Capital League)	06/03	h	2-2	-	112
Boston United	09/03	a	1-4	-	1243
Chelmsford City (E S C)	11/03	h	1-0	-	472
Weymouth	16/03	a	0-1	-	658

Chester City 1984-85 - Division 4

Peter Kitchen joined Chester after retuning from America in March 1985, he made 3+(2) League appearances, scoring1 goal

Opposition	Date	Venue	Score	Goals Scored	Att
Halifax Town (a sub)	22/03	a	4-0	-	1014
Aldershot	27/03	h	2-0	1	1534
Mansfield Town	30/03	h	0-3	-	1535
Peterborough United (a sub)	05/04	h	1-3	-	2020
Wrexham	06/04	a	0-2	-	3487

Margate 1991-92 - Southern League Southern Section

Peter Kitchen, aged thirty-nine joined Margate in August 1991, he made 11 + (7) League and Cup appearances, scoring 4 goals.

Opposition	Date	Venue	Score	Goals Scored	Att
Burnham	17/08	h	1-2	-	402
Hastings Town	20/08	a	0-4	-	201
Ashford Town (a sub)	26/08	h	2-2	1	510
Newport Isle of Wight	31/08	h	3-1	2	318
Sittingbourne	03/09	a	1-1	-	160
Gosport Borough	07/09	h	0-1	-	345
Weymouth (a sub)	05/10	h	1-1	-	262
Erith & Belvedere(Cup)	08/10	h	3-2	1	172
Havant Town	12/10	a	1-3	-	152
Buckingham Town (a sub)	16/11	a	2-0	-	161
Salisbury (a sub)	23/11	h	1-0	-	285
Hythe Town (Cup)	27/11	a	0-1	-	120
Slough Town (Cup)	30/11	a	0-0	-	663
Slough Town (Cup) (sub)	03/12	h	1-2	-	482
Sittingbourne (a sub)	07/12	h	0-0	-	348
Weymouth	14/12	a	0-3	-	770
Burnham	21/12	a	0-1	-	302
Canterbury City (a sub)	26/12	h	1-0	-	320

Scoring records by Orient players

Leading all-time goal scorers - 20 or more goals in a season

Player	Season	Goals scored
Tommy Johnston	1957-58	36 (35 League, 1 FA Cup)
PETER KITCHEN	1977-78	29 (21 League, 7 FA Cup, 1 FL Cup)
Ronnie Heckman	1955-56	29 (23 League, 6 FA Cup)
Tommy Johnston	1956-57	27 (27 League)
Tommy Johnston	1959-60	25 (25 League)
Frank Neary	1947-48	25 (25 League)
Ted Crawford	1935-36	25 (23 League, 2 FA Cup)
Carl Griffiths	1997-98	23 (18 League, 1 FA Cup, 3 FL Cup)
Johnny Hartburn	1955-56	23 (20 League, 3 FA Cup)
Ken Facey	1954-55	23 (22 League, 1 FA Cup)
David Dunmore	1961-62	22 (22 League)
Charlie Fletcher	1931-32	22 (20 League, 2 FA Cup)
Dennis Pacey	1953-54	21 (16 League, 5 FA Cup)
Richard McFadden	1914-15	21 (21 League)
Dennis Pacey	1952-53	20 (19 League, 1 FA Cup)

20 or more league goals in a season

Only 10 different players have scored 20 or more League goals in a season, since League entry in 1905-06 season.

Player	Season	Goals	Div
Richard McFadden	1914-15	21	2
Charlie Fletcher	1931-32	20	3s
Edmund Crawford	1935-36	23	3s
Frank Neary	1948-49	25	3s
Ken Facey	1954-55	22	3s
Ronnie Heckman	1955-56	23	3s
Johnny Hartburn	1955-56	20	3s
Tommy Johnston	1956-57	27	2
Tommy Johnston	1957-58	35	2
Tommy Johnston	1959-60	25	2
David Dunmore	1961-62	22	2
PETER KITCHEN	**1977-78**	**21**	**2**

40 goals or more
1905-06 to 2005-06

Player	League	FA Cup	L Cup	TOTAL Goals
Tommy Johnston	121	2	0	123
Ken Facey	74	5	0	79
Ted Crawford	67	6	0	73
Kevin Godfrey	63	5	4	72
Mickey Bullock	65	1	3	69
Richard McFadden	66	2	-	68
Steve Castle	56	6	5	67
Billy Rees	58	8	-	66
Reg Tricker	60	3	-	63
PETER KITCHEN	**49**	**9**	**3**	**61**
Carl Griffiths	51	6	3	60
David Dunmore	54	2	2	58
Dennis Pacey	46	12	-	58
Ian Juryeff	45	7	3	55
Mark Cooper *	48	4	2	54
Barrie Fairbrother	41	7	2	50
Alan Comfort	46	1	1	48
Matthew Lockwood**	40	2	2	44
Colin West	43	2	2	47
Ronnie Heckman	38	6	-	44
Frank Neary	44	0	-	44
Gary Alexander***	40	1	0	41
Joe Mayo	36	3	1	40

*Cooper's record includes 3 goals in play-off games in 1988-89
**Lockwood's record includes 1 goal in play-off game in 2000- 2001, he was still with the club for the 2006-07 season.
***Alexander was still with the club for the 2006-07 season.

Highest number of goals scored in a match
Five Goals

Ronnie Heckman (FA Cup)	(H)	Lovells Athletic	19 November 1955

Four Goals
(All in League)

Walter Leigh	(H)	Bradford City	13 April 1906
Albert Pape	(H)	Oldham Athletic	1 September 1924
Dennis Pacey	(H)	Colchester United	30 April 1953
Stan Morgan	(H)	Exeter City	26 March 1955
Johnny Hartburn	(H)	Queens Park Rangers	3 March 1956
Len Julians	(H)	Middlesbrough	28 September 1957
Tommy Johnston	(H)	Rotherham United	25 December 1957
Joe Elwood	(H)	Bristol City	29 November 1958
Eddie Brown	(H)	Sunderland	30 March 1959
PETER KITCHEN	(H)	Millwall	21 April 1984
Steve Castle	(A)	Rochdale	5 May 1986

Doncaster Rovers: Goal record holders
50 or More Goals
Doncaster Rovers FC. Leading scorers (all senior competitions)

Name	Total
Keetley, Thomas (Tom)	186
Jeffrey, Alick James	139
Tindill, Herbert (Bert)	134
Kitchen, Michael Peter (Peter)	**108**
O'callaghan, Brendan Richard	77
Booth, Colin	62
Douglas, Colin Francis	62
Snodin, Glynn	62
Doherty, Peter Dermot	59
Todd, Paul Raymond	56
Burton, Stanley (Stan)	54
Turner, Albert (Bert)	53
Harrison, Raymond William	50
Jordan, Clarence (Clarrie)	50

Doncaster Rovers FC. Leading scorers
(Football League Only)
50 or More League Goals

Name	Number Of Goals
Keetley, Thomas	180
Jeffrey, Alick James	127
Tindill, Herbert	125
Kitchen, Michael Peter (Peter)	**89**
O'callaghan, Brendan Richard	65
Snodin, Glynn	59
Booth, Colin	57
Doherty, Peter Dermot	56
Douglas, Colin Francis	53
Turner, Albert	51
Burton, Stanley	50

Doncaster Rovers FC
20 goals in a season

Football League Only

Tom Keetley	1923-24	21
Tom Keetley	1924-25	23
Tom Keetley	1925-26	24
Tom Keetley	1926-27	36
Tom Keetley	1927-28	36
Tom Keetley	1928-29	40
Archie Waterston	1932-33	24
Ronnie Dodd	1933-34	24
Bert Turner	1934-35	25
Reg Baines	1934-35	21
Eddie Perry	1937-38	24
Clarrie Jordan	1946-47	42
Paul Todd	1946-47	23
Peter Doherty	1949-50	27
Colin Booth	1962-63	34
Colin Booth	1963-64	23
Alfie Hale	1963-64	20
Alick Jeffrey	1964-65	36
Laurie Sheffield	1965-66	28
Alick Jeffrey	1965-66	22
PETER KITCHEN	**1974-75**	**21**
PETER KITCHEN	**1975-76**	**22**
Brendan O'Callaghan	1975-76	22
PETER KITCHEN	**1976-77**	**23**

20 goals in a season for Rovers

All senior competitions
(Football League & Conference seasons only).

Tom Keetley	1923-24	21 (FL-21)
Tom Keetley	1924-25	27 (FL-23, FAC 4)
Tom Keetley	1925-26	24 (FL-24)
Tom Keetley	1926-27	37 (FL-37, FAC-1)
Tom Keetley	1927-28	36 (FL-36)
Tom Keetley	1928-29	41(FL-40, FAC-1)
Archie Waterston	1932-33	24 (FL-24)
Ronnie Dodd	1933-34	24 (FL-24)
Bert Turner	1934-35	26 (FL-25, OTH-1)
Reg Baines	1934-35	21 (FL-21)
Eddie Perry	1937-38	24 (FL-24)
Clarrie Jordan	1946-47	44 (FL-42, FAC-2)
Paul Todd	1946-47	26 (FL-23, FAC-3)
Peter Doherty	1949-50	30 (FL-27, FAC-3)
Jim Fernie	1959-60	21 (FL-19, FAC- 2)
Colin Booth	1962-63	38 (FL-34, FAC-2, FLC-2)
Colin Booth	1963-64	24 (FL-23, FAC-1)
Alfie Hale	1963-64	21 (FL-20, FAC-1)
Alick Jeffrey	1964-65	39 (FL-36, FAC-2, FLC-1)
Laurie Sheffield	1965-66	28 (FL-28)
Alick Jeffrey	1965-66	22 (FL-22)
PETER KITCHEN	**1974-75**	**24 (FL-21, FAC-2, FLC-1)**
PETER KITCHEN	**1975-76**	**26 (FL-22, FLC-2, Other 2)**
Brendan O'Callaghan	1975-76	29 (FL-22, FLC-6, Other 1)
PETER KITCHEN	**1976-77**	**28 (FL-23, FAC-3, FLC-2)**
Colin Cramb	1996-97	21 (FL-18, FAC-1, FLC-1, Other 1)
Paul Barnes	2002-03	26 (Conf- 25, Conf Play-Off- 1)
Gregg Blundell	2003-04	20 (FL-18, FLC-2)

Goals in a game for Doncaster Rovers

Football League

6 Goals

Tom Keetley	v. Ashington (a)	16/2/1929	W 7-4

5 Goals

Albert Turner	v. New Brighton (h)	16/2/1935	W 7-1

4 Goals

Tom Keetley	v. Coventry City (h)	23/1/1926	W 8-1
Tom Keetley	v. Barrow (h)	7/5/1927	W 7-0
Tom Keetley	v. Nelson (h)	28/4/1928	W 4-2
Tom Keetley	v. Tranmere Rovers (h)	1/5/1928	W 5-2
Tom Keetley	v. Hartlepool United (h)	16/3/1929	W 4-1
Ronnie Dodd	v. Gateshead (h)	16/12/1933	W 5-2
Peter Clark	v. Hartlepool United (a)	19/3/1960	W 6-2
Alfie Hale	v. Darlington (h)	25/1/1964	W 10-0
Alick Jeffrey	v. Darlington (h)	29/9/1964	W 6-3

3 Goals

Ike Marsh	v. Chesterfield (h)	11/1/1901	W 4-1
John Murphy	v Newton Heath (h)	22/2/1902	W 4-0
Tom Keetley	v. Halifax Town (h)	22/3/1924	W 7-0
Sam Cowan	v. Halifax Town (h)	22/3/1924	W 7-0
Harold Keetley	v. Durham City (h)	19/12/1925	W 4-1
Harold Keetley	v. Southport (h)	26/12/1925	W 6-1
Harold Keetley	v. Wigan Borough (h)	9/10/1926	W 4-1
Tom Keetley	v. Tranmere Rovers (h)	13/11/1926	W 4-1
Tom Keetley	v. Bradford Park Avenue (h)	27/12/1926	W 4-1
Tom Keetley	v. Nelson (h)	22/1/1927	W 6-0
Tom Keetley	v. Rochdale (h)	26/3/1927	W 3-2
Tom Keetley	v. Durham City	9/4/1927	W 5-1

3 Goals (continued)

Allan Hall	v. Durham City	29/10/1927	W 5-0
Tom Keetley	v. Southport (h)	27/8/1928	W 4-2
Tom Keetley	v. Accrington Stanley (h)	27/10/1928	W 4-1
Tom Keetley	v. Darlington (h)	29/3/1929	W 3-1
Les Lievesley	v. Accrington Stanley (h)	8/11/1930	W 6-1
Wilf Bott	v. Rochdale (a)	15/11/1930	W 5-3
Wilf Bott	v. Tranmere Rovers (h)	6/12/1930	W 6-0
Fred Castle	v. Wigan Borough (h)	7/2/1931	W 5-1
Archie Waterston	v. Hartlepool (h)	8/10/1932	W 4-1
Archie Waterston	v. Halifax Town (h)	30/3/1933	W 5-1
Albert Turner	v. Rochdale (h)	7/4/1934	W 5-0
Reg Baines	v. Gateshead (h)	19/12/1935	W 5-1
Stan Burton	v. Hull City (a)	19/10/1935	W 3-2
Reg Baines	v. Hull City (h)	22/2/1936	W 6-1
Eddie Perry	v. Rochdale (h)	18/9/1937	W 5-0
George Little	v Chester (h)	19/11/1938	W 4-1
Eddie Perry	v. New Brighton (a)	11/3/1939	W 6-3
Leslie Owens	v Accrington Stanley (h)	7/4/1939	W 7-1
Herbert Tindill	v. New Brighton (a)	7/8/1946	W 5-2
Clarrie Jordan	v. Accrington Stanley (h)	28/9/1946	W 5-0
Clarrie Jordan	v. Bradford City (h)	12/10/1946	W 4-3
Clarrie Jordan	v. York City (a)	19/10/1946	W 4-1
Clarrie Jordan	v. Carlisle United (h)	25/2/1947	W 9-2
Paul Todd	v. Barrow (h)	13/3/1947	W 8-0
Ken Reeve	v. Darlington (a)	23/10/1948	W 5-1
Peter Doherty	v. Stockport County (h)	14/1/1950	W 3-0
Peter Doherty	v. Leeds United (h)	16/12/1950	D 4-4
Peter Doherty	v. West Ham United (h)	17/11/1951	W 4-1
Alick Jeffrey	v. Bury (a)	29/9/1956	D 4-4
Johnny Mooney	v. Fulham (h)	1/12/1956	W 4-0
Tony Leighton	v. Carlisle United	27/2/1960	W 4-1
John Ballagher	v. Crewe Alexandra (h)	29/4/1961	W 6-0
Colin Booth	v. Newport County (a)	27/4/1963	W 4-2
Colin Booth	v. Southport (h)	28/12/1964	W 4-0
Albert Broadbent	v. Millwall (h)	28/11/1964	W 4-0

Alfie Hale	v. Bradford City (a)	3/2/1965	W 3-0
Alick Jeffrey	v Halifax Town (h)	6/2/1965	W 4-0
Alick Jeffrey	v. Tranmere Rovers (h)	18/12/1965	W 3-1
Trevor Ogden	v. Darlington (h)	12/4/1966	W 6-3
Trevor Ogden	v. Mansfield Town (h)	15/11/1966	L 4-6
Alick Jeffrey	v. Peterborough United (h)	17/12/1966	W 3-1
Alick Jeffrey	v. Exeter City (h)	7/9/1968	W 3-1
Peter Kitchen	**v. Southport (h)**	**27/9/1975**	**W 5-2**
Brendan O'Callaghan	v. Bradford City (a)	22/10/1975	W 4-2
Ian Miller	v. Newport County (h)	15/11/1975	W 5-1
Peter Kitchen	v. Workington (h)	19/4/1977	W 6-3
Bobby Owen	v. Huddersfield Town (h)	25/2/1978	W 4-3
Jack Lewis	v. Grimsby Town (a)	5/5/1979	W 4-3
Ian Snodin	v. Reading (h)	25/9/1982	W 7-5
Alan Brown	v. Reading (a)	8/9/1984	W 4-1
Neville Chamberlain	v. Preston North End (h)	4/4/1988	W 3-2
Lee Turnbull	v. Hartlepool United (a)	30/9/1989	W 6-0
David Jones	v. Rochdale (a)	11/11/1989	W 3-1
Lee Turnbull	v. Aldershot (h)	1/12/1990	W 3-0
Micky Norbury	v. Scunthorpe United (a)	15/4/1995	W 5-0
Graeme Jones	v. Leyton Orient (h)	16/12/95	W 4-1
Colin Cramb	v. Hartlepool United (a)	18/1/1997	W 4-2
Michael McIndoe	v. Bristol Rovers (h)	4/10/2003	W 5-1

Football Conference - 3 Goals

Ian Duerden	v. Rushden & Diamonds (a)	23/1/1999	W 3-1
Ian Duerden	v. Northwitch Victoria (a)	16/3/1999	W 3-1
Ian Duerden	v. Forest Green Rovers (h)	14/8/2000	W 3-2

Fa Cup (Competition Proper)

4 Goals

Mike Kilourhy	v. Blythe Spartans (h) Round 1R	27/11/1937	W 7-0

1 Goal

Jackie Kirkaldie	v. Accrington Stanley (a) Round 1R	4/12/1946	W 5-0

League Cup

3 Goals

PETER KITCHEN	**v. Notts. County (a) Round 1**	**28/08/1973**	**W 4-0**
Brendan O'Callaghan	v. Grimsby Town (h) Round 1	20/08/1975	W 3-1

Peter Kitchen's Record
Most goals in a game
(Football League unless stated)

5 Goals

(h) Cardiff City v Cardiff Corinthians 3 December 1980 (Welsh Cup)

---

4 Goals

(h) Orient v Millwall 21 April 1984

---

3 Goals

(a) Notts County v Doncaster Rovers 28 August 1973 (League Cup)
(h) Doncaster Rovers v Southport 27 September 1975 (1 pen)
(h) Doncaster Rovers v Workington 19 April 1977
(h) Orient v Mansfield Town 3 December 1977
(h) Orient v Sheffield United 27 March 1978 (1 pen)
(h) Cardiff City v Wrexham 9 February 1982 (Welsh Cup)

2 Goals

(h) Doncaster Rovers v Bury 13 April 1971

(h) Doncaster Rovers v Workington 22 September 1973

(a) Swansea City v Doncaster Rovers 7 September 1974

(a) Ostwestry Town v Doncaster Rovers 23 November 1974 (FA Cup)

(a) Shrewsbury Town v Doncaster Rovers 1 February 1975

(h) Doncaster Rovers v Mansfield Town 22 February 1975

(h) Doncaster Rovers v Northampton Town 8 March 1975

(h) Doncaster Rovers v Bradford City 19 April 1975

(h) Doncaster Rovers v Hartlepool United 14 February 1976

(h) Doncaster Rovers v Darlington 27 February 1976 (I pen)

(a) Sheffield United v Doncaster Rovers 7 May 1976 (Sheffield County Cup Final)

(h) Doncaster Rovers v Darlington 25 September 1976

(h) Doncaster Rovers v Hartlepool United 5 November 1976

(h) Doncaster Rovers v Shrewsbury Town 20 November 1976 (League Cup)

(h) Doncaster Rovers v Crewe Alexandra 27 November 1976

(h) Doncaster Rovers v Scunthorpe United 11 April 1977

(h) Orient v Oldham Athletic 3 September 1977

(h) Orient v Cardiff City 15 October 1977

(h) Orient v Stoke City 27 December 1977

(h) Orient v Blackburn Rovers 28 January 1978 (FA Cup)

(a) Chelsea v Orient 27 February 1978 (FA Cup)

(h) Orient v Luton Town 28 October 1978

(h) Orient v Bury 9 January 1979 (FA Cup)

(a) Blackburn Rovers v Cardiff City 15 November 1980

(h) Cardiff City v Cambridge United 20 March 1982

(a) Doncaster Rovers v Orient 12 April 1983

(a) Brentford v Orient 21 February 1984 (Associate members Cup)

(h) Margate v Newport Isle of Wight 31 August 1991

1 Goal

(a) Shrewsbury Town v Doncaster Rovers 27 November 1970 – League debut

(h) Doncaster Rovers v Swansea City 5 December 1970 – Home debut

(h) Doncaster Rovers v Rochdale 27 April 1971

(a) Southend United v Doncaster Rovers 31 March 1972

(a) Barnsley v Doncaster Rovers 29 August 1972

(h) Doncaster Rovers v Stockport County 1 September 1972

(a) Crewe Alexandra v Doncaster Rovers 20 September 1972

(h) Doncaster Rovers v Northampton Town 6 October 1972

(h) Doncaster Rovers v Aldershot 21 October 1972

(h) Doncaster Rovers v Bury 18 November 1972 (FA Cup)

(h) Doncaster Rovers v Bury 25 November 1972

(a) Scarborough v Doncaster Rovers 9 December 1972 (FA Cup)

1 Goal
(Continued)

(a) Gillingham v Doncaster Rovers 29 September 1973

(h) Doncaster Rovers v Peterborough United 2 October 1973

(h) Doncaster Rovers v Hartlepool United 20 October 1973

(h) Doncaster Rovers v Swansea City 3 November 1973

(h) Doncaster Rovers v Tranmere Rovers 15 December 1973 (FA Cup)

(h) Doncaster Rovers v Gillingham 22 December 1973

(a) Scunthorpe United v Doncaster Rovers 26 December 1973

(a) Liverpool v Doncaster Rovers 5 January 1974

(h) Doncaster Rovers v Colchester United 27 January 1974

(a) Lincoln City v Doncaster Rovers 15 April 1974 (1 pen)

(h) Doncaster Rovers v Lincoln City 20 August 1974 (FL Cup)

(h) Doncaster Rovers v Rochdale 13 September 1974

(h) Doncaster Rovers v Lincoln City 15 October 1974

(a) Workington Town v Doncaster Rovers 26 October 1974

(h) Doncaster Rovers v Hartlepool United 7 December 1974

(h) Doncaster Rovers v Barnsley 24 January 1975

(a) Newport County v Doncaster Rovers 28 February 1975

(h) Doncaster Rovers v Swansea City 21 March 1975

(a) Cambridge United v Doncaster Rovers 28 March 1975

(a) Southport v Doncaster Rovers 31 March 1975

(h) Doncaster Rovers v Exeter City 22 April 1975

(a) Bournemouth v Doncaster Rovers 6 September 1975

(a) Stockport County v Doncaster Rovers 10 October 1975

(h) Doncaster Rovers v Swansea City 18 October 1975

(h) Doncaster Rovers v Huddersfield Town 4 November 1975

(h) Doncaster Rovers v Hull City 11 November 1975 (FL Cup)

(a) Tottenham Hotspur v Doncaster Rovers 3 December 1975 (FL Cup)

(h) Doncaster Rovers v Tranmere Rovers 13 December 1975

(a) Workington Town v Doncaster Rovers 20 December 1975

(h) Doncaster Rovers v Lincoln City 26 December 1975

(a) Scunthorpe United v Doncaster Rovers 27 December 1975

(a) Crewe Alexandra v Doncaster Rovers 10 January 1976

(h) Doncaster Rovers v Watford 17 January 1976

(h) Doncaster Rovers v Rochdale 20 January 1976

(a) Newport County v Doncaster Rovers 21 February 1976

(h) Doncaster Rovers v Stockport County 13 March 1976

(a) Torquay United v Doncaster Rovers 21 March 1976

(a) Cambridge United v Doncaster Rovers 3 April 1976

(h) Doncaster Rovers v Derby County 31 August 1976 (FL Cup)

(h) Doncaster Rovers v Aldershot 14 September 1976

(a) Swansea City v Doncaster Rovers 18 September 1976

(a) Stockport County v Doncaster Rovers 1 October 1976

1 Goal
(Continued)

(h) Doncaster Rovers v Barnsley 9 October 1976
(a) Huddersfield Town v Doncaster Rovers 16 October 1976
(h) Doncaster Rovers v Colchester United 25 October 1976
(h) Doncaster Rovers v Shrewsbury Town 20 November 1976 (FA Cup)
(h) Doncaster Rovers v Rochdale 11 January 1977
(h) Doncaster Rovers v Brentford 12 February 1977
(a)Newport County v Doncaster Rovers 1 March 1977
(a) Southend United v Doncaster Rovers 9 April 1977 (1 pen)
(h) Doncaster Rovers v Halifax Town 12 April 1977
(a) Crewe Alexandra v Doncaster Rovers 30 April 1977 *(last match for Doncaster Rovers)*
(a) Fulham v Orient 13 August 1977
(a) Sunderland v Orient 27 August 1977
(h) Orient v Bristol Rovers 17 September 1977 (1 pen)
(a) Notts. County v Orient 8 October 1977
(a) Fulham v Orient 22 October 1977
(a) Hull City v Orient 10 December 1977
(h) Orient v Norwich City 6 January 1978 (FA Cup)
(h) Orient v Sunderland 14 January 1978
(a) Norwich City v Orient 16 January 1978 (FA Cup)
(h) Orient v Middlesbrough 14 March 1978 (FA Cup)
(h) Orient v Hull City 22 April 1978
(a) Cardiff City v Orient 9 May 1978
(a)Sheffield United v Orient 19 August 1978
(h) Orient v Sheffield United 11 November 1978 (1 pen)
(h) Orient v Burnley 9 December 1978
(h) Orient v Newcastle United 3 February 1979
(a) Leicester City v Orient 10 February 1979
(a) Preston North End v Fulham 3 March 1979
(a) Wrexham v Fulham 24 March1979
(h) Fulham v Charlton Athletic 31 March 1979
(h) Fulham v Cardiff City 11 April 1979
(a) Blackburn Rovers v Fulham 9 May 1979
(a) Shrewsbury Town v Fulham 3 May 1980
(a) Chelsea v Cardiff City 3 September 1980 (FL Cup)
(a) Newcastle United v Cardiff City 6 September 1980
(a) Notts. County v Cardiff City 27 September 1980
(h) Cardiff City v Wrexham 12 November 1980 (1 pen)
(h) Cardiff City v Grimsby Town 6 December 1980 (1 pen)
(h) Cardiff City v Swansea City 27 December 1980

Breakdown of appearances and goals scored by Peter Kitchen against all the clubs he played against. With number of appeearances and goals scored

Club	Apps	Gls

A

Club	Apps	Gls
Aldershot	6(1)	4
Altrincham	1	0
Arsenal	1	0
Ashford Town	0(1)	1
Aston Villa	1	1

B

Club	Apps	Gls
Barnsley	11	3
Barrow	0(1)	0
Birmingham City	1(1)	0
Blackburn Rovers	9	5
Blackpool	2	0
Bolton Wanderers	6	1
Boston United	1	0
AFC Bournemouth	7	3 (1 pen)
Bradford City	9(1)	1
Brentford	11	5
Brighton & Hove Albion	3	0
Bristol City	2	1
Bristol Rovers	6	1 (1 pen)
Buckingham Town	0(1)	0
Burnham	2	0
Burnley	3(1)	1
Bury	7	6

Club	Apps	Gls
C		
Cambridge United	12	4
Canterbury City	0(1)	0
Cardiff City	5	4
Cardiff Corinthians	1	5
Charlton Athletic	5	1
Chelmsford City	1	0
Chelsea	9	4
Chester City	5	0
Chesterfield	4	2
Colchester United	4	2
Crewe Alexandra	10	5
Crystal Palace	7	0
D		
Darlington	8	4 (1 pen)
Derby County	5	1
Doncaster Rovers	1	2
E		
Enfield	1	0
Erith & Belvedere	1	1
Exeter City	13	1
F		
Fulham	6	3

Club	Apps	Gls
G		
Gillingham	7	2
Grimsby Town	5	1 (1 pen)
Gosport Borough	1	0
H		
Halifax Town	3(1)	1
Hartlepool United	10	6
Hastings United	1	0
Havant Town	1	0
Hereford United	4	0
Huddersfield Town	4	2
Hull City	5	4
Hythe United	1	0
I		
Ipswich Town	2	0
L		
Leicester City	8	2
Lincoln City	13(1)	4 (1 Pen)
Liverpool	2	1
Luton Town	7(2)	5 (1 pen)
M		
Mansfield Town	10(1)	6
Middlesbrough	2	1
Milton Keynes Dons	2	1
Millwall	7	5

Club	Apps	Gls
N		
Newcastle United	7(1)	3 (1 pen)
Newport County	9	3
Newport Isle of Wight	1	2
Northampton Town	7	3
Norwich City	5	2
Notts County	9	5
Nuneaton Borough	1	0
O		
Oldham Athletic	5	2
Orient	6(2)	1
Oxford United	2	1
Oswestry Town	1	2
P		
Peterborough United	3(1)	1
Plymouth Argyle	2	0
Port Vale	0(1)	0
Portsmouth	2	1
Preston North End	5(1)	3
Q		
Queens Park Rangers	3	0
R		
Reading	10	0
Rochdale	6	4
Rotherham United	7	1

Club	Apps	Gls	
S			
Salisbury	0(1)	0	
Scarborough	1	1	
Scunthorpe United	9	4	
Sheffield United	8	9 (2 pens)	
Sheffield Wednesday	3	0	
Shrewsbury Town	9	7	
Sittingbourne	1	0	
Slough Town	1(1)	0	
Southampton	2	0	
Southend United	5	2 (1 pen)	
Southport	7	4 (1 pen)	
Stockport County	9(1)	3	
Stoke City	4	2	
Sunderland	3	2	
Swansea City	10	9	
T			
Torquay United	12		1
Tottenham Hotspur	3		1
Tranmere Rovers	4		2
W			
Walsall	1	0	
Watford	7	2	
West Ham United	3	0	
Weymouth	1(2)	0	
Wigan Athletic	2	0	
Wimbledon (See Milton Keynes Dons)			
Workington	10(1)	7	
Wrexham	8	5 (1pen)	

The Goal Gourmet

Note: Peter Kitchen's most favourite teams to score against were on 9 goals each, Sheffield United from 9 appearances and Swansea City from 10 appearances, fol- lowed by 7 goals each against Shrewsbury Town 9(appearances) and Workington Town from 10(1) appearances.

The least favourite team was Exeter City with one goal from 13 appearances.

**Peter Kitchen with Joe Mayo, one of the stars in
O's great FA Cup run of 1978.**

About the Author
Neilson N Kaufman

Neilson N Kaufman was born in Barts' Hospital, Holborn, London on 3 October 1950 and first watched Leyton Orient Football Club back in the 1957-58 season. He has, despite mov- ing to South Africa during August 1981 served the club as its Honorary Historian for over 30 years, a position he has relinquished in order to write two books, the first for the South African market on the former Manchester United, West Ham United and Leyton Orient player Eddie Lewis, who has spent thirty years as top manager in South Africa, and also a book on the history of the Football League for their 120th anniver- sary, which he will be busy on for the next two years before giving up his writings on football altogether to spend more time with his familyand on helping expand a leading business publishing firm Succeed Publishing Group, which he manages.

Neil is author of seven other books related to the history, players and statistical record of Leyton Orient FC. He is a founder member of the Association of Football Statisticians - AFS and an honorary member of the Rec. Sport Soccer Statistics Foundation - R.S.S.S.F whose membership includes the top football historians and statisticians from around the world. His last two books being a biography on Tommy Johnston-The Happy Wanderer - O's greatest ever player, published in November 2004 and Leyton Orient FC - The Complete Record 1881 to 2006, the complete record 1881- 2006, published in August 2006 by Breedon Book Publishing Ltd, in celebration of the clubs 125th anniversary and on it's promotion to League One in May 2006.

In September 2012, Leyton Orient The Official Quiz Book 1881 - 2012 was published by DB Publishing, and in April 2015, The Pinnace Collection book Clapton Orient, was published by Roaring 20's Publishing. Currently Neil is working on a new website on the O's covering the history, profiles on all players, (first team, reserves, youth and trialists), managers, coaches, chairman and directors, backroom staff, officials and fans.

Lightning Source UK Ltd.
Milton Keynes UK
UKOW06f1449091015

260202UK00001B/42/P